SHAKESPEARE
A Selective Bibliography
of Modern Criticism

SHAKESPEARE
A Selective Bibliography
of Modern Criticism

Linda Woodbridge

LOCUST HILL PRESS
West Cornwall, CT
1988

Library of Congress Cataloging-in-Publication Data

Woodbridge, Linda, 1945-
Shakespeare, a selective bibliography of modern criticism.
Includes index.
1. Shakespeare, William, 1564-1616—Criticism and
interpretation—Bibliography.   I. Title.
Z8811.W85   1988   [PR2976]   822.3'3   87-31134
ISBN 0-933951-14-0 (lib. bdg. : alk. paper)

Printed on acid-free, 250-year-life paper
Manufactured in the United States of America

TABLE OF CONTENTS

PREFACE

Shakespeare: A Selective Bibliography of Modern Criticism is intended for beginning graduate students, senior undergraduate students, and teachers of Shakespeare at the university, college, and/or high school level. The bibliography is designed to introduce students to the wealth and variety of approaches to Shakespeare, and its principles of selection are catholic in this regard. The student will here find a number of traditional approaches—character study, imagery analysis, ritual and archetypal approaches, Freudian and Jungian approaches, source studies, history-of-ideas essays, Marxist approaches, analyses of structure, symbol, figurative language—alongside many essays employing state-of-the-art methodologies and theories—semiotic approaches, deconstructions, post-structuralist essays, reader-response and speech-act approaches, new historicism, feminist criticism. The period covered by the title's designation "modern" is roughly 1900 to 1985, with a couple of pre-1900 items and a few post-1985 items. The emphasis falls on the last several decades, but many books and essays from the earlier part of the century appear as well, some because they have never been superseded and some because it is valuable for students to have a sense of changing schools of criticism. Those who understand that every decade or so of critical time has its own flavour, its own critical fashions and assumptions, are less likely to accept present critical judgments as the "truth" or the last word about Shakespeare.

Until the appearance in 1986 of Larry Champion's *The Essential Shakespeare,* scholars wanting a selective bibliography covering the whole Shakespeare canon had to reach back to Bevington's Goldentree bibliography of 1978 or the McManaway/Roberts bibliography of 1975; Champion's useful bibliography does much to bring the student up to date, but it has serious limitations. Most noticeably, literary theory is but wanly represented in Champion's selection, possibly because Champion is unsympathetic to some theoretical approaches, possibly because it is only in the last several years that literary theory has taken hold firmly in Shakespeare studies, and Champion's cut-off date seems to be 1984. At any rate, one rues the absence from *The Essential Shakespeare* of stimulating new collections like Parker and Hartman's *Shakespeare and the Question of Theory* (1985) or Drakakis's *Alternative Shakespeares* (1985). Important work (at least, work that I consider important) by such critics as Stephen Orgel, Barbara Freedman, Meredith Skura, Lisa Jardine, Walter Cohen, Adena Rosmarin, and Karen Newman is similarly absent. The new historicism, undoubtedly the reigning critical movement in Shakespeare studies at the present time, is so slighted in *The Essential Shakespeare* that the name of its founder, Stephen Greenblatt, does not appear in Champion's index, though Greenblatt's influential book *Renaissance Self-Fashioning* appeared in 1980. And feminist criticism of Shakespeare, another major strain in current criticism, is very poorly represented in Champion's bibliography, a lack especially striking in the criticism selected for *The Rape of Lucrece* and *The Taming of the Shrew.* Any selective bibliography reflects the tastes of its compiler; my tastes are quite different from Champion's, and a student armed with both his bibliography and mine will have a better chance of lighting upon criticism useful to her or him than will a student armed with either bibliography alone.

This bibliography focuses on criticism, excluding for the most part studies which are purely textual or which establish or dispute about sources or dates. No lists of editions are included. The rationale for this is that the bibliography is designed primarily to serve the teaching situation: most instructors have in mind the edition of Shakespeare they want to use, and assign it to students, who have no choice and therefore pay no attention to a section of a bibliography devoted to editions; and once the student has a good edition, the edition itself will give her or him lots of information on dating, sources, and the text. (One exception is that I've included full references to the recent debate over *King Lear*'s text, since the debate raises issues central to the play's interpretation and is too recent to have been incorporated in most major editions.) Only works in English have been included, and I have tried to limit the selection to books available in most university and college libraries, at least through inter-library loan. No unpublished dissertations are listed. This bibliography is not designed for Ph.D. students doing a dissertation on Shakespeare: it is a nuts-and-bolts bibliography for people who want to get a handle on the criticism.

This is a "user-friendly" bibliography that tries to avoid features that drive so many bibliography users to distraction. With the exception of *SQ* for *Shakespeare Quarterly* and of *PMLA,* the bibliography uses no abbreviations for journals: every one is spelled out every time, so that the user is spared the irritation of constantly turning back to the abbreviations page in the front of most bibliographies—a great time-waster and very frustrating if one is already trying to hold the bibliography in one hand and operate an on-line terminal or make notes on an index card with the other. For the same reasons, users should appreciate the lack of irritating cross-references: an entry on an article in a *Festschrift* will not send the user to a list of *Festschriften*, and an entry on an article dealing with *Twelfth Night* and *As You Like It* will not send the user to the *Twelfth Night* section if s/he first looked under *As You Like It:* every entry is repeated in full, every time. The plays are listed in the most easily accessible order, that is, simple alphabetical order; a reader looking for *Troilus and Cressida* will not have to second-guess the compiler as to whether the play is grouped with the comedies or the tragedies or the satires, but can simply turn to "T"; no need to puzzle out whether *The Winter's Tale* comes under *Comedy* or *Romance:* one simply turns to "W." And the index lists *full* names of critics wherever possible, to spare the reader the time-wasting annoyance of looking through Charles Lawrence Barber, Catherine Lynn Barber, and twenty-five other Barbers before arriving at "the real" C.L. Barber in card catalogue, microfiche, or on-line entry.

The bibliography is not annotated: to annotate it properly would quadruple its length and frustrate one of its aims—to provide a portable, inexpensive working bibliography which a Shakespeare student might carry about all year. I am not as great an admirer of annotation as many scholars are: even the best annotations, by their very nature, distort a critical argument in the same way that even the best plot summary distorts a work of fiction. And omitting annotation permitted me to include many more items than I could otherwise have included—a total of 2460 items in 226 pages. If annotations are needed, a student can turn to Champion's bibliography or to one of the good single-play annotated bibliographies presently being published; but their price places them beyond the reach of most students and most teachers—they will be available in libraries for those doing more detailed and specialized work. And should the shrinking book budgets of so many libraries preclude the acquisition of the pricier bibliographies, the modest price of *Shakespeare: A Selective Bibliography* should keep it within range for all libraries; I strongly believe that Shakespeare of all authors should be kept accessible to libraries and individual book-buyers however remote, however impoverished.

As a university teacher of Shakespeare, one of my favorite opening assignments in a senior Shakespeare course is to send students out to find two critics whose interpretations of some facet of Shakespeare are in conflict with each other, to try to determine the grounds of the disagreement, and by close reference to the play to judge in favor of one or the other or to offer a new interpretation that will give a better account of the question than that of either critic. Such an assignment gets students into the library, gives them that first shock encounter with the massiveness of Shakespeare criticism, sets them thinking about the theoretical underpinnings of thought that make one critic's argument incompatible with another's, and gives students their first inkling of a central fact about Shakespeare: that his plays and poems encode incompatible value systems within a single work, a fact which may render mutually-exclusive interpretations almost equally valid. I have tried to make this bibliography creatively disjunctive enough to be hospitable to such assignments, by including for every genre and every play critics whose violent conflict with each other could only have been occasioned by Shakespeare.

Linda Woodbridge
University of Alberta
October 1987

ABBREVIATIONS FOR THE TITLES
OF SHAKESPEARE'S WORKS

Ado	*Much Ado About Nothing*
Ant	*Antony and Cleopatra*
AWW	*All's Well That Ends Well*
AYL	*As You Like It*
Cor	*Coriolanus*
Cym	*Cymbeline*
Err	*The Comedy of Errors*
Ham	*Hamlet*
1H4	*Henry IV, Part 1*
2H4	*Henry IV, Part 2*
1&2H4	*Henry IV, Parts 1 & 2*
H5	*Henry V*
1H6	*Henry VI, Part 1*
2H6	*Henry VI, Part 2*
3H6	*Henry VI, Part 3*
H8	*Henry VIII*
JC	*Julius Caesar*
Jn	*King John*
LLL	*Love's Labor's Lost*
Lr	*King Lear*
Luc	*The Rape of Lucrece*
Mac	*Macbeth*

MM	*Measure for Measure*
MND	*A Midsummer Night's Dream*
MV	*The Merchant of Venice*
Oth	*Othello*
Per	*Pericles*
PhT	*The Phoenix and the Turtle*
R2	*Richard II*
R3	*Richard III*
Rom	*Romeo and Juliet*
Shr	*The Taming of the Shrew*
Son	*Sonnets*
TGV	*The Two Gentlemen of Verona*
Tim	*Timon of Athens*
Tit	*Titus Andronicus*
TN	*Twelfth Night*
TNK	*The Two Noble Kinsmen*
Tmp	*The Tempest*
Tro	*Troilus and Cressida*
Ven	*Venus and Adonis*
Wiv	*The Merry Wives of Windsor*
WT	*The Winter's Tale*

Other Abbreviations

| *SQ* | *Shakespeare Quarterly* |
| *PMLA* | *Publications of the Modern Language Association of America* |

I. Bibliography

1

Berman, Ronald, comp. *A Reader's Guide to Shakespeare's Plays: A Discursive Bibliography.* New York: Scott, Foresman. 1973. Revised edition.

2

Bevington, David, comp. *Shakespeare (Goldentree Bibliographies).* Arlington Heights, Illinois: AHM. 1978.

3

Birmingham Public Libraries. *A Shakespeare Bibliography: The Catalogue of the Birmingham Shakespeare Library.* London: Mansell. 1971. 7 vols.

4

Champion, Larry S. *The Essential Shakespeare: An Annotated Bibliography of Major Modern Studies.* Boston: Hall. 1986.

5

Elton, W.R., comp. *Shakespeare's World: Renaissance Intellectual Contexts: A Selective, Annotated Guide, 1966-71.* New York and London: Garland. 1979.

6

McManaway, James G., and Roberts, Jeanne Addison, comps. *A Selective Bibliography of Shakespeare.* Charlottesville, Virginia: University Press of Virginia, for Folger Shakespeare Library. 1975.

7

McRoberts, Paul, comp. *Shakespeare and the Medieval Tradition: An Annotated Bibliography of Shakespearean Works from 1900-1980.* New York and London: Garland. 1985.

Shakespeare Quarterly. Annual annotated bibliography.

8

9

Shakespeare Survey. Annual description/review of the year's work in Shake-speare studies.

10

Smith, Gordon Ross, comp. *A Classified Shakespeare Bibliography 1936-58.* University Park, Pennsylvania: Pennsylvania State University Press. 1963.

11

Wells, Stanley, comp. *Shakespeare: Select Bibliographical Guides.* London: Oxford University Press. 1973.

See also bibliographies listed under individual plays.

II. General Studies

12

Allman, Eileen Jorge. *Player-King and Adversary: Two Faces of Play in Shakespeare.* Baton Rouge and London: Louisiana State University Press. 1980.

13

Altman, Joel B. *The Tudor Play of Mind: Rhetorical Inquiry and the Development of Elizabethan Drama.* Berkeley and Los Angeles: University of California Press. 1978.

14

Andrews, John F., ed. *William Shakespeare: His World, His Work, His Influence.* New York: Scribner. 1985. 3 vols.

15

Baldwin, T.W. *William Shakspere's Small Latine and Lesse Greeke.* Urbana: University of Illinois Press. 1944. 2 vols.

16

Bamber, Linda. *Comic Women, Tragic Men: A Study of Gender and Genre in Shakespeare.* Stanford: Stanford University Press. 1982.

17

Barish, Jonas. *The Antitheatrical Prejudice.* Berkeley and Los Angeles: University of California Press. 1981.

18

Bartlett, John. *A New and Complete Concordance to Shakespeare.* London: Macmillan. 1894.

19

Beckerman, Bernard. "Shakespeare Closing." *Kenyon Review.* 1985. 7: 79-95.

20

Bentley, Gerald Eades. *The Profession of Player in Shakespeare's Time, 1590-1642.* Princeton: Princeton University Press. 1984.

21

Berggren, Paula S. "'Imitari Is Nothing': A Shakespearean Complex Word." *Texas Studies in Literature and Language.* 1984. 26: 94-127.

22

Berry, Francis. "Pronoun and Verb in Shakespeare." *Poets' Grammar: Person, Time, and Mood in Poetry.* Westport, Conn.: Greenwood. 1974. 36-79.

23

Berry, Ralph. *Shakespeare and the Awareness of the Audience.* New York: St. Martin; London and Basingstoke: Macmillan. 1985.

24

Bethell, S.L. *Shakespeare and the Popular Dramatic Tradition.* Durham, N.C.: Duke University Press. 1944.

25

Bevington, David. *Action Is Eloquence: Shakespeare's Language of Gesture.* Cambridge, Massachusetts and London: Harvard University Press. 1984.

26

Bilton, Peter. "Shakespeare Criticism and the 'Choric Character'." *English Studies.* 1969. 50: 254-60.

27

Blake, N.F. *Shakespeare's Language: An Introduction.* New York: St. Martin's. 1983.

3

28

Bligh, John. "Shakespearean Character Study to 1800." *Shakespeare Survey.*
    1984. 36: 141-53.

29

Bristol, Michael D. *Carnival and Theater: Plebeian Culture and the Structure
    of Authority in Renaissance England.* New York and London: Methuen.
    1985.

30

Brown, John Russell. *Shakespeare's Plays in Performance.* London: Arnold.
    1966.

31

Bullough, Geoffrey. *Narrative and Dramatic Sources of Shakespeare.*
    London: Routledge and Kegan Paul; New York: Columbia University
    Press. 1957-75. 8 vols.

32

Burckhardt, Sigurd. *Shakespeare's Meanings.* Princeton: Princeton Univer-
    sity Press. 1968.

33

Bush, Douglas. "Classical Myth in Shakespeare's Plays." *Elizabethan and
    Jacobean Studies Presented to Frank Percy Wilson.* Davis, Herbert, and
    Gardner, Helen, eds. Oxford: Clarendon. 1959. 65-85.

34

Calderwood, James. *Shakespearean Metadrama.* Minneapolis: University of
    Minnesota Press. 1971.

35

Campbell, Oscar James. *Shakespeare's Satire.* Oxford: Oxford University
    Press. 1943.

36

Campbell, Oscar James, and Quinn, Edward G., eds. *The Reader's Encyclo-
    pedia of Shakespeare.* New York: Crowell. 1966.

37

Carlisle, Carol Jones. *Shakespeare from the Greenroom: Actors' Criticisms of
    Four Major Tragedies.* Chapel Hill: University of North Carolina Press.
    1969.

38

Chambers, E.K. *The Elizabethan Stage.* Oxford: Clarendon. 1923. 4 vols.
    Index to this volume, compiled by Beatrice White, Oxford: Clarendon,

1934.

39

Chambers, E.K. *William Shakespeare: A Study of Facts and Problems.*
    Oxford: Oxford University Press. 1930. 2 vols.

40

Chute, Marchette. *Shakespeare of London.* New York: Dutton. 1949.

41

Clemen, Wolfgang. *The Development of Shakespeare's Imagery.* Cambridge,
    Massachusetts: Harvard University Press; London: Methuen. 1951. Revised
    and augmented translation of *Shakespeares Bilder*, Bonn: Hanstein, 1936.

42

Clemen, Wolfgang. *English Tragedy Before Shakespeare.* Dorsch, T.S.,
    trans. London: Methuen. 1961. First published in German, 1955.

43

Cohen, Walter. *Drama of a Nation: Public Theatre in Renaissance England
    and Spain.* Ithaca and London: Cornell University Press. 1985.

44

Cook, Ann Jennalie. *The Privileged Playgoers of Shakespeare's London:
    1576-1642.* Princeton: Princeton University Press. 1981.

45

Cooke, Katharine. *A.C. Bradley and His Influence in Twentieth-Century
    Shakespeare Criticism.* Oxford: Clarendon. 1972.

46

Danby, John F. *Poets on Fortune's Hill: Studies in Sidney, Shakespeare,
    Beaumont and Fletcher.* London: Faber and Faber. 1952. Reprinted as
    Elizabethan and Jacobean Poets, 1964.

47

Dash, Irene. *Wooing, Wedding, and Power: Women in Shakespeare's Plays.*
    New York: Columbia University Press. 1981.

48

Dawson, Anthony B. *Indirections: Shakespeare and the Art of Illusion.*
    Toronto, Buffalo, and London: University of Toronto Press. 1978.

49

Dent, R.W. *Shakespeare's Proverbial Language: An Index.* Berkeley, Los
    Angeles, and London: University of California Press. 1981.

50

Dollimore, Jonathan. "Shakespeare, Cultural Materialism and the New
Historicism." *Political Shakespeare.* Dollimore, Jonathan, and Sinfield,
Alan, eds. Manchester: Manchester University Press. 1985. 2-17.

51

Donaldson, E. Talbot. *The Swan at the Well: Shakespeare Reading Chaucer.*
New Haven: Yale University Press. 1985.

52

Driscoll, James P. *Identity in Shakespearean Drama.* Lewisburg: Bucknell
University Press; London: Associated University Presses. 1983.

53

Eagleton, Terence. *Shakespeare and Society.* London: Chatto and Windus.
1967.

54

Eagleton, Terence. *William Shakespeare.* Oxford and New York: Blackwell.
1986.

55

Edens, Walter, et al, eds. *Teaching Shakespeare.* Princeton and Guildford,
Surrey: Princeton University Press. 1977.

56

Edwards, Paul C. "Elocution and Shakespeare: An Episode in the History of
Literary Taste." *SQ.* 1984. 35: 305-14.

57

Edwards, Philip. *Shakspeare and the Confines of Art.* London: Methuen;
New York: Barnes and Noble. 1968.

58

Elam, Keir. "'Understand Me by My Signs': On Shakespeare's Semiotics."
New Theatre Quarterly. 1985. 1: 84-96.

59

Erickson, Peter. *Patriarchal Structures in Shakespeare's Drama.* Berkeley,
Los Angeles, and London: University of California Press. 1985.

60

Erickson, Peter. "Shakespeare and the 'Author-Function'." *Shakespeare's
"Rough Magic": Renaissance Essays in Honor of C.L. Barber.* Erickson,
Peter, and Kahn, Coppélia, eds. Newark: University of Delaware Press;
London and Toronto: Associated University Presses. 1985. 245-55.

6

61

Evans, Malcolm. *Signifying Nothing: Truth's True Contents in Shakespeare's Text.* Brighton: Harvester; Athens: University of Georgia Press. 1986.

62

Fiedler, Leslie. *The Stranger in Shakespeare.* New York: Stein and Day. 1972.

63

Frazier, Harriet C. "'Like a Liar Gone to Burning Hell': Shakespeare and Dying Declarations." *Comparative Drama.* 1985. 19: 166-80.

64

French, Marilyn. *Shakespeare's Division of Experience.* New York: Summit Books, 1981.

65

Friesner, Donald Neil. "William Shakespeare, Conservative." *SQ.* 1969. 20: 165-78.

66

Garber, Marjorie. *Coming of Age in Shakespeare.* London and New York: Methuen. 1981.

67

Garber, Marjorie. "'The Rest is Silence': Ineffability and the 'Unscene' in Shakespeare's Plays." *Ineffability: Naming the Unnamable from Dante to Beckett.* Hawkins, Peter S., and Howland, Anne, eds. New York: AMS. 1984. 35-50.

68

Goldberg, Jonathan. "Shakespearean Inscriptions: The Voicing of Power." *Shakespeare and the Question of Theory.* Parker, Patricia, and Hartman, Geoffrey, eds. New York and London: Methuen. 1985. 116-37.

69

Goldman, Michael. *Shakespeare and the Energies of Drama.* Princeton: Princeton University Press. 1972.

70

Gordon, George. *Shakespeare's English.* Oxford: Clarendon. 1928.

71

Granville-Barker, Harley. *Prefaces to Shakespeare.* London: Sidgwick and Jackson. 1927-48. 6 vols.

7

72

Greenblatt, Stephen. "Invisible Bullets: Renaissance Authority and its Subversion." *Glyph (Johns Hopkins).* 1981. 8: 40-61.

73

Greenblatt, Stephen. "Murdering Peasants: Status, Genre, and the Representation of Rebellion." *Representations.* Feb., 1983. 1 (i): 1-29.

74

Greenblatt, Stephen. *Renaissance Self-Fashioning: From More to Shakespeare.* Chicago and London: University of Chicago Press. 1980.

75

Gurr, Andrew. *The Shakespearean Stage, 1574-1642.* Cambridge and New York: Cambridge University Press. 1970. Second edition, 1980.

76

Hapgood, Robert. "Shakespeare and the Ritualists." *Shakespeare Survey.* 1962. 15: 111-24.

77

Harbage, Alfred, ed. *Annals of English Drama, 975-1700.* Philadelphia: University of Pennsylvania Press. 1964. Revised by S. Schoenbaum.

78

Harbage, Alfred. *Conceptions of Shakespeare.* Cambridge: Harvard University Press; London: Oxford University Press. 1966.

79

Harbage, Alfred. *Shakespeare and the Rival Traditions.* New York: Macmillan. 1952.

80

Harbage, Alfred. *Shakespeare's Audience.* New York and London: Columbia University Press. 1941.

81

Harbage, Alfred. *William Shakespeare: A Reader's Guide.* New York: Farrar, Straus; Toronto: Ambassador. 1963.

82

Harris, Laurie Lanzen, and Scott, Mark W., eds. *Shakespearean Criticism: Excerpts from the Criticism of William Shakespeare's Plays and Poetry, from the First Published Appraisals to Current Evaluations.* Vol. 1. Detroit: Gale. 1984; Vol. 2. New York: Gale. 1985.

8

83

Hartwig, Joan. *Shakespeare's Analogical Scene.* Lincoln and London: University of Nebraska Press. 1983.

84

Hattaway, Michael. *Elizabethan Popular Theatre: Plays in Performance.* London and Boston: Routledge and Kegan Paul. 1982.

85

Hawkes, Terence. "Swisser-Swatter: Making a Man of English Letters." *Alternative Shakespeares.* Drakakis, John, ed. London and New York: Methuen. 1985. 26-46.

86

Hawkins, Harriett. *The Devil's Party: Critical Counter-Interpretations of Shakespearian Drama.* Oxford: Clarendon. 1985.

87

Henslowe, Philip. *Henslowe's Diary.* Foakes, R.A., and Rickert, R.T., eds. Cambridge: Cambridge University Press. 1961.

88

Hibbard, G.R. *The Making of Shakespeare's Dramatic Poetry.* Toronto: University of Toronto Press. 1986.

89

Hirsh, James E. *The Structure of Shakespearean Scenes.* New Haven and London: Yale University Press. 1981.

90

Holland, Norman. *Psychoanalysis and Shakespeare.* New York, Toronto, and London: McGraw-Hill. 1964.

91

Honigmann, E.A.J. *Shakespeare's Impact on His Contemporaries.* Totowa, N.J.: Barnes and Noble; London: Macmillan. 1982.

92

Howard, Jean E. *Shakespeare's Art of Orchestration.* Urbana and Chicago: University of Illinois Press. 1984.

93

Hulme, Hilda. *Explorations in Shakespeare's Language.* London: Longmans, Green. 1962. New York: Barnes and Noble. 1963.

94

Jardine, Lisa. *Still Harping on Daughters: Women and Drama in the Age of Shakespeare.* Brighton: Harvester; Totowa, N.J.: Barnes and Noble. 1983.

95

Jones, Emrys. *Scenic Form in Shakespeare.* Oxford: Clarendon. 1971.

96

Jorgens, Jack L. *Shakespeare on Film.* Bloomington, Indiana and London: Indiana University Press. 1977.

97

Kahn, Coppélia. *Man's Estate: Masculine Identity in Shakespeare.* Berkeley: University of California Press. 1981.

98

Kastan, David Scott. *Shakespeare and the Shapes of Time.* Hanover, N.H.: University Press of New England. 1982.

99

Kavanagh, James H. "Shakespeare in Ideology." *Alternative Shakespeares.* Drakakis, John, ed. London and New York: Methuen. 1985. 144-65.

100

Kay, Dennis. "'To Hear the Rest Untold': Shakespeare's Postponed Endings." *Renaissance Quarterly.* 1984. 37: 207-27.

101

Kirschbaum, Leo. *Character and Characterization in Shakespeare.* Detroit: Wayne State University Press. 1962.

102

Knight, G. Wilson. *The Shakespearian Tempest.* Oxford: Oxford University Press. 1932.

103

Knights, L.C. *How Many Children Had Lady Macbeth?* Cambridge: Minority Press. 1933. Reprinted in Knights' *Explorations.* London: Chatto and Windus, 1946.

104

Langbaum, Robert. "Character Versus Action in Shakespeare." *SQ.* 1957. 8: 57-69.

105

Lenz, Carolyn Ruth Swift, et al, eds. *The Woman's Part: Feminist Literary Criticism of Shakespeare.* Urbana, Chicago, and London: University of Illinois Press. 1980.

106

Levin, Richard L. *New Readings vs. Old Plays: Recent Trends in the Reinterpretation of English Renaissance Drama.* Chicago and London: University of Chicago Press. 1979.

107

Longhurst, Derek. "'Not for All Time, But for An Age': An Approach to Shakespeare Studies." *Re-Reading English*. Widdowson, Peter, ed. London and New York: Methuen. 1982. 150-63.

108

Mahood, M.M. *Shakespeare's Wordplay*. London: Methuen. 1957; New York: Barnes and Noble. 1965.

109

Marienstras, Richard. *New Perspectives on the Shakespearean World*. Lloyd, Janet, trans. Cambridge, New York, etc.: Cambridge University Press. 1985.

110

McGuire, Philip C. *Speechless Dialect: Shakespeare's Open Silences*. Berkeley and London: University of California Press. 1985.

111

Meagher, John C. "Economy and Recognition: Thirteen Shakespearean Puzzles." *SQ*. 1984. 35: 7-21.

112

Miola, Robert S. *Shakespeare's Rome*. Cambridge, New York, etc.: Cambridge University Press. 1983.

113

Miriam Joseph, Sister. *Shakespeare's Use of the Arts of Language*. New York: Columbia University Press, 1947. Abbreviated version, *Rhetoric in Shakespeare's Time*. New York: Harcourt, Brace, and World. 1962.

114

Muir, Kenneth. "Fifty Years of Shakespearean Criticism: 1900-1950." *Shakespeare Survey*. 1951. 4: 1-25.

115

Muir, Kenneth. *Shakespeare: Contrasts and Controversies*. Brighton: Harvester; Norman: University of Oklahoma Press. 1985.

116

Muir, Kenneth. *The Sources of Shakespeare's Plays*. London: Methuen. 1977; New Haven: Yale University Press. 1978.

117

Murray, John Tucker. *English Dramatic Companies, 1558-1642*. London: Constable; Boston: Houghton Mifflin. 1910. 2 vols.

11

118

Neely, Carol Thomas. *Broken Nuptials in Shakespeare's Plays.* New Haven and London: Yale University Press. 1985.

119

Norris, Christopher. "Post-structuralist Shakespeare: Text and Ideology." *Alternative Shakespeares.* Drakakis, John, ed. London and New York: Methuen. 1985. 47-66.

120

Novy, Marianne. *Love's Argument: Gender Relations in Shakespeare.* Chapel Hill: University of North Carolina Press. 1984.

121

Orgel, Stephen. "Shakespeare and the Kinds of Drama." *Critical Inquiry.* 1979. 6: 107-23.

122

Orrell, John. *The Quest for Shakespeare's Globe.* Cambridge, New York, etc.: Cambridge University Press. 1983.

123

Palmer, John. *Political and Comic Characters of Shakespeare.* London: Macmillan. 1962. (Two series of essays, originally published separately.)

124

Parker, Patricia, and Hartman, Geoffrey H., eds. *Shakespeare and the Question of Theory.* New York: Methuen. 1985.

125

Partridge, Eric. *Shakespeare's Bawdy.* London: Routledge and Kegan Paul. 1947. Revised edition, 1955. Revised and enlarged edition, 1968.

126

Rabkin, Norman. *Approaches to Shakespeare.* New York, Toronto, and London: McGraw-Hill. 1964.

127

Rabkin, Norman. *Shakespeare and the Common Understanding.* New York: Free Press. 1967.

128

Righter, Anne. *Shakespeare and the Idea of the Play.* London: Chatto and Windus. 1962.

129

Rose, Mark. *Shakespearean Design.* Cambridge, Massachusetts: Harvard University Press. 1972.

130

Rossiter, A.P. *Angel with Horns*. Storey, Graham, ed. New York: Theatre
  Arts Books; London: Longmans, Green. 1961.

131

Schoenbaum, Samuel. *Shakespeare and Others*. Washington, D.C.: Folger
  Shakespeare Library; Cranbury, N.J.: Associated University Presses;
  London: Scolar. 1985.

132

Schoenbaum, Samuel. "Shakespeare the Ignoramus." *The Drama of the Renaissance*. Blistein, Elmer M., ed. Providence, R.I.: Brown University
  Press. 1970. 154-64.

133

Schoenbaum, Samuel. *William Shakespeare: A Documentary Life*. New
  York: Oxford University Press. 1975.

134

Schücking, Levin L. *Character Problems in Shakespeare's Plays*. London:
  Harrap; New York: Holt. 1922. First published in German, 1919.

135

Serpieri, Alessandro. "Reading the Signs: Towards a Semiotics of Shakespearean Drama. Trans. Elam, Keir." *Alternative Shakespeares*. Drakakis,
  John, ed. London and New York: Methuen. 1985. 119-43.

136

Shaw, George Bernard. *Shaw on Shakespeare*. Wilson, Edwin, ed. New
  York: Dutton. 1961.

137

Sinfield, Alan. "Give An Account of Shakespeare and Education, Showing
  Why You Think They Are Effective and What You Have Appreciated
  About Them; Support Your Comments With Precise References." *Political
  Shakespeare*. Dollimore, Jonathan, and Sinfield, Alan, eds. Manchester:
  Manchester University Press. 1985.

138

Shakespeare Quarterly. 35 (5). Special issue on teaching Shakespeare. 1984.

139

Skura, Meredith. "Shakespeare's Psychology: Characterization in Shakespeare." *William Shakespeare: His World, His Work, His Influence*.
  Andrews, John F., ed. 3 vols. Vol. 2, 571-87.

13

140

Somerset, J.A.B. "Shakespeare's Great Stage of Fools, 1599-1607." *Mirror up to Shakespeare: Essays in Honour of G.R. Hibbard.* Gray, J.C., ed. Toronto, Buffalo, and London: University of Toronto Press. 1984. 68-81.

141

Soyinka, Wole. "Shakespeare and the Living Dramatist." *Shakespeare Survey.* 1983. 36: 1-10.

142

Spencer, Theodore. *Shakespeare and the Nature of Man.* New York: Macmillan. 1942.

143

Spevack, Marvin. *A Complete and Systematic Concordance to the Works of Shakespeare.* Hildesheim: G. Olms. 1968-80. 9 vols.

144

Spevack, Marvin. *The Harvard Concordance to Shakespeare.* Cambridge: Belknap Press of Harvard University Press. 1969.

145

Spivack, Bernard. *Shakespeare and the Allegory of Evil.* New York and London: Columbia University Press. 1958.

146

Sprague, Arthur Colby. "Shakespeare's Unnecessary Characters." *Shakespeare Survey.* 1967. 20: 75-82.

147

Spurgeon, Caroline F.E. *Shakespeare's Imagery and What It Tells Us.* Cambridge: Cambridge University Press; New York: Macmillan. 1935.

148

Stewart, J.I.M. *Character and Motive in Shakespeare.* London, New York, and Toronto: Longmans, Green. 1949.

149

Stoll, E.E. *Shakespeare Studies, Historical and Comparative in Method.* New York: Macmillan. 1927.

150

Summers, Joseph H. *Dreams of Love and Power: On Shakespeare's Plays.* Oxford: Clarendon; London and New York: Oxford University Press. 1984.

14

151

Taylor, Gary. *To Analyze Delight: A Hedonist Criticism of Shakespeare.* Newark: University of Delaware Press. 1985. English title: *Moment by Moment By Shakespeare.* London: Macmillan. 1985.

152

Taylor, Mark. *Shakespeare's Darker Purpose: A Question of Incest.* New York: AMS Press. 1982.

153

Tennenhouse, Leonard. *Power on Display: The Politics of Shakespeare's Genres.* London: Methuen. 1986.

154

Thomson, Peter. *Shakespeare's Theatre.* London and Boston: Routledge and Kegan Paul. 1983.

155

Traversi, Derek. *An Approach to Shakespeare: "1H6" to "TN".* London: Sands. 1938. Revised, 1957. Third revised and enlarged edition, 2 vols., London: Hollis and Carter, 1968.

156

Van Den Berg, Kent. *Playhouse and Cosmos: Shakespearean Theatre as Metaphor.* Newark: University of Delaware Press. 1985.

157

Vickers, Brian. *The Artistry of Shakespeare's Prose.* London: Methuen; New York: Barnes and Noble. 1968.

158

Vickers, Brian, ed. *Shakespeare: The Critical Heritage.* London and Boston: Routledge and Kegan Paul. 1974-81. 6 vols.

159

Watson, Robert N. *Shakespeare and the Hazards of Ambition.* Cambridge and London: Harvard University Press. 1984.

160

Weimann, Robert. *Shakespeare and the Popular Tradition in the Theater.* Schwartz, Robert, ed. Baltimore and London: Johns Hopkins University Press. 1978. First published in German, 1967.

161

Wells, Stanley. "Experiencing Shakespeare." *Caliban.* 1984. 21: 211-26.

162

Wells, Stanley. *Shakespeare: An Illustrated Dictionary.* London: Kaye and Ward; New York: Oxford University Press. 1978.

163

Whigham, Frank. *Ambition and Privilege: The Social Tropes of Elizabethan Courtesy Theory.* Berkeley and London: University of California Press. 1984.

164

Whitaker, Virgil K. *Shakespeare's Use of Learning.* San Marino, California: Huntington Library Press. 1953.

165

Woodbridge, Linda. *Women and the English Renaissance.* Urbana and Chicago: University of Illinois Press; Brighton: Harvester. 1984.

166

Wright, George T. "The Play of Phrase and Line in Shakespeare's Iambic Pentameter." *SQ.* 1983. 34: 147-58.

III. Comedy: General Studies

167

Adelman, Janet. "Male Bonding in Shakespeare's Comedies." *Shakespeare's "Rough Magic": Renaissance Essays in Honor of C.L. Barber.* Erickson, Peter, and Kahn, Coppélia, eds. Newark: University of Delaware Press; London and Toronto: Associated University Presses. 1985. 73-103.

168

Barber, C.L. *Shakespeare's Festive Comedy.* Princeton: Princeton University Press. 1959.

169

Barton, Anne. "Shakespeare and Jonson." *Shakespeare, Man of the Theater.* Muir, K. et al, eds. Associated University Presses. 1983. 155-72.

170

Belsey, Catherine. "Disrupting Sexual Difference: Meaning and Gender in the Comedies." *Alternative Shakespeares.* Drakakis, John, ed. London and New York: Methuen. 1985. 166-90.

171

Bennett, Kenneth C. "The Affective Aspect of Comedy." *Genre.* 1981. 14: 191-205.

172

Berry, Edward. *Shakespeare's Comic Rites*. Cambridge: Cambridge University Press. 1984.

173

Berry, Ralph. *Shakespeare's Comedies: Explorations in Form*. Princeton: Princeton University Press. 1972.

174

Bradbury, Malcolm, and Palmer, David. *Shakespearian Comedy*. London: Arnold. 1972. Stratford-upon-Avon Studies 14.

175

Brown, John Russell. *Shakespeare and His Comedies*. London: Methuen. 1957.

176

Carroll, William C. *The Metamorphoses of Shakespearean Comedy*. Princeton and Guildford, Surrey: Princeton University Press. 1985.

177

Champion, Larry S. *The Evolution of Shakespeare's Comedies*. Cambridge, Massachusetts: Harvard University Press. 1970.

178

Charlton, H.B. *Shakespearian Comedy*. London: Methuen. 1938.

179

Cole, Douglas. "Shakespearean Pastoral: Review Article." *Renaissance Drama*. 1972. 5: 213-24.

180

Coulter, Cornelia C. "The Plautine Tradition in Shakespeare." *Journal of English and Germanic Philology*. 1919. 18: 66-83.

181

Coursen, H.R. "Shakespearean Comedy and the Moral Limits of Art." *Christianity and Literature*. 1977. 26 (iv): 4-12.

182

Elam, Keir. *Shakespeare's Universe of Discourse: Language-Games in the Comedies*. Cambridge, New York, etc.: Cambridge University Press. 1984.

183

Evans, Bertrand. *Shakespeare's Comedies*. Oxford: Clarendon. 1960.

184

Evans, Malcolm. "Deconstructing Shakespeare's Comedies." *Alternative Shakespeares*. Drakakis, John, ed. London and New York: Methuen. 1985.

17

67-94.

185

Farnham, Willard. *The Shakespearean Grotesque: Its Genesis and Transformations.* Oxford: Clarendon. 1971.

186

Fiedler, Leslie A. "Shakespeare's Commodity-Comedy: A Meditation on the Preface to the 1609 Quarto of *Tro.*" *Shakespeare's "Rough Magic": Renaissance Essays in Honor of C.L. Barber.* Erickson, Peter, and Kahn, Coppélia, eds. Newark: University of Delaware Press; London and Toronto: Associated University Presses. 1985. 50-60.

187

Frye, Northrop. *Anatomy of Criticism.* Princeton: Princeton University Press. 1957.

188

Frye, Northrop. "Characterization in Shakespearean Comedy." *SQ.* 1953. 4: 271-7.

189

Frye, Northrop. *A Natural Perspective: The Development of Shakespearean Comedy and Romance.* New York: Columbia University Press. 1965.

190

Garber, Marjorie. "'Wild Laughter in the Throat of Death': Darker Purposes in Shakespearean Comedy." *New York Literary Forum.* 1980. 5-6: 121-6.

191

Gordon, George. *Shakespearean Comedy and Other Studies.* Oxford: Oxford University Press; London: Milford. 1944.

192

Grene, Nicholas. *Shakespeare, Jonson, Molière: the Comic Contract.* London: Macmillan; Totowa, N.J.: Barnes and Noble. 1980.

193

Hawkins, Sherman. "The Two Worlds of Shakespearean Comedy." *Shakespeare Studies.* 1967. 3: 62-80.

194

Hunter, Robert Grams. *Shakespeare and the Comedy of Forgiveness.* New York and London: Columbia University Press. 1965.

195

Kantak, V.Y. "An Approach to Shakespearian Comedy." *Shakespeare Survey.* 1969. 22: 7-13.

196

Kermode, Frank. "The Mature Comedies." *Early Shakespeare.* Brown, John Russell, and Harris, Bernard, eds. London: E. Arnold. 1961. 211-27. Stratford-upon-Avon Studies 3.

197

Krieger, Elliott R. *A Marxist Study of Shakespeare's Comedies.* London: Macmillan; New York: Barnes and Noble. 1979.

198

Lerner, Laurence, ed. *Shakespeare's Comedies: An Anthology of Modern Criticism.* Harmondsworth: Penguin. 1967.

199

Levin, Richard A. *Love and Society in Shakespearean Comedy: A Study of Dramatic Form and Content.* Newark: University of Delaware Press; London and Toronto: Associated University Presses. 1985.

200

MacCary, W. Thomas. *Friends and Lovers: The Phenomenology of Desire in Shakespearean Comedy.* New York: Columbia University Press. 1985.

201

Martz, William J. *Shakespeare's Universe of Comedy.* London: Methuen, 1970; New York: David Lewis, 1971.

202

McFarland, Thomas. *Shakespeare's Pastoral Comedy.* Chapel Hill: University of North Carolina Press. 1972.

203

Merrill, Robert. "The Generic Approach in Recent Criticism of Shakespeare's Comedies and Romances: A Review-Essay." *Texas Studies in Literature and Language.* 1978. 20: 474-87.

204

Muir, Kenneth. *Shakespeare's Comic Sequence.* Liverpool: Liverpool University Press; New York: Barnes and Noble. 1979.

205

Nevo, Ruth. *Comic Transformations in Shakespeare.* London and New York: Methuen. 1980.

19

206

Newman, Karen. *Shakespeare's Rhetoric of Comic Character*. London and
   New York: Methuen. 1985.

207

Novy, Marianne L. "'And You Smile Not, He's Gagged': Mutuality in
   Shakespearean Comedy." *Philological Quarterly*. 1976. 55: 178-94.

208

Ornstein, Robert. *Shakespeare's Comedies: From Roman Farce to Romantic
   Mystery*. Newark: University of Delaware Press. 1986.

209

Ornstein, Robert. "Shakespearian and Jonsonian Comedy." *Shakespeare
   Survey*. 1969. 22: 43-6.

210

Parrott, Thomas Marc. *Shakespearean Comedy*. New York: Oxford University Press. 1949.

211

Pettet, E.C. *Shakespeare and the Romance Tradition*. New York and
   London: Staples. 1949.

212

Rebhorn, Wayne A. "After Frye: A Review-Article on the Interpretation of
   Shakespearean Comedy and Romance." *Texas Studies in Literature and
   Language*. 1979. 21: 553-82.

213

Richmond, Hugh M. *Shakespeare's Sexual Comedy: A Mirror for Lovers*.
   Indianapolis and New York: Bobbs-Merrill. 1971.

214

Riemer, A.P. *Antic Fables: Patterns of Evasion in Shakespeare's Comedies*.
   Manchester: Manchester University Press; New York: St. Martin's;
   Sydney: Sydney University Press. 1980.

215

Roberts, Jeanne Addison. "American Criticism of Shakespeare's Comedies."
   Shakespeare Studies. 1976. 9: 1-10.

216

Roberts, Jeanne Addison. "Animals as Agents of Revelation: The Horizon-
   talizing of the Chain of Being in Shakespeare's Comedies." *New York
   Literary Forum*. 1980. 5-6: 79-96.

217

Salingar, Leo. *Shakespeare and the Traditions of Comedy.* London and New York: Cambridge University Press. 1974.

218

Scott, William O. *The God of Arts: Ruling Ideas in Shakespeare's Comedies.* Lawrence: University of Kansas Press. 1977.

219

Shaaber, M.A. "The Comic View of Life in Shakespeare's Comedies." *The Drama of the Renaissance.* Blistein, Elmer M., ed. Providence, R.I.: Brown University Press. 1970. 165-78.

220

Shakespeare Survey 22. 1969. 11 essays on comedies.

221

Sider, John W. "The Serious Elements of Shakespeare's Comedies." *SQ.* 1973. 24: 1-11.

222

Snyder, Susan. *The Comic Matrix of Shakespeare's Tragedies.* Princeton and Guildford, Surrey: Princeton University Press. 1979.

223

Somerset, J.A.B. "Shakespeare's Great Stage of Fools, 1599-1607." *Mirror up to Shakespeare: Essays in Honour of G.R. Hibbard.* Gray, J.C., ed. Toronto, Buffalo, and London: University of Toronto Press. 1984. 68-81.

224

Sprague, Arthur Colby. "The Moments of Seriousness in Shakespearian Comedy." *Shakespeare-Jahrbuch.* (Heidelberg) 1965: 240-7.

225

Stevenson, David Lloyd. *The Love-Game Comedy.* New York: Columbia University Press. 1946.

226

Stoll, E.E. "The Comic Method." *Shakespeare Studies, Historical and Comparative in Method.* New York: Macmillan. 1927. 147-86.

227

Swinden, Patrick. *An Introduction to Shakespeare's Comedies.* London: Macmillan. 1973; New York: Barnes and Noble. 1974.

228

Tillyard, E.M.W. *The Nature of Comedy and Shakespeare.* London: English Association. 1958.

229

Trousdale, Marion. "Semiotics and Shakespeare's Comedies." *New York Literary Forum.* 1980. 5-6: 245-55.

230

Walker, Marshall. "Shakespeare's Comedy (Or Much Ado About Bergson)." *Interpretations.* 1971. 3: 1-12.

231

Wilson, John Dover. *Shakespeare's Happy Comedies.* London: Faber; Evanston: Northwestern University Press. 1962.

IV. Comedy: The Early Comedies

232

Bergeron, David M. "Plays within Plays in Shakespeare's Early Comedies." *Teaching Shakespeare.* Edens, Walter, et al, eds. Princeton and Guildford, Surrey: Princeton University Press. 1977. 153-73.

233

Bonazza, Blaze Odell. *Shakespeare's Early Comedies: A Structural Analysis.* London, The Hague, and Paris: Mouton. 1966.

234

Cody, Richard. *The Landscape of the Mind: Pastoralism and Platonic Theory in Tasso's "Aminta" and Shakespeare's Early Comedies.* Oxford: Clarendon. 1969.

235

Coghill, Nevill. "The Basis of Shakespearian Comedy." *Shakespeare Criticism 1935-60.* Ridler, Anne, ed. London: Oxford University Press. 1963. 201-27.

236

Hamilton, A.C. *The Early Shakespeare.* San Marino: Huntington Library Press. 1967.

237

Hunter, G.K. *John Lyly: The Humanist as Courtier.* London: Routledge and Kegan Paul. 1962. Chapter VI.

238

Huston, J. Dennis. *Shakespeare's Comedies of Play.* New York: Columbia University Press. 1981.

239

Miola, Robert. "Early Shakespearean Comedy: *sub specie ludi*." *Thoth*. 1974. 14: 23-36.

240

Talbert, Ernest William. *Elizabethan Drama and Shakespeare's Early Plays*. Chapel Hill: University of North Carolina Press. 1963.

241

Tillyard, E.M.W. *Shakespeare's Early Comedies*. London: Chatto and Windus; Toronto: Clarke, Irwin; New York: Barnes and Noble. 1965.

242

Traversi, Derek. *Shakespeare: The Early Comedies*. London: Longmans, Green. 1960. Revised edition, 1964.

243

Turner, Robert Y. *Shakespeare's Apprenticeship*. Chicago and London: University of Chicago Press. 1974.

244

Von Rosador, K. Tetzeli. "Plotting the Early Comedies: *Err, LLL, TGV*." *Shakespeare Survey*. 1984. 37: 13-22.

245

Weller, Barry. "Identity and Representation in Shakespeare." *English Literary History*. 1982. 49: 339-62. (*Err, Shr, TGV*).

246

White, R.S. "Criticism of the Comedies up to *The Merchant of Venice*." *Shakespeare Survey*. 1984. 37: 1-11.

V. Comedy: The Middle and Romantic Comedies

247

Felheim, Marvin, and Traci, Philip. *Realism in Shakespeare's Romantic Comedies: "O Heavenly Mingle"*. Lanham, Md.: University Press of America. 1980.

248

Hassel, R. Chris, Jr. *Faith and Folly in Shakespeare's Romantic Comedies*. Athens: University of Georgia Press. 1980.

249

Hyland, Peter. "Shakespeare's Heroines: Disguise in the Romantic Comedies." *Ariel*. 1978. 9: 23-39.

250

Leggatt, Alexander. *Shakespeare's Comedy of Love*. London: Methuen; New York: Barnes and Noble. 1974.

251

Lewis, C.S. *The Allegory of Love*. Oxford: Clarendon. 1936.

252

Mahood, M.M. "Shakespeare's Middle Comedies: A Generation of Criticism." *Shakespeare Survey*. 1979. 32: 1-13.

253

Phialas, Peter G. *Shakespeare's Romantic Comedies: The Development of Their Form and Meaning*. Chapel Hill: University of North Carolina Press. 1966.

254

Vyvyan, John. *Shakespeare and Platonic Beauty*. New York: Barnes and Noble. 1961.

255

Westlund, Joseph. *Shakespeare's Reparative Comedies: A Psychoanalytic View of the Middle Plays*. Chicago and London: University of Chicago Press. 1984.

256

Wilcher, Robert. "The Art of the Comic Duologue in Three Plays by Shakespeare." *Shakespeare Survey*. 1982. 35: 87-100. (*AYL, TN, Ham.*)

VI. Comedy: The Problem Comedies

257

Foakes, R.A. *Shakespeare: The Dark Comedies to the Last Plays*. London: Routledge and Kegan Paul. 1971.

258

Frye, Northrop. *The Myth of Deliverance: Reflections on Shakespeare's Problem Comedies*. Toronto, Buffalo and London: University of Toronto Press. 1983.

259

Jamieson, Michael. "The Problem Plays, 1920-1970: A Retrospect." *Shakespeare Survey*. 1972. 25: 1-10.

24

260

Lawrence, W.W. *Shakespeare's Problem Comedies*. New York: Macmillan. 1931; Harmondsworth: Penguin. 1969.

261

Ornstein, Robert, ed. *Discussions of Shakespeare's Problem Comedies*. Boston: Heath. 1961.

262

Rossiter, A.P. *Angel with Horns*. Storey, Graham, ed. New York: Theatre Arts Books; London: Longmans, Green. 1961.

263

Schanzer, Ernest. *The Problem Plays of Shakespeare*. New York: Schocken; London: Routledge and Kegan Paul. 1963.

264

Sisson, C.J. *The Mythical Sorrows of Shakespeare*. London: Milford. 1934.

265

Tillyard, E.M.W. *Shakespeare's Problem Plays*. Cambridge: Cambridge University Press; Toronto: University of Toronto Press. 1949.

266

Toole, William B. *Shakespeare's Problem Plays: Studies in Form and Meaning*. The Hague: Mouton. 1966.

267

Westlund, Joseph. *Shakespeare's Reparative Comedies: A Psychoanalytic View of the Middle Plays*. Chicago and London: University of Chicago Press. 1984.

268

Wheeler, Richard P. *Shakespeare's Development and the Problem Comedies*. Berkeley, Los Angeles, and London: University of California Press. 1981.

VII. Comedy: The Late Romances

269

Barber, C.L. "'Thou that beget'st him that did thee beget': Transformation in *Pericles* and *The Winter's Tale*." *Shakespeare Survey*. 1969. 22: 59-67.

270

Bentley, G.E. "Shakespeare and the Blackfriars Theatre." *Shakespeare Survey*. 1948. 1: 38-50.

271

Bergeron, David M. *Shakespeare's Romances and the Royal Family.*
  Lawrence: University Press of Kansas. 1985.

272

Cruttwell, Patrick. *The Shakespearean Moment and its Place in the Poetry of
  the Seventeenth Century.* London: Chatto and Windus. 1954; New York:
  Columbia University Press. 1955. 73-106.

273

Dean, John. *Restless Wanderers: Shakespeare and the Pattern of Romance.*
  Hogg, James, ed. Atlantic Highlands, N.J.: Humanities Press. 1979.

274

Edwards, Philip. "Shakespeare's Romances: 1900-1957." *Shakespeare
  Survey.* 1958. 11: 1-18.

275

Felperin, Howard. *Shakespearean Romance.* Princeton: Princeton University
  Press. 1972.

276

Frank, Mike. "Shakespeare's Existential Comedy." *Shakespeare's Late
  Plays.* Tobias, Richard C., and Zolbrod, Paul G., eds. Athens: Ohio University Press. 1974. 142-65.

277

Frye, Northrop. *The Secular Scripture: A Study of the Structure of Romance.*
  Cambridge, Massachusetts and London: Harvard University Press. 1976.

278

Gesner, Carol. *Shakespeare and the Greek Romance: A Study of Origins.*
  Lexington: University of Kentucky Press. 1970.

279

Hartwig, Joan. *Shakespeare's Tragicomic Vision.* Baton Rouge: Louisiana
  State University Press. 1972.

280

Homan, Sidney R. "*The Tempest* and Shakespeare's Last Plays: The Aesthetic Dimensions." *SQ.* 1973. 24: 69-76.

281

Hunter, G.K. *William Shakespeare: The Late Comedies.* London: Longmans, Green. 1962.

282

James, D.G. *Scepticism and Poetry*. London: Allen and Unwin. 1937. 205-41.

283

Kastan, David Scott. "'More Than History Can Pattern': Notes Towards an Understanding of Shakespeare's Romances." *Cithara*. 1977. 17: 29-44.

284

Kay, Carol McGinnis, and Jacobs, Henry E., eds. *Shakespeare's Romances Reconsidered*. Lincoln and London: University of Nebraska Press. 1978.

285

Kermode, Frank. *William Shakespeare: The Final Plays*. London: Longman's. 1963.

286

Knight, G. Wilson. *The Crown of Life: Essays in Interpretation of Shakespeare's Final Plays*. London: Oxford University Press. 1947.

287

Knight, G. Wilson. *The Shakespearian Tempest*. London: H. Milford, Oxford University Press. 1932.

288

Leavis, F.R. "The Criticism of Shakespeare's Late Plays: A Caveat." *Scrutiny*. 1942. 10: 339-45. Reprinted in *The Common Pursuit*, New York: G.W. Stewart, 1952, 731-81; and in *Shakespeare Criticism 1935-60*, ed. Anne Ridler, London: Oxford University Press, 1963, 132-41.

289

Mowat, Barbara. *The Dramaturgy of Shakespeare's Romances*. Athens: University of Georgia Press. 1976.

290

Muir, Kenneth. *Last Periods of Shakespeare, Racine, Ibsen*. Detroit: Wayne State University Press; Liverpool: University of Liverpool Press; Toronto: Ambassador. 1961.

291

Palmer, D.J., ed. *Shakespeare's Later Comedies: An Anthology of Modern Criticism*. Harmondsworth: Penguin. 1971.

292

Quiller-Couch, Arthur. *Shakespeare's Workmanship*. London: Unwin. 1918. 221-362.

293

Ristine, Frank Humphrey. *English Tragicomedy: Its Origin and History.*
New York: Columbia University Press. 1910.

294

Semon, Kenneth J. "Fantasy and Wonder in Shakespeare's Last Plays." *SQ.*
1974. 25: 89-102.

295

Shakespeare Survey 11. 1958. 7 essays on the last plays.

296

Strachey, Lytton. "Shakespeare's Final Period." *Books and Characters,*
French and English. London: Chatto and Windus; New York: Harcourt,
Brace. 1922. 49-69. First published 1906.

297

Tanner, Tony. *Adultery in the Novel.* Baltimore and London: Johns Hopkins
University Press. 1979. 39-52.

298

Thorndike, Ashley H. *The Influence of Beaumont and Fletcher on Shakspere.*
Worcester, Mass.: O.B. Wood. 1901.

299

Tillyard, E.M.W. *Shakespeare's Last Plays.* London: Chatto and Windus.
1938.

300

Traversi, Derek. *Shakespeare: The Last Phase.* London: Hollis and Carter.
1954; New York: Harcourt, Brace. 1955.

301

Uphaus, Robert W. *Beyond Tragedy: Structure and Experience in*
Shakespeare's Romances. Lexington: University Press of Kentucky. 1981.

302

Wells, Stanley. "Shakespeare and Romance." *Later Shakespeare.* Brown,
John Russell, and Harris, Bernard, eds. London: E. Arnold. 1966. 49-79.
Reprinted in *Shakespeare's Later Comedies*, ed. D.J. Palmer. Har-
mondsworth: Penguin, 1971. 117-42.

303

White, R.S. *"Let Wonder Seem Familiar": Endings in Shakespeare's*
Romance Vision. Atlantic Highlands, N.J.: Humanities Press; London:
Athlone. 1985.

304

Wincor, Richard. "Shakespeare's Festival Plays." *SQ* . 1950. 1: 219-40.

305

Yates, Frances. "Magic in Shakespeare's Last Plays." *Encounter*. 1975. April: 14-22.

VIII. History Plays

306

Armstrong, William A. "The Elizabethan Conception of the Tyrant." *Review of English Studies.* 1946. 22: 161-81.

307

Armstrong, William A. "The Influence of Seneca and Machiavelli on the Elizabethan Tyrant." *Review of English Studies.* 1948. 24: 19-35.

308

Berger, Harry, Jr. "Psychoanalyzing the Shakespeare Text: The First Three Scenes of the *Henriad.*" *Shakespeare and the Question of Theory.* Parker, Patricia, and Hartman, Geoffrey, eds. New York and London: Methuen. 1985. 210-29.

309

Berry, Edward I. *Patterns of Decay: Shakespeare's Early Histories.* Charlottesville, Va.: University Press of Virginia. 1975.

310

Bethell, Samuel L. "The Comic Element in Shakespeare's Histories." *Anglia.* 1952. 71: 82-101.

311

Blanpied, John W. *Time and the Artist in Shakespeare's English Histories.* Newark: University of Delaware Press; London and Toronto: Associated University Presses. 1983.

312

Boris, Edna Zwick. *Shakespeare's English Kings, the People, and the Law.* Rutherford, Madison, and Teaneck: Fairleigh Dickinson University Press; London: Associated University Presses. 1978.

313

Bullough, Geoffrey. "The Uses of History." *Shakespeare's World.* Sutherland, James, and Hurstfield, Joel, eds. New York: St. Martin's. 1964. 96-115.

314

Bulman, James C. "Shakespeare's Georgic Histories." *Shakespeare Survey.* 1985. 38: 37-47.

315

Burden, Dennis H. "Shakespeare's History Plays: 1952-1983." *Shakespeare Survey*. 1985. 38: 1-18.

316

Calderwood, James L. *Metadrama in Shakespeare's Henriad*. Berkeley, Los Angeles, and London: University of California Press. 1979.

317

Campbell, Lily B. *Shakespeare's "Histories": Mirrors of Elizabethan Policy*. San Marino, California: Huntington Library Press. 1947.

318

Champion, Larry S. *Perspective in Shakespeare's English Histories*. Athens: University of Georgia Press. 1980.

319

Chapman, Raymond. "The Wheel of Fortune in Shakespeare's Historical Plays." *Review of English Studies*. 1950. 1: 1-7.

320

Charlton, H.B. *Shakespeare, Politics and Politicians*. Oxford: English Association. 1929.

321

Clemen, Wolfgang H. "Anticipation and Foreboding in Shakespeare's Early Histories." *Shakespeare Survey*. 1953. 6: 25-35.

322

Coursen, Herbert R. *The Leasing Out of England: Shakespeare's Second Henriad*. Lanham, Md.: University Press of America. 1982.

323

Craig, Hardin. "Shakespeare and the History Play." *Joseph Quincy Adams Memorial Studies*. McManaway, James G., et al, eds. Washington, D.C.: Folger Shakespeare Library. 1948. 55-64.

324

Crane, Mary Thomas. "The Shakespearean Tetralogy." *SQ* . 1985. 36: 282-99.

325

David, Richard. "Shakespeare's History Plays: Epic or Drama?" *Shakespeare Survey*. 1953. 6: 129-39.

326

Dean, Leonard F. "*Richard II* to *Henry V:* A Closer View." *Studies in Honor of DeWitt T. Starnes*. Harrison, Thomas P., et al, eds. Austin:

31

University of Texas Press. 1967. 37-52.

327
Dorius, R.J., ed. *Discussions of Shakespeare's Histories:* Richard II *to* Henry V. Boston: Heath. 1964.

328
Forker, Charles R. "Shakespeare's Chronicle Plays as Historical-Pastoral." *Shakespeare Studies.* 1965. 1: 85-104.

329
Frye, Northrop. *Spiritus Mundi: Essays on Literature, Myth, and Society.* Bloomington and London: Indiana University Press. 1976.

330
Hapgood, Robert. "Shakespeare's Thematic Modes of Speech: *Richard II* to *Henry V.*" *Shakespeare Survey.* 1967. 20: 41-9.

331
Hapgood, Robert. *Shakespeare's Histories and "The Emotion of Multitude".* Oxford: Oxford University Press. 1968.

332
Holderness, Graham. *Shakespeare's History.* Dublin: Gill and Macmillan; New York: St. Martin. 1985.

333
Hunter, G.K. "Shakespeare's Politics and the Rejection of Falstaff." *Critical Quarterly.* 1959. 1: 229-36.

334
Jenkins, Harold. "Shakespeare's History Plays: 1900-1951." *Shakespeare Survey.* 1953. 6: 1-15.

335
Jochum, K.P.S. *Discrepant Awareness: Studies in English Renaissance Drama.* Frankfurt am Main, Bern, Las Vegas: Lang. 1979.

336
Jorgensen, Paul A. *Shakespeare's Military World.* Berkeley and Los Angeles: University of California Press. 1956.

337
Kantorowicz, Ernst H. *The King's Two Bodies: A Study in Mediaeval Political Theology.* Princeton: Princeton University Press. 1957.

338
Kelly, Henry A. *Divine Providence in the England of Shakespeare's Histories.* Cambridge, Mass.: Harvard University Press. 1970.

339

Kernan, Alvin B. "The Henriad: Shakespeare's Major History Plays." *Yale Review*. 1969. 59: 3-32.

340

Knights, L.C. "Shakespeare and Political Wisdom: A Note on the Personalism of *JC* and *Cor*." *Sewanee Review*. 1953. 61: 43-55.

341

Knights, L.C. "Shakespeare's Politics: With Some Reflections on the Nature of Tradition." *Proceedings of the British Academy*. 1957. 43: 115-32.

342

Knights, L.C. *William Shakespeare: The Histories*. London: Longmans, Green. 1962.

343

LaGuardia, Eric. "Ceremony and History: The Problem of Symbol from *Richard II* to *Henry V*." *Pacific Coast Studies in Shakespeare*. McNeir, Waldo F., and Greenfield, Thelma N., eds. Eugene: University of Oregon Press. 1966. 68-88.

344

Law, Robert A. "Links between Shakespeare's History Plays." *Studies in Philology*. 1953. 50: 168-87.

345

Leech, Clifford. *Shakespeare: The Chronicles*. London: Longmans, Green. 1962.

346

Lindenberger, Herbert. *Historical Drama: The Relation of Literature and Reality*. Chicago and London: University of Chicago Press. 1975.

347

MacDonald, Ronald R. "Uneasy Lies: Language and History in Shakespeare's Lancastrian Tetralogy." *SQ*. 1984. 35: 22-39.

348

Maclean, Hugh. "Time and Horsemanship in Shakespeare's Histories." *University of Toronto Quarterly*. 1965-6. 35: 229-45.

349

Manheim, Michael. *The Weak King Dilemma in the Shakespearean History Play*. Syracuse: Syracuse University Press. 1973.

350

Morton, A.L. "Shakespeare's Historical Outlook." *Shakespeare-Jahrbuch.*
1965. (Weimar), 100/101: 208-26.

351

Mroz, Mary B. *Divine Vengeance: A Study in the Philosophical Backgrounds
of the Revenge Motif as It Appears in Shakespeare's Chronicle History
Plays.* Washington, D.C.: Catholic University of America Press. 1941.

352

Ornstein, Robert. *A Kingdom for a Stage.* Cambridge, Massachusetts: Harvard University Press. 1972.

353

Palmer, Barbara D. "'Ciphers to This Great Accompt': Civic Pageantry in
the Second Tetralogy." *Pageantry in the Shakespearean Theater.* Bergeron,
David M., ed. Athens: University of Georgia Press. 1985. 114-29.

354

Porter, Joseph A. *The Drama of Speech Acts: Shakespeare's Lancastrian
Tetralogy.* Berkeley and Los Angeles: University of California Press. 1979.

355

Prior, Moody E. *The Drama of Power: Studies in Shakespeare's History
Plays.* Evanston: Northwestern University Press. 1973.

356

Quinn, Michael. "Providence in Shakespeare's Yorkist Plays." *SQ.* 1959. 10:
45-52.

357

Reed, Robert Rentoul, Jr. *Crime and God's Judgement in Shakespeare.* Lexington: University Press of Kentucky. 1984.

358

Reese, Max M. *The Cease of Majesty: A Study of Shakespeare's History
Plays.* London: E. Arnold. 1961.

359

Ribner, Irving. *The English History Play in the Age of Shakespeare.* Princeton: Princeton University Press. 1957. Revised and enlarged edition, New
York: Barnes and Noble; London: Methuen, 1965.

360

Richmond, Hugh M. *Shakespeare's Political Plays.* New York: Random
House. 1967.

361

Riggs, David. *Shakespeare's Heroical Histories.* Cambridge, Massachusetts: Harvard University Press. 1971.

362

Rogers, William Hudson. *Shakespeare and English History.* Totowa, N.J.: Littlefield, Adams. 1966.

363

Rossiter, A.P. "Ambivalence: The Dialectic of the Histories." *Talking of Shakespeare.* Garrett, John, ed. London: Hodder and Stoughton. 1954. 149-72. Reprinted in Rossiter's *Angel with Horns*, ed. Graham Storey. New York: Theatre Arts Books, 1961.

364

Saccio, Peter. *Shakespeare's English Kings: History, Chronicle, and Drama.* New York: Oxford University Press. 1977.

365

Sanders, Norman. "American Criticism of Shakespeare's History Plays." *Shakespeare Studies.* 1976. 9: 11-23.

366

Sanders, Wilbur. "Shakespearian History: Critique of 'Elizabethan Policy'." *The Dramatist and the Received Idea.* London: Cambridge University Press. 1968. 143-57.

367

Schelling, Felix E. *The English Chronicle Play: A Study in the Popular Historical Literature Environing Shakespeare.* New York: Macmillan. 1902.

368

Smidt, Kristian. *Unconformities in Shakespeare's History Plays.* Atlantic Highlands, N.J.: Humanities Press. 1982.

369

Smith, Gordon Ross. "A Rabble of Princes: Considerations Touching Shakespeare's Political Orthodoxy in the Second Tetralogy." *Journal of the History of Ideas.* 1980. 41: 29-48.

370

Sprague, Arthur C. *Shakespeare's Histories: Plays for the Stage.* London: Society for Theatre Research. 1964.

371

Szenczi, Miklos. "The Nature of Shakespeare's Realism." *Shakespeare-Jahrbuch* (Weimar). 1966. 102: 37-59.

372

Talbert, Ernest W. *The Problem of Order*. Chapel Hill: University of North Carolina Press. 1962.

373

Thayer, C.G. *Shakespearean Politics: Government and Misgovernment in the Great Histories*. Athens, Ohio, and London: Ohio University Press. 1983.

374

Tillyard, E.M.W. "Shakespeare's Historical Cycle: Organism or Compilation?" *Studies in Philology*. 1954. 51: 34-9.

375

Tillyard, E.M.W. *Shakespeare's History Plays*. London: Chatto and Windus. 1944.

376

Traversi, Derek A. *Shakespeare, from* Richard II *to* Henry V. Stanford: Stanford University Press. 1957.

377

Turner, Robert Y. "Characterization in Shakespeare's Early History Plays." *English Literary History*. 1964. 31: 241-58.

378

Turner, Robert Y. "Shakespeare and the Public Confrontation Scene in Early History Plays." *Modern Philology*. 1964. 62: 1-12.

379

Turner, Robert Y. *Shakespeare's Apprenticeship*. Chicago and London: University of Chicago Press. 1974.

380

Waith, Eugene M., ed. *Shakespeare: The Histories. A Collection of Critical Essays*. Englewood Cliffs, N.J.: Prentice-Hall. 1965.

381

Watson, Robert N. "Horsemanship in Shakespeare's Second Tetralogy." *English Literary Renaissance*. 1983. 13: 274-300.

382

Webber, Joan. "The Renewal of the King's Symbolic Role: From *Richard II* to *Henry V*." *Texas Studies in Literature and Language*. 1962-3. 4: 530-8.

383

Wells, Robin Headlam. "The Fortunes of Tillyard: Twentieth-Century Critical Debate on Shakespeare's History Plays." *English Studies*. 1985. 66: 391-403.

384

Wilders, John. *The Lost Garden: A View of Shakespeare's English and Roman History Plays.* London: Macmillan; Totowa, N.J.: Rowman and Littlefield. 1978.

385

Wilson, F.P. "The English History Play." *Shakespearean and Other Studies.* Gardner, Helen, ed. Oxford: Clarendon. 1969.

386

Wilson, F.P. *Marlowe and the Early Shakepeare.* Oxford: Clarendon. 1953.

387

Winny, James. *The Player King: A Theme of Shakespeare's Histories.* New York: Barnes and Noble; London: Chatto and Windus. 1968.

388

Zeeveld, W. Gordon. "The Influence of Hall on Shakespeare's English Historical Plays." *English Literary History.* 1936. 3: 317-53.

IX. Tragedy

389

Adams, Robert P. "Shakespeare's Tragic Vision." *Pacific Coast Studies in Shakespeare.* McNeir, Waldo F., and Greenfield, Thelma N., eds. Eugene: University of Oregon Press. 1966. 225-33.

390

Allen, M.J.B. "Toys, Prologues and the Great Amiss: Shakespeare's Tragic Openings." *Shakespearian Tragedy.* Bradbury, Malcolm, and Palmer, David, eds. (Stratford-upon-Avon Studies 20.) New York: Holmes and Meier. 1984. 3-30.

391

Bayley, John. *Shakespeare and Tragedy.* London: Routledge and Kegan Paul. 1981.

392

Belsey, Catherine. *The Subject of Tragedy: Identity and Difference in Renaissance Drama.* London and New York: Methuen. 1985.

393

Berlin, Normand. *The Secret Cause: A Discussion of Tragedy.* Amherst: University of Massachusetts Press. 1981.

394

Black, Matthew W. "Aristotle's Mythos and the Tragedies of Shakespeare." *Shakespeare-Jahrbuch.* (Heidelberg). 1968. 43-55.

395

Black, Matthew W. "*Hamartia* in Shakespeare." *Library Chronicle* (U. of Penn.) 1964. 30: 100-16.

396

Bowers, Fredson T. "Death in Victory." *South Atlantic Bulletin.* 1965. 30: 1-7. Expanded version in *Studies in Honor of DeWitt Starnes.* Ed. Thomas P. Harrison, et al. Austin: University of Texas Press, 1967. 53-76.

397

Braden, Gordon. *Renaissance Tragedy and the Senecan Tradition: Anger's Privilege.* New Haven and London: Yale University Press. 1985.

398

Bradley, A.C. *Shakespearean Tragedy.* London: Macmillan. 1904.

399

Brereton, Geoffrey. *Principles of Tragedy: A Rational Examination of the Tragic Concept in Life and Literature.* London: Routledge and Kegan Paul. 1968; Miami: University of Miami Press. 1969.

400

Brooke, Nicholas. *Shakespeare's Early Tragedies.* London: Methuen. 1968.

401

Brower, Reuben A. *Hero and Saint: Shakespeare and the Graeco-Roman Heroic Tradition.* New York and Oxford: Oxford University Press. 1971.

402

Bulman, James C. *The Heroic Idiom of Shakespearean Tragedy.* Newark: University of Delaware Press; London and Toronto: Associated University Presses. 1985.

403

Brown, John Russell, and Harris, Bernard, eds. *Early Shakespeare.* London: E. Arnold. 1961. Stratford-upon-Avon Studies 3.

404

Cantor, Paul A. *Shakespeare's Rome: Republic and Empire.* Ithaca and London: Cornell University Press. 1976.

405

Champion, Larry S. *Tragic Patterns in Jacobean and Caroline Drama.* Knoxville: University of Tennessee Press. 1977.

406

Charlton, H.B. *Shakespearean Tragedy*. Cambridge: Cambridge University Press. 1948.

407

Charney, Maurice, ed. *Discussions of Shakespeare's Roman Plays*. Boston: Heath. 1964.

408

Charney, Maurice, ed. *Shakespeare's Roman Plays: The Function of Imagery in the Drama*. Cambridge, Massachusetts: Harvard University Press. 1961.

409

Cole, Susan Letzler. *The Absent One: Mourning Ritual, Tragedy, and the Performance of Ambivalence*. University Park and London: Penn. State University Press. 1985.

410

Cunliffe, John W. *The Influence of Seneca on Elizabethan Tragedy*. New York: Macmillan. 1893.

411

Cunningham, J.V. *Woe or Wonder: The Emotional Effect of Shakespearean Tragedy*. Denver: University of Denver Press. 1951.

412

Danson, Lawrence. *Tragic Alphabet: Shakespeare's Drama of Language*. New Haven and London: Yale University Press. 1974.

413

Dickey, Franklin M. *Not Wisely but Too Well: Shakespeare's Love Tragedies*. San Marino, California: Huntington Library Press. 1957.

414

Diehl, Huston. "The Iconography of Violence in English Renaissance Tragedy." *Renaissance Drama*. 1980. 11: 27-44.

415

Dollimore, Jonathan. *Radical Tragedy: Religion, Ideology, and Power in the Drama of Shakespeare and His Contemporaries*. Chicago and London: University of Chicago Press; Brighton: Harvester. 1984.

416

Eliot, T.S. *Shakespeare and the Stoicism of Seneca*. London: Oxford University Press. 1927.

417

Evans, Bertrand. *Shakespeare's Tragic Practice.* Oxford: Clarendon; New York: Oxford University Press. 1979.

418

Farnham, Willard E. *The Medieval Heritage of Elizabethan Tragedy.* Berkeley and Los Angeles: University of California Press; Oxford: Blackwell. 1936.

419

Farnham, Willard E. *Shakespeare's Tragic Frontier.* Berkeley and Los Angeles: University of California Press. 1950.

420

Felperin, Howard. *Shakespearean Representation.* Princeton: Princeton University Press. 1977.

421

Foakes, R.A. "Shakespeare's Later Tragedies." *Shakespeare, 1564-1964.* Bloom, Edward A., ed. Providence, R.I.: Brown University Press. 1964. 95-109.

422

Foreman, Walter C., Jr. *The Music of the Close: The Final Scenes of Shakespeare's Tragedies.* Lexington, Ky.: University Press of Kentucky. 1978.

423

Forker, Charles R. "The Green Underworld of Early Shakespearean Tragedy." *Shakespeare Studies.* 1985. 17: 25-47.

424

Frye, Northrop. *Fools of Time: Studies in Shakespearean Tragedy.* Toronto: University of Toronto Press. 1967.

425

Gohlke, Madelon. "'And When I Love Thee Not': Women and the Psychic Integrity of the Tragic Hero." *Hebrew University Studies in Literature.* 1980. 8: 44-65.

426

Gohlke, Madelon. "'I Wooed Thee With My Sword': Shakespeare's Tragic Paradigms." *The Woman's Part.* Lenz, Carolyn Ruth Swift, et al, eds. Urbana, Chicago, and London: University of Illinois Press. 1980. 150-70. Reprinted in *Representing Shakespeare.* Ed. Murray M. Schwartz and Coppélia Kahn. Baltimore and London: Johns Hopkins University Press,

40

1980. 170-87.

427

Golden, Leon. "*Othello, Hamlet*, and Aristotelian Tragedy." *SQ*. 1984. 35: 142-56.

428

Goldman, Michael. *Acting and Action in Shakespearean Tragedy*. Princeton: Princeton University Press. 1985.

429

Grudin, Robert. *Mighty Opposites: Shakespeare and Renaissance Contrariety*. Berkeley and Los Angeles: University of California Press. 1979.

430

Hallett, Charles A., and Hallett, Elaine S. *The Revenger's Madness: A Study of Revenge Tragedy Motifs*. Lincoln: University of Nebraska Press. 1980.

431

Hankiss, Elemér. "A Comparative Study of Tragic Catharsis." *Actes du VIIe congrès de l'Association Internationale de Littérature Comparée/Proceedings of the 7th Congress of the International Comparative Literature Association*. Dimić, Milan V., and Kushner, Eva, eds. Stuttgard: Erich Bieber. 1979. 2 vols. 565-71.

432

Hapgood, Robert. "Shakespeare's Maimed Rites: The Early Tragedies." *Centennial Review*. 1965. 9: 494-508.

433

Harbage, Alfred, ed. *Shakespeare: The Tragedies, a Collection of Critical Essays*. Englewood Cliffs, N.J.: Prentice-Hall. 1964.

434

Hardison, O.B. "Three Types of Renaissance Catharsis." *Renaissance Drama*. 1969. 2: 3-22.

435

Hawkes, Terence. *Shakespeare and the Reason: A Study of the Tragedies and the Problem Plays*. London: Routledge and Kegan Paul. 1964.

436

Herndl, George C. *The High Design: English Renaissance Tragedy and the Natural Law*. Lexington, Ky.: University Press of Kentucky. 1970.

437

Herrick, Marvin T. *Italian Tragedy in the Renaissance*. Urbana: University of Illinois Press. 1965.

438

Hill, R.F. "Shakespeare's Early Tragic Mode." *SQ*. 1958. 9: 455-69.

439

Holland, Norman N. "Shakespearean Tragedy and the Three Ways of Psychoanalytic Criticism." *Hudson Review*. 1962. 15: 217-27.

440

Holloway, John. *The Story of the Night*. London: Routledge and Kegan Paul. 1961.

441

Honigmann, E.A.J. *Shakespeare: Seven Tragedies. The Dramatist's Manipulation of Response*. London: Macmillan; New York: Barnes and Noble. 1976.

442

Hunter, G.K. "The Last Tragic Heroes." *Later Shakespeare*. Brown, John Russell, and Harris, Bernard, eds. London: Arnold. 1966. 11-30. Stratford-upon-Avon Studies 8.

443

Hunter, G.K. "Tyrant and Martyr: Religious Heroisms in Elizabethan Tragedy." *Poetic Traditions of the English Renaissance*. Mack, Maynard, and Lord, George deForest, eds. New Haven and London: Yale University Press. 1982. 85-102.

444

Hunter, Robert Grams. *Shakespeare and the Mystery of God's Judgments*. Athens, Georgia: University of Georgia Press. 1976.

445

Hyde, Thomas. "Identity and Acting in Elizabethan Tragedy." *Renaissance Drama*. 1985. 15: 93-114.

446

Jenkins, Harold. *The Catastrophe in Shakespearean Tragedy*. Edinburgh: Edinburgh University Press. 1969.

447

Jenkins, Harold. "The Tragedy of Revenge in Shakespeare and Webster." *Shakespeare Survey*. 1961. 14: 45-55.

448

Kettle, Arnold. "From *Hamlet* to *Lear*." *Shakespeare in a Changing World*. Kettle, Arnold, ed. London: Lawrence and Wishart. 1964.

449

Kiefer, Frederick. *Fortune and Elizabethan Tragedy.* San Marino, Califor-
    nia: Huntington Library. 1983.

450

Kirschbaum, Leo. "Shakespeare's Stage Blood and its Critical Significance."
    PMLA. 1949. 64: 517-29.

451

Koelb, Clayton. "'Tragedy' and 'The Tragic': The Shakespearean Connec-
    tion." *Genre.* 1980. 13: 275-86.

452

Lawlor, John J. *The Tragic Sense in Shakespeare.* London: Chatto and
    Windus. 1960.

453

Leech, Clifford, ed. *Shakespeare: The Tragedies, a Collection of Critical
    Essays.* Chicago and London: University of Chicago Press. 1965.

454

Lerner, Laurence, ed. *Shakespeare's Tragedies: An Anthology of Modern
    Criticism.* Harmondsworth: Penguin. 1963.

455

Lloyd-Evans, Gareth. "Shakespeare, Seneca, and the Kingdom of Violence."
    Roman Drama. Dorey, T.A., and Dudley, Donald R., eds. London: Rout-
    ledge and Kegan Paul. 1965. 123-59.

456

Long, Michael. *The Unnatural Scene: A Study of Shakespearean Tragedy.*
    London: Methuen. 1976.

457

McElroy, Bernard. *Shakespeare's Mature Tragedies.* Princeton: Princeton
    University Press. 1973.

458

McFarland, Thomas. *Tragic Meanings in Shakespeare.* New York: Random
    House. 1966.

459

Mack, Maynard. "The Jacobean Shakespeare: Some Observations on the
    Construction of the Tragedies." *Jacobean Theatre.* Brown, John Russell,
    and Harris, Bernard, eds. London: E. Arnold. 1960. 11-42.
    Stratford-upon-Avon Studies 1.

460

Mack, Maynard. *Killing the King: Three Studies in Shakespeare's Tragic Structure.* New Haven and London: Yale University Press. 1973.

461

MacLure, Millar. "Shakespeare and the Lonely Dragon." *University of Toronto Quarterly.* 1955. 24: 109-20.

462

McNeal, Thomas H. "Shakespeare's Cruel Queens." *Huntington Library Quarterly.* 1958-9. 22: 41-50.

463

Margeson, John M.R. *The Origins of English Tragedy.* Oxford: Oxford University Press. 1967.

464

Marsh, Derick R.C. *Passion Lends Them Power: A Study of Shakespeare's Love Tragedies.* Manchester: Manchester University Press; New York: Barnes and Noble. 1976.

465

Mason, Harold A. *Shakespeare's Tragedies of Love.* London: Chatto and Windus; New York: Barnes and Noble. 1970.

466

Maxwell, James C. "Shakespeare's Roman Plays: 1900-1956." *Shakespeare Survey.* 1957. 10: 1-11.

467

Mincoff, Marco. "Shakespeare, Fletcher, and Baroque Tragedy." *Shakespeare Survey.* 1967. 20: 1-15.

468

Mincoff, Marco. "The Structural Pattern of Shakespeare's Tragedies." *Shakespeare Survey.* 1950. 3: 58-65.

469

Morris, Harry. *Last Things in Shakespeare.* Tallahassee: Florida State University Press. 1985.

470

Muir, Kenneth. *Shakespeare and the Tragic Pattern.* Oxford: Oxford University Press. 1958.

471

Muir, Kenneth. *Shakespeare's Tragic Sequence.* London: Hutchinson. 1972; New York: Barnes and Noble. 1979.

44

472

Muir, Kenneth. *William Shakespeare: The Great Tragedies*. London: Longmans, Green. 1961.

473

Nicoll, Allardyce. *Studies in Shakespeare*. London: Hogarth Press. 1927.

474

Neill, Michael. "'Exeunt with a Dead March': Funeral Pageantry on the
Shakespearean Stage." *Pageantry in the Shakespearean Theater*. Bergeron,
David M., ed. Athens: University of Georgia Press. 1985. 153-93.

475

Novy, Marianne. "Shakespeare's Female Characters as Actors and Audience." *The Woman's Part*. Lenz, Carolyn Ruth Swift, et al, eds. Urbana,
Chicago, and London: University of Illinois Press. 1980. 256-70.

476

Ornstein, Robert. "Can We Define the Nature of Shakespearean Tragedy?"
Comparative Drama. 1985. 19: 258-69.

477

Phillips, James Emerson, Jr. *The State in Shakespeare's Greek and Roman
Plays*. New York: Columbia University Press. 1940.

478

Prior, Moody E. *The Language of Tragedy*. New York: Columbia University
Press. 1947.

479

Proser, Matthew N. *The Heroic Image in Five Shakespearean Tragedies*.
Princeton: Princeton University Press. 1965.

480

Rabkin, Norman. "Stumbling Toward Tragedy." *Shakespeare's "Rough
Magic": Renaissance Essays in Honor of C.L. Barber*. Erickson, Peter, and
Kahn, Coppélia, eds. Newark: University of Delaware Press; London and
Toronto: Associated University Presses. 1985. 28-49.

481

Rackin, Phyllis. *Shakespeare's Tragedies*. New York: Frederick Ungar.
1978.

482

Reiss, Timothy J. *Tragedy and Truth: Studies in the Development of a Renaissance and Neoclassical Discourse*. New Haven and London: Yale University Press. 1980.

483

Rosen, William. *Shakespeare and the Craft of Tragedy.* Cambridge, Massachusetts: Harvard University Press. 1960.

484

Rosenberg, Marvin. "Shakespeare's Tragic World of *If.*" *Shakespeare Jahrbuch* (Heidelberg). 1980. 109-17.

485

Rozett, Martha Tuck. *The Doctrine of Election and the Emergence of Elizabethan Tragedy.* Princeton: Princeton University Press. 1984.

486

Sanders, Wilbur, and Jacobson, Howard. *Shakespeare's Magnanimity: Four Tragic Heroes, Their Friends, and Families.* New York: Oxford University Press; London: Chatto and Windus. 1978.

487

Schücking, Levin L. *The Baroque Character of the Elizabethan Tragic Hero.* Oxford: Oxford University Press. 1938.

488

Schwartz, Elias. "The Idea of the Person and Shakespearean Tragedy." *SQ.* 1965. 16: 39-47.

489

Schwindt, John. "Luther's Paradoxes and Shakespeare's God: The Emergence of the Absurd in Sixteenth-Century Literature." *Modern Language Studies.* 1985. 15: 4-12.

490

Siegel, Paul N. *Shakespearean Tragedy and the Elizabethan Compromise: A Marxist Study.* New York: New York University Press. 1957. Revised ed., Lanham, Md.: University Press of America, 1983.

491

Simmons, J.L. *Shakespeare's Pagan World: The Roman Tragedies.* Charlottesville, Va.: University Press of Virginia. 1973.

492

Sisson, C.J. *Shakespeare's Tragic Justice.* London: Methuen. 1962.

493

Speaight, Robert. *Nature in Shakespearean Tragedy.* London: Hollis and Carter. 1955.

494

Spencer, T.J.B. "Shakespeare and the Elizabethan Romans." *Shakespeare Survey.* 1957. 10: 27-38.

495

Spencer, T.J.B. *Shakespeare: The Roman Plays.* London: Longmans, Green. 1963.

496

Spencer, Theodore. *Death and Elizabethan Tragedy.* Cambridge, Massachusetts: Harvard University Press. 1936.

497

Spevack, Marvin. "Hero and Villain in Shakespeare: On Dualism and Tragedy." *Tennessee Studies in Literature.* 1967. 12: 1-11.

498

Spivack, Bernard. *Shakespeare and the Allegory of Evil.* New York: Columbia University Press. 1958.

499

Stampfer, Judah. *The Tragic Engagement: A Study of Shakespeare's Classical Tragedies.* New York: Funk and Wagnalls. 1968.

500

States, Bert O. "The Persistence of the Archetype." *Critical Inquiry.* 1980. 7: 333-44.

501

Stirling, Brents. *Unity in Shakespearean Tragedy.* New York: Columbia University Press. 1956.

502

Traversi, Derek A. *Shakespeare: The Roman Plays.* Stanford: Stanford University Press; London: Hollis and Carter. 1963.

503

Velz, John W. "The Ancient World in Shakespeare: Authenticity or Anachronism? A Retrospect." *Shakespeare Survey.* 1978. 31: 1-12.

504

Velz, John W. *Shakespeare and the Classical Tradition: A Critical Guide to Commentary, 1660-1960.* Minneapolis: University of Minnesota Press. 1968.

505

Waith, Eugene M. *The Herculean Hero in Marlowe, Chapman, Shakespeare, and Dryden.* New York: Columbia University Press; London: Chatto and

Windus. 1962.

506

Watson, Curtis B. "T.S. Eliot and the Interpretation of Shakespearean Tragedy in Our Time." *Etudes Anglaises*. 1964. 17: 502-21.

507

Weidhorn, Manfred. "The Relation of Title and Name to Identity in Shakespearean Tragedy." *Studies in English Literature*. 1969. 9: 303-19.

508

Weisinger, Herbert. "The Study of Shakespearean Tragedy since Bradley." *SQ*. 1955. 6: 387-96.

509

Whitaker, Virgil K. *The Mirror Up to Nature: The Technique of Shakespeare's Tragedies*. San Marino, California: Huntington Library Press. 1965.

510

White, R.S. *Innocent Victims: Poetic Injustice in Shakespearean Tragedy*. Newcastle upon Tyne: Tyneside Free Press. 1982.

511

Willson, Robert F., Jr. "Shakespeare's Tragic Prefigurers." *Shakespeare Studies*. 1983. 16: 143-51.

512

Wilson, Harold S. *On the Design of Shakespearean Tragedy*. Toronto: University of Toronto Press. 1957.

513

Wood, Frederick T. "Shakespeare and the Plebs." *Essays and Studies by Members of the English Association*. 1933. 18: 53-73.

X. Individual Plays and Poems

All's Well That Ends Well

514

Adams, John F. "*AWW*: The Paradox of Procreation." *SQ*. 1961. 12: 261-70.

515

Arthos, John. "The Comedy of Generation." *Essays in Criticism*. 1955. 5: 97-117.

516

Bennett, Josephine W. "New Techniques of Comedy in *AWW*." *SQ*. 1967. 18: 337-62.

517

Bergeron, David M. "The Structure of Healing in *AWW*." *South Atlantic Bulletin*. 1972. 37: 25-34.

518

Bradbrook, Muriel C. "Virtue Is the True Nobility: A Study of the Structure of *AWW*." *Review of English Studies*. 1950. 1: 289-301.

519

Calderwood, James L. "The Mingled Yarn of *AWW*." *Journal of English and Germanic Philology*. 1963. 62: 61-76.

520

Calderwood, James L. "Styles of Knowing in *AWW*." *Modern Language Quarterly*. 1964. 25: 272-94.

521

Cartelli, Thomas. "Shakespeare's 'Rough Magic': Ending as Artifice in *AWW*." *Centennial Review*. 1983. 27: 117-34.

522

Carter, Albert H. "In Defense of Bertram." *SQ*. 1956. 7: 21-31.

523

Cole, Howard C. *The All's Well Story from Boccaccio to Shakespeare*. Urbana, Chicago, and London: University of Illinois Press. 1981.

524

Donaldson, Ian. "*AWW*: Shakespeare's Play of Endings." *Essays in Criticism*. 1977. 27: 34-55.

525

Godshalk, William Leigh. "*AWW* and the Morality Play." *SQ*. 1974. 25: 61-70.

526

Halio, Jay L. "*AWW*." *SQ*. 1964. 15: 33-43.

527

Hapgood, Robert. "The Life of Shame: Parolles and *AWW*." *Essays in Criticism*. 1965. 15: 269-78.

528

Kastan, David Scott. "*AWW* and the Limits of Comedy." *English Literary History*. 1985. 52: 575-89.

529

King, Walter N. "Shakespeare's 'Mingled Yarn'." *Modern Language Quarterly*. 1960. 21: 33-44.

530

Lecercle, Ann. "Anatomy of a Fistula, Anatomy of a Drama." *AWW: Nouvelles Perspectives Critiques*. Fuzier, Jean, and Laroque, Francois, eds. Montpellier: Pubs. de l'Univ. Paul Valéry. 1985. 105-24.

531

Leech, Clifford. "The Theme of Ambition in *AWW*." *English Literary History*. 1954. 21: 17-29.

532

Leggatt, Alexander. "*AWW*: The Testing of Romance." *Modern Language Quarterly*. 1971. 32: 21-41.

533

Levin, Richard A. "*AWW*, and 'All Seems Well'." *Shakespeare Studies*. 1980. 13: 131-44.

534

Nagarajan, S. "The Structure of *AWW*." *Essays in Criticism*. 1960. 10: 24-31.

535

Parker, R.B. "War and Sex in *AWW*." *Shakespeare Survey*. 1984. 37: 99-113.

536

Price, Joseph G. *The Unfortunate Comedy: A Study of* AWW *and Its Critics.* Liverpool: Liverpool University Press, 1968. Toronto: University of Toronto Press, 1969.

537

Schoff, Francis G. "Claudio, Bertram, and a Note on Interpretation." *SQ.* 1959. 10: 11-23.

538

Taylor, Michael. "Persecuting Time with Hope: The Cynicism of Romance in *AWW*." *English Studies in Canada*. 1985. 11: 282-94.

539

Turner, Robert Y. "Dramatic Conventions in *AWW*." *PMLA*. 1960. 75: 497-502.

540

Warren, Roger. "Why Does It End Well? Helena, Bertram, and *Son*." *Shakespeare Survey*. 1969. 22: 79-92.

541

Welsh, Alexander. "The Loss of Men and Getting of Children: *AWW* and *MM*." *Modern Language Review*. 1978. 73: 17-28.

542

Wilson, Harold S. "Dramatic Emphasis in *AWW*." *Huntington Library Quarterly*. 1949-50. 13: 217-40.

See also works listed under *Comedy: General Studies*, above, especially by R.G. Hunter and Salingar, and under *Comedy: The Problem Comedies,* above, especially by Lawrence and Wheeler.

Antony and Cleopatra

543

Adelman, Janet. *The Common Liar: An Essay on "Ant"*. New Haven and London: Yale University Press. 1973.

544

Barroll, J. Leeds. *Shakespearean Tragedy: Genre, Tradition, and Change in* Ant. Washington, D.C.: Folger Shakespeare Library; London: Associated University Presses. 1984.

545

Bono, Barbara J. *Literary Transvaluation: From Vergilian Epic to Shakespearean Tragicomedy.* Berkeley, Los Angeles, and London: University of California Press. 1984.

546

Booth, Stephen. "Poetic Richness: A Preliminary Audit." *Pacific Coast Philology.* 1984. 19: 68-78.

547

Bowers, Fredson. "The Concept of Single or Dual Protagonists in Shakespeare's Tragedies." *Renaissance Papers.* 1982. (published 1983). 27-33.

548

Bradley, A.C. "*Ant.*" *Oxford Lectures on Poetry.* London: Macmillan. 1904.

549

Brand, Alice Glarden. "Antony and Cleopatra and the Nature of Their Sexuality." *The Bard* (London). 1976. 1 (iii): 98-107.

550

Burke, Kenneth. "Shakespearean Persuasion: *Ant.*" *Language as Symbolic Action: Essays on Life, Literature and Method.* Berkeley and Los Angeles: University of California Press. 1966. 101-14.

551

Caputi, Anthony. "Shakespeare's *Ant*: Tragedy without Terror." *SQ.* 1965. 16: 183-91.

552

Charney, Maurice. "Shakespeare's Antony: A Study of Image Themes." *Studies in Philology.* 1957. 54: 149-61.

553

Couchman, Gordon W. "*Ant* and the Subjective Convention." *PMLA.* 1961. 76: 420-25.

554

Danby, John F. "*Ant:* A Shakespearean Adjustment." *Poets on Fortune's Hill.* London: Faber and Faber. 1952. 128-51. Reprinted as *Elizabethan and Jacobean Poets,* 1964.

555

Danby, John F. "The Shakespearean Dialectic." *Scrutiny*. 1949. 16: 196-213.

556

Davies, H. Neville. "Jacobean *Ant*." *Shakespeare Studies*. 1985. 17: 123-58.

557

Donno, Elizabeth S. "Cleopatra Again." *SQ*. 1956. 7: 227-33.

558

Doran, Madeleine. "'High Events as These': The Language of Hyperbole in *Ant*." *Queen's Quarterly*. 1965. 72: 26-51.

559

Estrin, Barbara L. "'Behind a Dream': Cleopatra and Sonnet 129." *Women's Studies*. 1982. 9: 177-88.

560

Fitch, Robert E. "No Greater Crack?" *SQ*. 1968. 19: 3-17.

561

Fitz, L.T. "Egyptian Queens and Male Reviewers: Sexist Attitudes in *Ant* Criticism." *SQ*. 1977. 28: 297-316.

562

Grindon, Rosa. *A Woman's Study of "Ant"*. Manchester: Sherratt and Hughes. 1909.

563

Hamilton, Donna B. "*Ant* and the Tradition of Noble Lovers." *SQ*. 1973. 24: 245-52.

564

Harbage, Alfred. (pseud. Thomas Kyd). "Cosmic Card Game." *American Scholar*. 1951. 20: 325-33.

565

Jorgensen, Paul A. "Antony and the Protesting Soldiers: A Renaissance Tradition for the Structure of *Ant*." *Essays on Shakespeare*. Smith, Gordon Ross, ed. University Park and London: Pennsylvania State University Press. 1965. 163-81.

566

Kaula, David. "The Time Sense of *Ant*." *SQ*. 1964. 15: 211-23.

567

Leavis, Frank R. "*Ant* and [Dryden's] *All for Love*: A Critical Exercise." *Scrutiny*. 1936-7. 5: 158-69.

568

Lloyd, Michael. "Antony and the Game of Chance." *Journal of English and Germanic Philology*. 1962. 61: 548-54.

569

Lloyd, Michael. "Cleopatra as Isis." *Shakespeare Survey*. 1959. 12: 88-94.

570

Lloyd, Michael. "The Roman Tongue." *SQ*. 1959. 10: 461-8.

571

MacDonald, Ronald R. "Playing Till Doomsday: Interpreting *Ant*." *English Literary Renaissance*. 1985. 15: 78-99.

572

Mack, Maynard. "*Ant:* The Stillness and the Dance." *Shakespeare's Art: Seven Essays*. Crane, Milton, ed. Chicago and London: University of Chicago Press. 1973. 79-113.

573

Markels, Julian. *The Pillar of the World:* Ant *in Shakespeare's Development*. Columbus: Ohio State University Press. 1968.

574

Mills, Laurens J. *The Tragedies of Shakespeare's* Ant. Bloomington: Indiana University Press. 1964.

575

Moore, John R. "The Enemies of Love: The Examples of Antony and Cleopatra." *Kenyon Review*. 1969. 31: 646-74.

576

Nevo, Ruth. "The Masque of Greatness." *Shakespeare Studies*. 1967. 3: 111-28.

577

Ornstein, Robert T. "The Ethic of the Imagination: Love and Art in *Ant*." *Later Shakespeare*. Stratford-upon-Avon Studies 8. London: E. Arnold. 1966. 31-48.

578

Plutarch. *The Life of Marcus Antonius*. Trans. North, Thomas. *Shakespeare's Plutarch*. Spencer, T.J.B., ed. Harmondsworth: Penguin. 1964.

579

Riemer, A.P. *A Reading of Shakespeare's* Ant. Sydney: Sydney University Press. 1968.

580

Rose, Paul L. "The Politics of *Ant*." *SQ*. 1969. 20: 379-89.

581

Rozett, Martha Tuck. "The Comic Structures of Tragic Endings: The Suicide Scenes in *Rom* and *Ant*." *SQ*. 1985. 36: 152-64.

582

Shapiro, Michael. "Boying Her Greatness: Shakespeare's Use of Coterie Drama in *Ant*." *Modern Language Review*. 1982. 77: 1-15.

583

Shapiro, Stephen A. "The Varying Shore of the World: Ambivalence in *Ant*." *Modern Language Quarterly*. 1966. 27: 18-32.

584

Simmons, Joseph L. "The Comic Pattern and Vision in *Ant*." *English Literary History*. 1969. 36: 493-510.

585

Simpson, Lucie. "Shakespeare's 'Cleopatra'." *Fortnightly Review*. March 1928. NS 123: 332-42.

586

Snyder, Susan. "Patterns of Motion in *Ant*." *Shakespeare Survey*. 1980. 33: 113-22.

587

Stempel, Daniel. "The Transmigration of the Crocodile." *SQ*. 1956. 7: 59-72.

588

Steppat, Michael. *The Critical Reception of Shakespeare's* Ant *from 1607 to 1905*. Amsterdam: Grüner. 1980.

589

Stirling, Brents. "Cleopatra's Scene with Seleucus: Plutarch, Daniel, and Shakespeare." *SQ*. 1964. 15: 299-311.

590

Stoll, Elmer E. "Cleopatra." *Modern Language Review*. 1928. 23: 145-63.

591

Stroup, Thomas B. "The Structure of *Ant*." *SQ* . 1964. 15: 289-98.

592

Traci, Philip J. *The Love Play of Antony and Cleopatra*. The Hague: Mouton. 1970.

593

Vincent, Barbara C. "Shakespeare's *Ant* and the Rise of Comedy." *English Literary Renaissance*. 1982. 12: 53-86.

594

Williamson, Marilyn L. *Infinite Variety: Antony and Cleopatra in Renaissance Drama and Earlier Tradition*. Mystic, Connecticut: Lawrence Verry. 1974.

595

Wilson, Elkin Calhoun. "Shakespeare's Enobarbus." *Joseph Quincy Adams Memorial Studies*. McManaway, James G., et al, eds. Washington, D.C.: Folger Shakespeare Library. 1948. 391-408.

596

Wimsatt, William K. "Poetry and Morals: A Relation Reargued." *Thought*. 1948. 23: 281-99. Reprinted in Wimsatt, *The Verbal Icon*. Lexington, Ky.: University of Kentucky Press, 1954. 85-100.

597

Woodbridge, Linda. *Women and the English Renaissance*. Urbana and Chicago: University of Illinois Press; Brighton: Harvester. 1984. 152-62, 195-6, 294-7, passim.

See also works listed under *Tragedy*, above, especially by Brower, Cantor, Charney, Farnham, Holloway, Mack, Maxwell, Proser, Rosen, Simmons, Spencer, and Traversi.

As You Like It

598

Alpers, Paul. "What is Pastoral?" *Critical Inquiry*. 1982. 8: 437-60.

599

Babb, Lawrence. *The Elizabethan Malady: A Study of Melancholia in English Literature, from 1580-1642*. East Lansing, Michigan: Michigan State College Press. 1951.

600

Barber, C.L. "The Use of Comedy in *AYL*." *Philological Quarterly*. 1942. 21: 353-67.

601

Barnet, Sylvan. "'Strange Events': Improbability in *AYL*." *Shakespeare Studies*. 1968. 4: 119-31.

602

Barton, Anne. "*AYL* and *TN:* Shakespeare's Sense of an Ending." *Shakespearean Comedy*. Bradbury, Malcolm, and Palmer, D.J., eds. London and New York: E. Arnold. 1972. 160-80. Stratford-upon-Avon Studies 14.

603

Bennett, Robert B. "The Reform of a Malcontent: Jaques and the Meaning of *AYL*." *Shakespeare Studies*. 1976. 9: 183-204.

604

Berry, Edward I. "Rosalynde and Rosalind." *SQ*. 1980. 31: 42-52.

605

Bracher, Mark. "Contrary Notions of Identity in *AYL*." *Studies in English Literature*. 1984. 24: 225-40.

606

Burns, Margie. "Odd and Even in *AYL*." *Allegorica*. 1980. 5: 119-40.

607

Chew, Samuel C. "'This Strange Eventful History'." *Joseph Quincy Adams Memorial Studies*. McManaway, James G., et al, eds. Washington, D.C.: Folger Shakespeare Library. 1948. 157-82.

608

Cirillo, Albert R. "*AYL*: Pastoralism Gone Awry." *English Literary History*. 1971. 38: 19-39.

609

Doebler, John. *Shakespeare's Speaking Pictures: Studies in Iconic Imagery*. Albuquerque, N.M.: University of New Mexico Press. 1974.

610

Doran, Madeleine. "'Yet Am I Inland Bred'." *SQ*. 1964. 15: 99-114.

611

Draper, R.P. "Shakespeare's Pastoral Comedy." *Etudes Anglaises*. 1958. 11: 1-17.

612

Erickson, Peter B. "Sexual Politics and the Social Structure in *AYL*." *Massachusetts Review*. 1982. 23: 65-83.

613

Fink, Zera S. "Jaques and the Malcontent Traveler." *Philological Quarterly.* 1935. 14: 237-52.

614

Fortin, René E. "'Tongues in Trees': Symbolic Patterns in *AYL.*" *Texas Studies in Literature and Language.* 1973. 14: 569-82.

615

Frail, David. "To the Point of Folly: Touchstone's Function in *AYL.*" *Massachusetts Review.* 1981. 22: 695-717.

616

Halio, Jay L. "'No Clock in the Forest': Time in *AYL.*" *Studies in English Literature.* 1962. 2: 197-207.

617

Halio, Jay L., and Millard, Barbara C., comps. AYL: *An Annotated Bibliography, 1940-1980.* New York: Garland. 1985.

618

Iser, Wolfgang. "The Dramatization of Double Meaning in Shakespeare's *AYL.*" *Theatre Journal* (Columbia, Missouri). 1983. 35: 307-32.

619

Jamieson, Michael. *Shakespeare:* AYL. London: E. Arnold. 1965.

620

Jenkins, Harold. "*AYL.*" *Shakespeare Survey.* 1955. 8: 40-51.

621

Kernan, Alvin B. *The Cankered Muse: Satire of the English Renaissance.* New Haven: Yale University Press. 1959.

622

Kimbrough, Robert. "Androgyny Seen Through Shakespeare's Disguise." *SQ.* 1982. 33: 17-33.

623

Knowles, Richard. "Myth and Type in *AYL.*" *English Literary History.* 1966. 33: 1-22.

624

Kreider, Paul V. "Genial Literary Satire in the Forest of Arden." *Shakespeare Association Bulletin.* 1935. 10: 212-31.

625

Lerner, Laurence. "The Pastoral World: Arcadia and the Golden Age." *The Pastoral Mode: A Casebook.* Loughrey, Bryan, ed. London: Macmillan.

1984.

626

Marx, Steven. "'Fortunate Senex': The Pastoral of Old Age." *Studies in English Literature*. 1985. 25: 21-44.

627

Mincoff, Marco. "What Shakespeare Did to *Rosalynde*." *Shakespeare-Jahrbuch*. 1960. 96: 78-89.

628

Morris, Harry. "*AYL*: Et in Arcadia Ego." *SQ* . 1975. 26: 269-75.

629

Palmer, D.J. "Art and Nature in *AYL*." *Philological Quarterly*. 1970. 49: 30-40.

630

Park, Clara Claiborne. "As We Like It: How a Girl Can be Smart and Still Popular." *American Scholar*. 1973. 42: 262-78. Revised version reprinted in *The Woman's Part*. Ed. Carolyn Ruth Swift Lenz et al. Urbana, Chicago, and London: University of Illinois Press, 1980. 100-16.

631

Shaw, John. "Fortune and Nature in *AYL*." *SQ* . 1955. 6: 45-50.

632

Smith, James C. "*AYL*." *Scrutiny*. 1940-41. 9: 9-32.

633

Spencer, Theodore. "The Elizabethan Malcontent." *Joseph Quincy Adams Memorial Studies*. McManaway, James G., et al, eds. Washington, D.C.: Folger Shakespeare Library. 1948. 523-35.

634

Staebler, Warren. "Shakespeare's Play of Atonement." *Shakespeare Association Bulletin*. 1949. 24: 91-105.

635

Stoll, Elmer E. "Jaques and the Antiquaries." *Modern Language Notes*. 1939. 54: 79-84.

636

Tolman, Albert H. "Shakespeare's Manipulation of His Sources in *AYL*." *Modern Language Notes*. 1922. 37: 65-76.

637

Traci, Philip. "*AYL*: Homosexuality in Shakespeare's Play." *College Language Association Journal*. 1981. 25: 91-105.

59

638

Van den Berg, Kent. "Theatrical Fiction and the Reality of Love in *AYL*." *PMLA*. 1975. 90: 885-93.

639

Whall, Helen M. "*AYL*: The Play of Analogy." *Huntington Library Quarterly*. 1984. 47: 33-46.

640

Williamson, Marilyn L. "The Masque of Hymen in *AYL*." *Comparative Drama*. 1968. 2: 248-58.

641

Wilson, Rawdon. "The Way to Arden: Attitudes toward Time in *AYL*." *SQ*. 1975. 26: 16-24.

642

Young, David. *The Heart's Forest: A Study of Shakespeare's Pastoral Plays*. New Haven: Yale University Press. 1972.

See also works listed under *Comedy: General Studies*, especially by Brown, R. G. Hunter, McFarland, Salingar, and under *Comedy: The Middle and Romantic Comedies*, especially by Leggatt and Mahood.

The Comedy of Errors

643

Arthos, John. "Shakespeare's Transformation of Plautus." *Comparative Drama*. 1967. 1: 239-53.

644

Baldwin, T.W. *On the Compositional Genetics of "Err"*. Urbana: University of Illinois Press. 1965.

645

Barber, C.L. "Shakespearean Comedy in *Err*." *College English*. 1964. 25: 493-7.

646

Brooks, Harold. "Themes and Structure in *Err*." *Early Shakespeare*. Brown, John Russell, and Harris, Bernard, eds. London: E. Arnold. 1961. 55-71. Stratford-upon-Avon Studies 3.

647

Clubb, Louise G. "Italian Comedy and *Err.*" *Comparative Literature.* 1967. 19: 240-51.

648

Coulter, Cornelia C. "The Plautine Tradition in Shakespeare." *Journal of English and Germanic Philology.* 1919. 18: 66-83.

649

Crewe, Jonathan V. "God or the Good Physician: The Rational Playwright in *Err.*" *Genre.* 1982. 15: 203-23.

650

Elliott, George R. "Weirdness in *Err.*" *University of Toronto Quarterly.* 1939. 9: 95-106.

651

Freedman, Barbara. "Egeon's Debt: Self-Division and Self-Redemption in *Err.*" *English Literary Renaissance.* 1980. 10: 360-83.

652

Girard, René. "Comedies of Errors: Plautus-Shakespeare-Molière." *American Criticism in the Poststructuralist Age.* Konigsberg, Ira, ed. Ann Arbor: University of Michigan Press. 1981. 66-86.

653

Knight, W. Nicholas. "Equity in Shakespeare and His Contemporaries." *Iowa State Journal of Research.* 1981. 56: 67-77.

654

Lea, K.M. *Italian Popular Comedy: A Study in the Commedia dell' Arte, 1560-1620, with Special Reference to the English Stage.* Oxford: Clarendon. 1934.

655

Parker, Patricia. "Elder and Younger: The Opening Scene of *Err.*" *SQ.* 1983. 34: 325-7.

656

Salgado, Gamini. "'Time's Deformed Hand': Sequence, Consequence, and Inconsequence in *Err.*" *Shakespeare Survey.* 1972. 25: 81-91.

657

Shaw, Catherine M. *"The Conscious Art of* Err." Shakespearean Comedy. Charney, Maurice, ed. *New York Literary Forum.*, 1980. 17-28.

61

658

Trousdale, Marion. "Semiotics and Shakespeare's Comedies." *Shakespearean Comedy*. Charney, Maurice, ed. *New York Literary Forum*. 1980. 245-55.

659

Williams, Gwyn. "*Err* Rescued from Tragedy." *Review of English Literature*. 1964. 5: 63-71.

See also works listed under *Comedy: General Studies*, especially by Berry, Charleton, Evans, Pettet, Richmond, Salingar, Tillyard, and under *Comedy: The Early Comedies*, especially by Cody, Traversi, and Turner.

660

Adelman, Janet. "'Anger's My Meat': Feeding, Dependency, and Aggression in *Cor.*" *Shakespeare, Pattern of Excelling Nature.* Bevington, David, and Halio, Jay L., eds. Newark, Del.: University of Delaware Press; London: Associated University Presses. 1978. 108-24.

661

Alvis, John. "Coriolanus and Aristotle's Magnanimous Man Reconsidered." *Interpretation: A Journal of Political Philosophy.* 1978. 7: 4-28.

662

Barton, Anne. "Livy, Machiavelli, and Shakespeare's *Cor.*" *Shakespeare Survey.* 1985. 38: 115-29.

663

Berry, Ralph. "The Metamorphoses of *Cor.*" *SQ* . 1975. 26: 172-83.

664

Berry, Ralph. "Sexual Imagery in *Cor.*" *Studies in English Literature.* 1973. 13: 301-16.

665

Bradley, A.C. *Coriolanus.* Oxford and New York: Oxford University Press. 1912.

666

Brittin, Norman A. "*Cor*, Alceste, and Dramatic Genres." *PMLA.* 1956. 71: 799-807.

667

Brockman, B.A., ed. *Shakespeare's "Cor": A Casebook.* London: Macmillan. 1977.

668

Browning, Ivor R. "*Cor*: Boy of Tears." *Essays In Criticism.* 1955. 5: 13-31.

669

Burton, Dolores M. "Odds Beyond Arithmetic: Comparative Clauses in *Cor.*" *Style.* 1980. 14: 299-317.

670

Calderwood, James L. "*Cor*: Wordless Meanings and Meaningless Words." *Studies in English Literature.* 1966. 6: 211-24.

671

Carr, W.I. "'Gracious Silence'--A Selective Reading of *Cor.*" *English Studies.* 1965. 46: 221-34.

672

Cavell, Stanley. "'Who Does the Wolf Love?' Reading *Cor.*" *Representations.* 1983. 1 (3): 1-20.

673

Charney, Maurice. "The Dramatic Use of Imagery of Shakespeare's *Cor.*" *English Literary History.* 1956. 23: 183-93.

674

Colman, E.A.M. "The End of Coriolanus." *English Literary History.* 1967. 34: 1-20.

675

Craig, Hardin. "*Cor:* Interpretation." *Pacific Coast Studies in Shakespeare.* McNeir, Waldo F., and Greenfield, Thelma N., eds. Eugene: University of Oregon Press. 1966. 199-209.

676

Dean, Leonard F. "Voice and Deed in *Cor.*" *University Review.* 1955. 21: 177-84.

677

DuBois, Page. "A Disturbance of Syntax at the Gates of Rome." *Stanford Literature Review.* 1985. 2: 185-208.

678

Enright, D.J. "*Cor*: Tragedy or Debate?" *Essays in Criticism.* 1954. 4: 1-19.

679

Faber, M.D. "Freud and Shakespeare's Mobs." *Literature and Psychology.* 1965. 15: 238-55.

680

Fish, Stanley. "How to Do Things with Austin and Searle: Speech Act Theory and Literary Criticism." *Modern Language Notes.* 1976. 91: 983-1025.

681

Frye, Dean. "Commentary in Shakespeare: The Case of *Cor.*" *Shakespeare Studies.* 1965. 1: 105-17.

682

Goldman, Michael. "Characterizing Coriolanus." *Shakespeare Survey.* 1981. 34: 73-84.

683

Gordon, D.J. "Name and Fame: Shakespeare's Coriolanus." *Papers Mainly Shakespearean.* Duthie, G.I., ed. Edinburgh: Oliver and Boyd. 1964. 40-57.

684

Hill, R.F. "*Cor*: Violentest Contrariety." *Essays and Studies by Members of the English Association.* 1964. 17: 12-23.

685

Hofling, Charles K. "An Interpretation of Shakespeare's Coriolanus." *American Imago.* 1957. 14: 407-35.

686

Holstun, James. "Tragic Superfluity in *Cor*." *English Literary History.* 1983. 50: 485-507.

687

Honig, Edwin. "*Sejanus* and *Cor*: A Study in Alienation." *Modern Language Quarterly.* 1951. 12: 407-21.

688

Huffman, Clifford Chalmers. Cor *in Context.* Lewisburn, Pa.: Bucknell University Press. 1971.

689

Hutchings, W. "Beast or God: The *Cor* Controversy." *Critical Quarterly.* 1982. 24: 35-50.

690

Jorgensen, Paul A. "Shakespeare's Coriolanus: Elizabethan Soldier." *PMLA.* 1949. 64: 221-35.

691

Knights, L.C. "Shakespeare and Political Wisdom: A Note on the Personalism of *JC* and *Cor*." *Sewanee Review.* 1953. 61: 43-55.

692

McCanles, Michael. "The Dialectic of Transcendence in Shakespeare's *Cor*." *PMLA.* 1967. 82: 44-53.

693

MacIntyre, Jean. "Word, Acts, and Things: Visual Language in *Cor*." *English Studies in Canada.* 1984. 10: 1-10.

65

694

MacLure, Millar. "Shakespeare and the Lonely Dragon." *University of Toronto Quarterly*. 1955. 24: 109-120.

695

Maxwell, J.C. "Animal Imagery in *Cor*." *Modern Language Review*. 1947. 42: 417-21.

696

Mitchell, Charles. "*Cor*: Power as Honor." *Shakespeare Studies*. 1965. 1: 199-226.

697

Muir, Kenneth. "The Background of *Cor*." *SQ*. 1959. 10: 137-45.

698

Münch, W. "Aufidius." *Shakespeare-Jahrbuch*. 1906. 42: 127-47.

699

Murry, John Middleton. "*Coriolanus*." *Discoveries*. London: Collins. 1924.

700

Neumeyer, Peter F. "Ingratitude is Monstrous: An Approach to *Cor*." *College English*. 1964. 25: 192-8.

701

Oliver, Harold J. "Coriolanus as Tragic Hero." *SQ*. 1959. 10: 53-60.

702

Proser, Matthew N. "*Cor*: The Constant Warrior and the State." *College English*. 1963. 24: 507-12.

703

Rabkin, Norman. "*Cor*: The Tragedy of Politics." *SQ*. 1966. 17: 195-212.

704

Rackin, Phyllis. "*Cor*: Shakespeare's Anatomy of *Virtus*." *Modern Language Studies*. 1983. 13: 68-79.

705

Rouda, F.H. "*Cor* -- A Tragedy of Youth." *SQ* . 1961. 12: 103-6.

706

Simonds, Peggy Muñoz. "*Cor* and the Myth of Juno and Mars." *Mosaic*. 1985. 18: 33-50.

707

Stockholder, Katherine. "The Other Coriolanus." *PMLA*. 1970. 85: 228-36.

708

Taylor, Michael. "Playing the Man He Is: Role-Playing in Shakespeare's *Cor.*" *Ariel: Review of International English Literature.* 1984. 15: 19-28.

709

Traversi, Derek A. "*Cor.*" *Scrutiny.* 1937-38. 6: 43-58.

710

Wilson, Emmett. "Coriolanus: The Anxious Bridegroom." *American Imago.* 1968. 25: 224-41.

711

Zeeveld, W. Gordon. "*Cor* and Jacobean Politics." *Modern Language Review.* 1962. 57: 321-34.

See also works listed under *Tragedy*, especially by Brower, Cantor, Charney, Danson, Farnham, Holloway, and Rosen.

Cymbeline

712

Bergeron, David M. "Sexuality in *Cym.*" *Essays in Literature.* (Western Illinois University) 1983. 10: 159-68.

713

Brockbank, J.P. "History and Histrionics in *Cym.*" *Shakespeare Survey.* 1958. 11: 42-9.

714

Camden, Carroll C. "The Elizabethan Imogen." *Rice Institute Pamphlet.* 1951. 38: 1-17.

715

Dusinberre, Juliet. *Shakespeare and the Nature of Women.* London: Macmillan. 1975. 263-5, passim.

716

Foakes, R.A. "Character and Dramatic Technique in *Cym and WT.*" *Studies in the Arts: Proceedings of the St. Peter's College Literary Society.* Warner, Francis, ed. Oxford: Blackwell. 1968. 116-30.

717

Geller, Lila. "*Cym* and the Imagery of Covenant Theology." *Studies in English Literature.* 1980. 20: 241-55.

718

Gesner, Carol. "*Cym* and the Greek Romances." *Studies in English Renaissance Literature Dedicated to John Earle Uhler.* McNeir, Waldo, ed. Baton Rouge: Louisiana State University Press. 1962. 105-31.

719

Gilliland, Joan F. "*Cym* as Folk Tale." *Bulletin of the West Virginia Association of College English Teachers.* 1981. 6: 13-18.

720

Harris, Bernard. "'What's Past is Prologue': *Cym* and *H8*." *Later Shakespeare.* Brown, John Russell, and Harris, Bernard, eds. London: E. Arnold. 1966. 203-34. Stratford-upon-Avon Studies 8.

721

Hoeniger, F.D. "Irony and Romance in *Cym*." *Studies in English Literature.* 1962. 2: 219-28.

722

Hofling, Charles K. "Notes on Shakespeare's *Cym*." *Shakespeare Studies.* 1965. 1: 118-36.

723

Hunt, Maurice. "Shakespeare's Empirical Romance: *Cym* and Modern Knowledge." *Texas Studies in Literature and Language.* 1980. 22: 322-42.

724

Jacobs, Henry E., comp. Cym*: An Annotated Bibliography.* New York: Garland. 1982.

725

Jones, Emrys. "Stuart Cymbeline." *Essays in Criticism.* 1961. 11: 84-99.

726

Kay, Carol McGinnis. "Generic Sleight-of-Hand in *Cym*." *South Atlantic Review.* 1981. 46: 34-40.

727

Kirsch, Arthur C. "*Cym* and Coterie Dramaturgy." *English Literary History.* 1967. 34: 285-306.

728

Kirsch, Arthur C. "Jacobean Theatrical Self-Consciousness." *Research Opportunities in Renaissance Drama.* 1980. 23: 9-13.

729

Landry, D.E. "Dreams as History: The Strange Unity of *Cym*." *SQ.* 1982. 33: 68-79.

730

Lawrence, Judiana. "Natural Bonds and Artistic Coherence in the Ending of *Cym.*" *SQ.* 1984. 35: 440-60.

731

Leggatt, Alexander. "The Island of Miracles: An Approach to *Cym.*" *Shakespeare Studies.* 1977. 10: 191-209.

732

Marsh, D.R.C. *The Recurring Miracle: A Study of* Cym *and the Last Plays.* Pietermaritzburg: University of Natal Press. 1962.

733

Marx, Joan C. "The Encounter of Genres: *Cym's* Structure of Juxtaposition." *The Analysis of Literary Texts: Current Trends in Methodology.* Pope, Randolph D, ed. Ypsilanti, Michigan: Bilingual Press. 1980. 138-44.

734

Moffet, Robin. "*Cym* and the Nativity." *SQ.* 1962. 13: 207-18.

735

Mowat, Barbara A. "*Cym*: Crude Dramaturgy and Aesthetic Distance." *Renaissance Papers 1966.* 1967. 39-48.

736

Nosworthy, J.M. "The Integrity of Shakespeare: Illustrated from *Cym.*" *Shakespeare Survey.* 1955. 8: 52-6.

737

Ribner, Irving. "Shakespeare and Legendary History: *Lr* and *Cym.*" *SQ.* 1956. 7: 47-52.

738

Shaheen, Naseeb. "The Use of Scripture in *Cym.*" *Shakespeare Studies.* 1969. 4: 294-315.

739

Skura, Meredith. "Interpreting Posthumus' Dream from Above and Below: Families, Psychoanalysts, and Literary Critics." *Representing Shakespeare.* Schwartz, Murray M., and Kahn, Coppélia, eds. Baltimore and London: Johns Hopkins University Press. 1980. 203-16.

740

Smith, Warren D. "Cloten with Caius Lucius." *Studies in Philology.* 1952. 49: 185-94.

741

Stamm, Rudolf. "George Bernard Shaw and Shakespeare's *Cym.*" *Studies in Honor of T.W. Baldwin.* Allen, Don Cameron, ed. Urbana: University of Illinois Press. 1958. 254-66.

742

Stephenson, A.A. "The Significance of *Cym.*" *Scrutiny.* 1941-42. 10: 329-38.

743

Swander, Homer D. "*Cym* and the 'Blameless Hero'." *English Literary History.* 1964. 31: 259-70.

744

Swander, Homer D. "*Cym:* Religious Idea and Dramatic Design." *Pacific Coast Studies in Shakespeare.* McNeir, Waldo F., and Greenfield, Thelma N., eds. Eugene: University of Oregon Press. 1966. 248-62.

745

Taylor, Michael. "The Pastoral Reckoning in *Cym.*" *Shakespeare Survey.* 1983. 36: 97-106.

746

Thorne, William B. "*Cym*: 'Lopp'd Branches' and the Concept of Regeneration." *SQ.* 1969. 20: 143-59.

747

Tinkler, F.C. "*Cym.*" *Scrutiny.* 1938-39. 7: 5-20.

748

Turner, Robert Y. "Slander in *Cym* and Other Jacobean Tragicomedies." *English Literary Renaissance.* 1983. 13: 182-202.

749

Warren, Roger. "Theatrical Virtuosity and Poetic Complexity in *Cym.*" *Shakespeare Survey.* 1976. 29: 41-50.

750

Wickham, Glynne. "Riddle and Emblem: A Study in the Dramatic Structure of *Cym.*" *English Renaissance Studies Presented to Dame Helen Gardner.* Carey, John, ed. Oxford: Clarendon. 1980. 94-113.

751

Wilson, Harold S. "*Philaster* and *Cym.*" *English Institute Essays 1951.* 1952. 146-67.

See also works listed under *Comedy: The Late Romances*, especially by Felperin, Frye, Gesner, Kay, and Mowat.

752

Aldus, P.J. *Mousetrap: Structure and Meaning in* Ham. Toronto and Buffalo: University of Toronto Press. 1977.

753

Alexander, Peter. *Hamlet: Father and Son.* Oxford: Clarendon. 1955.

754

Altick, Richard D. "*Ham* and the Odor of Mortality." *SQ.* 1954. 5: 167-76.

755

Andrews, Michael Cameron. "*Ham* and the Satisfactions of Revenge."
Hamlet Studies. 1981. 3: 83-102.

756

Baldo, Jonathan. "'He That Plays the King': The Problem of Pretending in
Ham." *Criticism.* 1983. 25: 13-26.

757

Battenhouse, Roy W. "The Ghost in *Ham*: A Catholic 'Linchpin'?" *Studies
in Philology.* 1951. 48: 161-92.

758

Bennett, Josephine W. "Characterization in Polonius' Advice to Laertes."
SQ. 1953. 4: 3-9.

759

Berry, Ralph. "Hamlet: Nationhood and Identity." *University of Toronto
Quarterly.* 1980. 49: 283-303.

760

Bonjour, Adrien. "Hamlet and the Phantom Clue." *English Studies.* 1954.
35: 253-9.

761

Bonjour, Adrien. "The Question of Hamlet's Grief." *English Studies.* 1962.
43: 336-43.

762

Booth, Stephen. "On the Value of *Ham.*" *Reinterpretations of Elizabethan
Drama.* Rabkin, Norman, ed. London and New York: Columbia University Press. 1969. 137-76. Selected Papers from the English Institute.

763

Bowers, Fredson T. "The Death of Hamlet: A Study in Plot and Character."
Studies in English Renaissance Drama in Memory of Karl Julius

Holzknecht. New York: New York University Press. 1959. 28-42.

764

Bowers, Fredson T. *Elizabethan Revenge Tragedy, 1587-1642*. Princeton: Princeton University Press. 1940.

765

Braddy, Haldeen. *Hamlet's Wounded Name*. El Paso: Texas Western College Press. 1964.

766

Brashear, William R. "Nietzsche and Spengler on Hamlet." *The Gorgon's Head: A Study in Tragedy and Despair*. Athens: University of Georgia Press. 1977. 15-26.

767

Brown, John Russell, and Harris, Bernard, eds. *Ham*. London: Arnold; New York: Schocken. 1963. Stratford-upon-Avon Studies 5.

768

Brucher, Richard T. "Fantasies of Violence: *Ham* and *The Revenger's Tragedy*." *Studies in English Literature*. 1981. 21: 257-70.

769

Calderwood, James L. "Hamlet's Readiness." *SQ*. 1984. 35: 267-73.

770

Calderwood, James L. *To Be and Not to Be: Negation and Metadrama in Ham*. New York and London: Columbia University Press. 1983.

771

Camden, Carroll C. "On Ophelia's Madness." *SQ*. 1964. 15: 247-55.

772

Charney, Maurice. *Style in Ham*. Princeton: Princeton University Press. 1969.

773

Childs, Herbert E. "On the Elizabethan Staging of *Ham*." *SQ*. 1962. 13: 463-74.

774

Clifton, Charles H. "Hamlet *Ludens*: The Importance of Playing in *Ham*." *Shakespeare and Renaissance Association of West Virginia: Selected Papers*. 1981. 6: 35-41.

775

Conklin, Paul. *A History of Ham Criticism, 1601-1821*. Oxford: Oxford University Press; New York: King's Crown. 1947.

72

776

Cooperman, Stanley. "Shakespeare's Anti-Hero: Hamlet and the Underground Man." *Shakespeare Studies.* 1965. 1: 37-63.

777

Craig, Hardin. "Hamlet as a Man of Action." *Huntington Library Quarterly.* 1963-64. 27: 229-37.

778

Craig, Hardin. "Hamlet's Book." *Huntington Library Bulletin.* 1934. 6: 17-37.

779

Davidson, H.R. Ellis. "The Hero as Fool: The Northern Hamlet." *The Hero in Tradition and Folklore.* Davidson, H.R.E., and Blacker, Carmen, eds. London: Folklore Society. 1984. 30-45.

780

Deats, Sara M. "The Once and Future Kings: Four Studies of Kingship in *Ham.*" *Essays in Literature.* (Western Illinois University) 1982. 9: 15-30.

781

Doebler, Bettie Anne. "*Ham*: A Grave Scene and Its Audience." *Hamlet Studies.* 1981. 3: 68-82.

782

Doran, Madeleine. "The Language of *Ham.*" *Huntington Library Quarterly.* 1963-64. 27: 259-78.

783

Draper, John W. *The Ham of Shakespeare's Audience.* Durham: Duke University Press. 1938.

784

Edwards, Philip. "Tragic Balance in *Ham.*" *Shakespeare Survey.* 1983. 36: 43-52.

785

Eliot, T.S. "Hamlet and His Problems." *The Sacred Wood.* London: Methuen. 1920. 95-103.

786

Elliott, G.R. *Scourge and Minister: A Study of Ham as Tragedy of Revengefulness and Justice.* Durham: Duke University Press. 1951.

787

Empson, William. "*Ham* When New." *Sewanee Review.* 1953. 61: 15-42, 185-205.

788

Falk, Doris V. "Proverbs and the Polonius Destiny." *SQ* . 1967. 18: 23-36.

789

Ferguson, Margaret W. "*Ham:* Letters and Spirits." *Shakespeare and the Question of Theory.* Parker, Patricia, and Hartman, Geoffrey, eds. New York and London: Methuen. 1985. 292-309.

790

Fleming, Keith. "*Hamlet* and *Oedipus* Today: Jones and Lacan." *Hamlet Studies.* 1982. 4: 54-71.

791

Foakes, R.A. "*Ham* and the Court of Elsinore." *Shakespeare Survey.* 1956. 9: 35-43.

792

Forker, Charles R. "Shakespeare's Theatrical Symbolism and Its Function in *Ham.*" *SQ.* 1963. 14: 215-29.

793

Frye, Roland M. *The Renaissance* Ham: *Issues and Responses in 1600.* Princeton: Princeton University Press. 1984.

794

Gardner, Helen. "The Historical Approach." *The Business of Criticism.* Oxford: Oxford University Press. 1959. 25-51.

795

Gomez, Christine. "Hamlet--An Early Existential Outsider?" *Hamlet Studies.* 1983. 5: 27-39.

796

Graves, Michael. "Hamlet as Fool." *Hamlet Studies.* 1982. 4: 72-88.

797

Guilfoyle, Cherrell. "'Ower Swete Sokor': The Role of Ophelia in *Ham.*" *Comparative Drama.* 1980. 14: 3-17.

798

Gurr, Andrew. Ham *and the Distracted Globe.* Edinburgh: Scottish Academic Press. 1978.

799

Halio, Jay L. "Hamlet's Alternative." *Texas Studies in Literature and Language.* 1966. 8: 169-88.

800

Hamilton, William. "Hamlet and Providence." *Christian Scholar*. 1964. 47: 193-207.

801

Hapgood, Robert. "*Ham* Nearly Absurd: The Dramaturgy of Delay." *The Drama Review*. 1965. 9: 132-45.

802

Hardison, O.B. "The Dramatic Triad in *Ham.*" *Studies in Philology*. 1960. 57: 144-64.

803

Hawkes, Terence. *Shakespeare's Talking Animals: Language and Drama in Society*. London: E. Arnold. 1973.

804

Hawkes, Terence. "*Telmah.*" *Shakespeare and the Question of Theory*. Parker, Patricia, and Hartman, Geoffrey, eds. New York and London: Methuen. 1985. 310-32.

805

Hedrick, Donald K. "'It is No Novelty for a Prince to be a Prince': An Enantiomorphous Hamlet." *SQ*. 1984. 35: 62-76.

806

Hertzbach, Janet S. "Hamlet and the Integrity of Majesty." *Hamlet Studies*. 1983. 5: 40-51.

807

Hirsh, James E. "The 'To Be or Not To Be' Scene and the Conventions of Shakespearean Drama." *Modern Language Quarterly*. 1981. 42: 115-36.

808

Hunter, G.K. "Isocrates' Precepts and Polonius' Character." *SQ*. 1957. 8: 501-6.

809

Jenkins, Harold. *Hamlet and Ophelia*. Oxford: Oxford University Press. 1964.

810

Jewkes, W.T. "'To Tell My Story': The Function of Framed Narrative and Drama in *Ham.*" *Shakespearian Tragedy*. Bradbury, Malcolm, and Palmer, David, eds. New York: Holmes and Meier. 1984. 31-46. Stratford upon Avon Studies 20.

811

Jones, Ernest. *Hamlet and Oedipus.* London: V. Gollancz; Garden City, N.Y.: Doubleday. 1949.

812

Jones-Davies, Marie-Thérèse. "'The Players . . . Will Tell All,' or the Actor's Role in Renaissance Drama." *Shakespeare, Man of the Theater.* Muir, Kenneth, et al, eds. Newark: University of Delaware Press; London and Toronto: Associated University Presses. 1983. 76-85.

813

Jorgensen, Paul A. "*Ham* and the Restless Renaissance." *Shakespearean Essays.* Thaler, Alwin, and Sanders, Norman, eds. Knoxville: University of Tennessee Press. 1964. 131-43.

814

Jorgensen, Paul A. "Hamlet's Therapy." *Huntington Library Quarterly.* 1963-64. 27: 239-58.

815

Joseph, Bertram. *Conscience and the King: A Study of* Ham. London: Chatto and Windus. 1953.

816

Joseph, Bertram. "*The Spanish Tragedy* and *Ham:* Two Exercises in English Seneca." *Classical Drama and Its Influence: Essays Presented to H.D.F. Kitto.* Anderson, M.J, ed. London: Methuen; New York: Barnes and Noble. 1965. 119-34.

817

Jump, John D., ed. *Shakespeare:* Ham, *a Casebook.* London: Macmillan. 1968.

818

Kerrigan, William. "Psychoanalysis Unbound." *New Literary History.* 1980. 12: 199-206.

819

King, Walter N. *Hamlet's Search for Meaning.* Athens: University of Georgia Press. 1982.

820

Kirsch, Arthur C. "Hamlet's Grief." *English Literary History.* 1981. 48: 17-36.

821

Kitto, H.D.F. Ham. *Form and Meaning in Drama.* London: Methuen. 1956. 246-337.

822

Knights, L.C. *An Approach to* Ham. London: Chatto and Windus, 1960; Stanford: Stanford University Press, 1961.

823

Knights, L.C. Ham *and Other Shakespearean Essays.* London: Cambridge University Press. 1979.

824

Knights, L.C. "*Ham* and the Perplexed Critics." *Sewanee Review.* 1984. 92: 225-38.

825

Kott, Jan. "Hamlet and Orestes."Taborski, Boleslaw, trans. *PMLA.* 1967. 82: 303-13.

826

Lacan, Jacques. "Desire and the Interpretation of Desire in *Ham.*"Hulbert, James, trans. *Yale French Studies.* 1977. 55-6: 11-52.

827

Lawlor, John J. "The Tragic Conflict in *Ham.*" *Review of English Studies.* 1950. N.S. 1: 97-113.

828

Leech, Clifford. "Studies in *Ham,* 1901-1955." *Shakespeare Survey.* 1956. 9: 1-15.

829

Lee-Riffe, Nancy M. "What Fortinbras and Laertes Tell Us about Hamlet." *Hamlet Studies.* 1981. 3: 103-9.

830

Leverenz, David. "The Woman in Hamlet: An Interpersonal View." *Representing Shakespeare.* Schwartz, Murray M., and Kahn, Coppélia, eds. Baltimore and London: Johns Hopkins University Press. 1980. 110-28.

831

Lewis, C.S. *Hamlet: The Prince or the Poem?* Oxford: Oxford University Press. 1942.

832

Lorant, André. "*Ham* and Mythical Thought." *Diogenes.* 1982. 118: 49-76.

77

833

Lu-Gu-Sun. "Hamlet Across Space and Time." *Shakespeare Survey*. 1983.
36: 53-6.

834

McDonald, Russ. "Osric." *Hamlet Studies*. 1983. 5: 59-65.

835

MacIntyre, Alasdair. "Epistemological Crises, Dramatic Narrative, and the
Philosophy of Science." *Paradigms and Revolutions*. Butting, Gary, ed.
Notre Dame: University of Notre Dame Press. 1980. 54-74.

836

MacIntyre, Jean. "Hamlet and the Comic Heroine." *Hamlet Studies*. 1982. 4:
6-18.

837

Mack, Maynard. "The World of Hamlet." *Yale Review*. 1952. 41: 502-23.

838

Miller, David L. "*Ham*: The Lie as an Image of the Fall." *Renaissance
Papers 1979*. 1980. 1-8.

839

Mills, John A. *Hamlet on Stage: The Great Tradition*. New York: Greenwood. 1985.

840

Miriam Joseph, Sister. "Discerning the Ghost in *Ham*." *PMLA*. 1961. 76:
493-502.

841

Miriam Joseph, Sister. "*Ham*, A Christian Tragedy." *Studies in Philology*.
1962. 59: 119-40.

842

Muir, Kenneth. "Imagery and Symbolism in *Ham*." *Etudes Anglaises*. 1964.
17: 253-63.

843

Muller, John P. "Psychosis and Mourning in Lacan's *Ham*." *New Literary
History*. 1980. 12: 147-65.

844

Murray, Gilbert. *Hamlet and Orestes*. New York: Oxford University Press.
1914.

845

Myrick, Kenneth. "Kittredge on Hamlet." *SQ*. 1964. 15: 219-34.

846

Nardo, Anna K. "Hamlet, 'A Man to Double Business Bound'." *SQ*. 1983. 34: 181-99.

847

Neill, Michael. "Remembrance and Revenge: *Ham, Mac, Tmp.*" *Jonson and Shakespeare.* Donaldson, Ian, ed. Canberra: Australian National University; Atlantic Highlands, N.J.: Humanities Press. 1983. 35-56.

848

Newell, Alex. "The Dramatic Context and Meaning of Hamlet's 'To Be or Not to Be' Soliloquy." *PMLA*. 1965. 80: 38-50.

849

Newman, Karen. "Hayman's Missing *Ham.*" *SQ*. 1983. 34: 73-8.

850

Ornstein, Robert T. "Historical Criticism and the Interpretation of Shakespeare." *SQ*. 1959. 10: 3-9.

851

Ornstein, Robert T. "The Mystery of *Ham*: Notes toward an Archetypal Solution." *College English*. 1959. 21: 30, 35-6.

852

Phialas, Peter G. "Hamlet and the Grave-Maker." *Journal of English and Germanic Philology*. 1964. 63: 226-34.

853

Pollin, Burton R. "Hamlet, a Successful Suicide." *Shakespeare Studies*. 1965. 1: 240-60.

854

Prior, Moody E. "The Thought of *Ham* and the Modern Temper." *English Literary History*. 1948. 15: 261-85.

855

Proser, Matthew N. "Hamlet and the Name of Action." *Essays on Shakespeare*. Smith, Gordon Ross, ed. University Park and London: Pennsylvania State University Press. 1965. 84-114.

856

Prosser, Eleanor A. Ham *and Revenge.* Stanford: Stanford University Press. 1967.

79

857

Reynolds, George F. "*Ham* at the Globe." *Shakespeare Survey*. 1956. 9: 49-53.

858

Robertson, D.W., Jr. "A Medievalist Looks at *Ham.*" *Essays in Medieval Culture*. Princeton: Princeton University Press. 1980. 312-31.

859

Robinson, Randal F., comp. Ham *in the 1950s: An Annotated Bibliography*. New York: Garland. 1984.

860

Rose, Jacqueline. "Sexuality in the Reading of Shakespeare*: Ham and MM.*" *Alternative Shakespeares*. Drakakis, John, ed. London and New York: Methuen. 1985. 95-118.

861

Rose, Mark. "*Ham* and the Shape of Revenge." *English Literary Renaissance*. 1971. 1: 132-43.

862

Salingar, Leo. "The Players in *Ham.*" *Aligarh Journal of English Studies*. 1981. 6: 168-83.

863

Sanford, Wendy C. *Theater as Metaphor in* Ham. Cambridge, Massachusetts: Harvard University Press. 1967.

864

Scheff, Thomas J. "A Theory of Catharsis in Drama." *Catharsis in Healing, Ritual, and Drama*. Berkeley and Los Angeles: University of California Press. 1979. 149-79.

865

Schwartz, Robert. "Coming Apart at the 'Seems': More on the Complexity of *Ham.*" *Pacific Coast Philology*. 1982. 17: 40-9.

866

Seng, Peter J. "Ophelia's Songs in *Ham.*" *Durham University Journal*. 1964. 25: 77-85.

867

Shakespeare Survey 9. Eight essays on *Ham*. 1956.

868

Showalter, Elaine. "Representing Ophelia: Women, Madness, and the Responsibilities of Feminist Criticism." *Shakespeare and the Question of*

Theory. Parker, Patricia, and Hartman, Geoffrey, eds. New York and London: Methuen. 1985. 77-94.

869

Sinfield, Alan. "Hamlet's Special Providence." *Shakespeare Survey.* 1980. 33: 89-97.

870

Sisson, C.J. "The Mouse-trap Again." *Review of English Studies.* 1940. 16: 129-36.

871

Skulsky, Harold. "Revenge, Honor, and Conscience in *Ham.*" *PMLA.* 1970. 85: 78-87.

872

Smith, Rebecca. "A Heart Cleft in Twain: The Dilemma of Shakespeare's Gertrude." *The Woman's Part.* Lenz, Carolyn Ruth Swift, et al, eds. Urbana, Chicago, and London: University of Illinois Press. 1980. 194-210.

873

Southall, Raymond. "The Hamlet Syndrome." *Hamlet Studies.* 1981. 3: 3-12.

874

Spencer, Theodore. "Hamlet and the Nature of Reality." *English Literary History.* 1938. 5: 253-77.

875

Spevack, Marvin. "Hamlet and Imagery: The Mind's Eye." *Die Neueren Sprachen.* 1966. 25: 203-12.

876

States, Bert O. "Phenomenology of the Curtain Call." *Hudson Review.* 1981. 34: 371-80.

877

Stockholder, Kay. "Sex and Authority in *Ham*, *Lr*, and *Per.*" *Mosaic.* 1985. 18: 17-29.

878

Suhamy, Henri. "The Metaphorical Fallacy: Some Remarks on the Sickness Imagery in *Ham.*" *Cahiers Elisabéthains.* 1983. 24: 27-32.

879

Taylor, Michael. "The Case of Rosencrantz and Guildenstern." *Dalhousie Review.* 1983-84. 63: 645-53.

880

Teodorescu, Anda. "An Elizabethan Model: Marlowe's 'Titan' and Its
   Downgraded Versions: Shakespeare's Hamlet and Prospero." *Synthesis.*
   (Bucharest) 1980. 7: 239-47.

881

Traschen, Isadore. "*Hamlet*'s Modernity." *Southern Review.* 1982. 18:
   517-27.

882

Walker, Roy. *The Time is Out of Joint: A Study of* Ham. London: Dakers.
   1948.

883

Warhaft, Sidney. "The Mystery of *Ham.*" *English Literary History.* 1963.
   30: 193-208.

884

Weigand, Hermann J. "Hamlet's Consistent Inconsistency." *The Persistence
   of Shakespeare's Idolatry.* Schueller, Herbert M., ed. Detroit: Wayne State
   University Press. 1964. 135-72.

885

Weimann, Robert. "Mimesis in *Ham.*" *Shakespeare and the Question of
   Theory.* Parker, Patricia, and Hartman, Geoffrey, eds. New York and
   London: Methuen. 1985. 275-91.

886

Weisinger, Herbert. "'Is There No Offense In't?': The Place of Poetry in
   Society." *Centennial Review.* 1981. 25: 363-79.

887

Welsh, Alexander. "The Task of Hamlet." *Yale Review.* 1980. 69: 481-502.

888

Wentersdorf, Karl P. "Hamlet's Encounter with the Pirates." *SQ.* 1983. 34:
   434-40.

889

Williamson, Claude C.H., ed. *Readings on the Character of Hamlet,
   1661-1947.* London: Allen and Unwin. 1950.

890

Wilson, J. Dover. *What Happens in* Ham. Cambridge: Cambridge University
   Press. 1935. Revised edition 1951.

891

Wilson, Robert R. "Narratives, Narrators and Narratees in *Ham.*" *Hamlet Studies.* 1984. 6: 30-40.

892

Wilt, Judith. "Comment on David Leverenz's 'The Woman in *Ham*'." *Women's Studies.* 1981. 9: 93-7.

893

Wormhoudt, Arthur. *Hamlet's Mousetrap: A Psychoanalytic Study of the Drama.* New York: Philosophical Library. 1956.

894

Wray, William R. "You, Claudius: An Anatomy of a Name." *Publications of the Arkansas Philological Association.* 1980. 6: 78-94.

895

Wynne, Lorraine. "The Poetic Function of the State Audience and Embedded Performance in Drama." *Semiotics* 1980. Herzfeld, Michael, and Lenhart, Margot D., eds. New York: Plenum Press, 1982. 571-6.

896

Young, David. "Hamlet, Son of Hamlet." *Perspectives on* Ham. Holzberger, William G., and Waldock, Peter B., eds. Lewisburg, Pa.: Bucknell University Press. 1975. 184-206.

897

Ziegelman, Lois. "*Ham:* Shakespeare's Mannerist Tragedy." *Shakespeare and the Arts.* Cary, Cecile Williamson, and Limouze, Henry S., eds. Washington, D.C.: University Press of America. 1982. 57-71.

898

Zitner, Sheldon P. "*Ham* and *Hamartia.*" Hamartia: *The Concept of Error in the Western Tradition.* Stump, Donald V., et al, eds. New York and Toronto: Edwin Mellen Press. 1983. 193-210.

See also works listed under *Tragedy*, especially by Bradley, Brower, Felperin, Holloway, Mack, Rosen, and Whitaker.

899

Alvis, John. "A Little Touch of the Night in Harry: The Career of Henry Monmouth." *Shakespeare as Political Thinker.* Alvis, John, and West, Thomas G., eds. Durham, N.C.: Carolina Academic Press. 1981. 95-125.

900

Auden, W.H. "The Prince's Dog." *The Dyer's Hand.* New York: Random House. 1948. 182-208.

901

Barber, C.L. "Rule and Misrule in *H4.*" *Shakespeare's Festive Comedy.* Princeton: Princeton University Press. 1959. 192-221.

902

Barber, Charles L. "Prince Hal, Henry V, and the Tudor Monarchy." *The Morality of Art: Essays Presented to G. Wilson Knight.* Jefferson, D.W, ed. New York: Barnes and Noble; London: Routledge and Kegan Paul. 1969. 67-75.

903

Barish, Jonas A. "The Turning Away of Prince Hal." *Shakespeare Studies.* 1965. 1: 9-17.

904

Bass, Eben. "Falstaff and the Succession." *College English.* 1963. 24: 502-6.

905

Beck, Richard J. *Shakespeare:* H4. London: E. Arnold. 1965.

906

Berger, Harry, Jr. "Sneak's Noise or Rumor and Detextualization in *2H4.*" *Kenyon Review.* 1984. 6: 58-78.

907

Berkeley, David, and Eidson, Donald. "The Theme of *1H4.*" *SQ.* 1968. 19: 25-31.

908

Berry, Edward I. "The Rejection Scene in *2H4.*" *Studies in English Literature.* 1977. 17: 201-18.

909

Black, James. "Henry IV's Pilgrimage." *SQ.* 1983. 34: 18-26.

910

Blanpied, John W. "'Unfathered Heirs and Loathly Births of Nature':
Bringing History to Crisis in *2H4*." *English Literary Renaissance*. 1975. 5:
212-31.

911

Boughner, Daniel C. "Traditional Elements in Falstaff." *Journal of English
and Germanic Philology*. 1944. 43: 417-28.

912

Boughner, Daniel C. "Vice, Braggart, and Falstaff." *Anglia*. 1954. 72:
35-61.

913

Bowers, Fredson T. "Theme and Structure in *1H4*." *The Drama of the Renaissance: Essays for Leicester Bradner*. Blistein, Elmer M., ed. Providence,
R.I.: Brown University Press. 1970. 42-68.

914

Bradley, A.C. "The Rejection of Falstaff." *Oxford Lectures on Poetry*.
London: Macmillan. 1909. 247-75.

915

Bryant, J.A. "Prince Hal and the Ephesians." *Sewanee Review*. 1959. 67:
204-19.

916

Burrow, J.A. "'Young Saint, Old Devil': Reflections on a Medieval Pro-
verb." *Review of English Studies*. 1979. 30 N.S.: 385-96.

917

Cain, H. Edward. "Further Light on the Relation of *1* and *2H4*." *SQ*. 1952.
3: 21-38.

918

Campbell, Josie P. "Farce as Function in Medieval and Shakespearean
Drama." *Upstart Crow*. Fall, 1980. 3: 11-18.

919

Candido, Joseph. "The Name of King: Hal's 'Titles' in the 'Henriad'."
Texas Studies in Literature and Language. 1984. 26: 61-73.

920

Charlton, H.B. "Falstaff." *Bulletin of the John Rylands Library*. 1935. 19:
46-89.

921

Cohen, Derek. "The Rite of Violence in *1H4*." *Shakespeare Survey*. 1985. 38: 77-84.

922

Cross, Gerald. "The Justification of Prince Hal." *Texas Studies in Literature and Language*. 1968. 10: 27-35.

923

Dessen, Alan C. "The Intemperate Knight and the Politic Prince: Late Morality Structure in *1H4*." *Shakespeare Studies*. 1974. 7: 147-71.

924

Dickinson, Hugh. "The Reformation of Prince Hal." *SQ* . 1961. 12: 33-46.

925

Doran, Madeleine. "Imagery in *R2* and *H4*." *Modern Language Review*. 1942. 37: 113-22.

926

Draper, John W. "Sir John Falstaff." *Review of English Studies*. 1932. 8: 414-24.

927

Empson, William. "Falstaff and Mr. Dover Wilson." *Kenyon Review*. 1953. 15: 213-62.

928

Empson, William. "They That Have Power." *Some Versions of Pastoral*. London: Chatto and Windus. 1950. 89-118.

929

Evans, Gareth Lloyd. "The Comical-Tragical-Historical Method: *H4*." *Early Shakespeare*. Brown, John Russell, and Harris, Bernard, eds. (Stratford-upon-Avon Studies 3.) London: E. Arnold. 1961. 145-63.

930

Finke, Laurie A. "Falstaff, the Wife of Bath, and the Sweet Smoke of Rhetoric." *Chaucerian Shakespeare: Adaptation and Transformation*. Donaldson, E. Talbot, and Kollmann, Judith J., eds. Detroit: Michigan Consortium for Medieval and Early Modern Studies. 1983. 7-24.

931

Fish, Charles. "*H4*: Shakespeare and Holinshed." *Studies in Philology*. 1964. 61: 205-18.

932

Freund, Elizabeth. "Strategies of Inconclusiveness in *1H4*." *New York Literary Forum.* 1980. 5-6: 207-16.

933

Goldman, Michael. *Shakespeare and the Energies of Drama.* Princeton: Princeton University Press. 1972. 45-57.

934

Goodman, Alice. "Falstaff and Socrates." *English.* 1985. 34: 97-112.

935

Grund, Gary R. "Rhetoric as Metaphor: Some Notes on Dramatic Method." *Etudes Anglaises.* 1980. 33: 282-95.

936

Hapgood, Robert. "Falstaff's Vocation." *SQ.* 1965. 16: 91-8.

937

Hawkins, Sherman H. "*H4*: The Structural Problem Revisited." *SQ.* 1982. 33: 278-301.

938

Hemingway, Samuel B. "On Behalf of that Falstaff." *SQ* . 1952. 3: 307-11.

939

Henkle, Roger B. "The Social Dynamics of Comedy." *Sewanee Review.* 1982. 90: 200-16.

940

Hotson, Leslie. "Ancient Pistol." *Yale Review.* 1948. 38: 51-66.

941

Hunter, G.K. "*H4* and the Elizabethan Two-Part Play." *Review of English Studies.* 1954. 5: 236-48.

942

Hunter, G.K. "Shakespeare's Politics and the Rejection of Falstaff." *Critical Quarterly.* 1959. 1: 229-36.

943

Jenkins, Harold. *The Structural Problem in Shakespeare's* H4. London: Methuen. 1956.

944

Jorgensen, Paul. "The 'Dastardly Treachery' of Prince John of Lancaster." *PMLA.* 1961. 76: 488-92.

87

945

Kernan, Alvin. "*The Henriad*: Shakespeare's Major History Plays." *Yale Review.* 1969. 59: 3-32.

946

Kiernan, Michael. 1H4: *A Bibliography to Supplement the New Variorum Edition of 1936 and the Supplement of 1956.* New York: Modern Language Association. 1977.

947

Kleinstück, Johannes. "The Problem of Order in Shakespeare's Histories." *Neophilologus.* 1954. 38: 268-77.

948

Knoepflmacher, U.C. "The Humors as Symbolic Nucleus in *1H4.*" *College English.* 1963. 24: 497-501.

949

Knowles, Richard. "Unquiet and the Double Plot of *2H4.*" *Shakespeare Studies.* 1967. 2: 133-40.

950

Knowlton, Edgar C. "Falstaff Redux." *Journal of English and Germanic Philology.* 1926. 25: 193-215.

951

Kris, Ernst. "Prince Hal's Conflict." *Psychoanalytical Quarterly.* 1948. 17: 487-506.

952

La Branche, Anthony. "'If Thou Wert Sensible of Courtesy': Private and Public Virtue in *1H4.*" *SQ.* 1966. 17: 371-82.

953

Landt, D.B. "The Ancestry of Sir John Falstaff." *SQ* . 1966. 17: 69-76.

954

Law, R.A. "Structural Unity in the Two Parts of *H4.*" *Studies in Philology.* 1927. 24: 223-42.

955

Lawry, Jon S. "'Born to Set It Right': Hal, Hamlet, and Prospero." *Ball State University Forum.* 1964. 5: 16-25.

956

Leech, Clifford. "The Unity of *2H4.*" *Shakespeare Survey.* 1953. 6: 16-24.

957

Leslie, Nancy T. "The Worthy Wife and the Virtuous Knight: Survival of the Wittiest." *Chaucerian Shakespeare: Adaptation and Transformation.* Donaldson, E. Talbot, and Kollmann, Judith J., eds. Detroit: Michigan Consortium for Medieval and Early Modern Studies. 1983. 25-41.

958

Levin, Harry. "Falstaff's Encore." *SQ.* 1981. 32: 5-17.

959

McGuire, Richard L. "The Play-within-the-Play in *1H4*." *SQ.* 1967. 18: 47-52.

960

McLaverty, J. "No Abuse: The Prince and Falstaff in the Tavern Scenes of *H4*." *Shakespeare Survey.* 1981. 34: 105-10.

961

McLuhan, Herbert M. "*H4*, a Mirror for Magistrates." *University of Toronto Quarterly.* 1947. 17: 152-60.

962

McNamara, Anne M. "*H4*: The King as Protagonist." *SQ.* 1959. 10: 423-31.

963

McNeir, Waldo F. "Structure and Theme in the First Tavern Scene (II.iv) of *1H4*." *Pacific Coast Studies in Shakespeare.* McNeir, Waldo F., and Greenfield, Thelma N, eds. Eugene: University of Oregon Press. 1966. 89-105.

964

Manley, Frank. "The Unity of Betrayal in *2H4*." *Studies in the Literary Imagination.* 1972. 5: 91-110.

965

Marsh, Derick R.C. "Hal and Hamlet: The Loneliness of Integrity." *Jonson and Shakespeare.* Donaldson, Ian, ed. Canberra: Australian National University; Atlantic Highlands, N.J.: Humanities Press; London: Macmillan. 1983. 18-34.

966

Merrix, Robert P., and Palacas, Arthur. "Gadshill, Hotspur, and the Design of Proleptic Parody." *Comparative Drama.* 1980-81. 14: 299-311.

967

Mitchell, Giles R., and Wright, Eugene P. "Hotspur's Poor Memory." *South Central Bulletin.* (now South Central Review). 1983. 43: 121-3.

968

Monaghan, James. "Falstaff and His Forebears." *Studies in Philology.* 1921. 18: 353-61.

969

Mullaney, Steven. "Strange Things, Gross Terms, Curious Customs: The Rehearsal of Cultures in the Late Renaissance." *Representations.* 1983. 1, 3: 40-67.

970

Murry, John Middleton. "The Creation of Falstaff." *John Clare and Other Studies.* London and New York: Nevill. 1950.

971

Newman, Franklin B. "The Rejection of Falstaff and the Rigorous Charity of the King." *Shakespeare Studies.* 1967. 2: 153-61.

972

Osborne, Laurie E. "Crisis of Degree in Shakespeare's Henriad." *Studies in English Literature.* 1985. 25: 337-59.

973

Palmer, D.J. "Casting off the Old man: History and St. Paul in *H4*." *Critical Quarterly.* 1970. 12: 267-83.

974

Pechter, Edward. "Falsifying Men's Hopes: The Ending of *1H4*." *Modern Language Quarterly.* 1980. 41: 211-30.

975

Reno, Raymond. "Hotspur: The Integration of Character and Theme." *Renaissance Papers 1962.* 1963. 17-26.

976

Riemer, A.P. "'A World of Figures': Language and Character in *1H4*." *Sydney Studies in English.* 1980-81. 6: 62-74.

977

Salingar, Leo. "Falstaff and the Life of Shadows." *New York Literary Forum.* 1980. 5-6: 185-205.

978

Scoufos, Alice L. "Gads Hill and the Structure of Comic Satire." *Shakespeare Studies.* 1970. 5: 25-52.

979

Scoufos, Alice L. "The 'Martyrdom' of Falstaff." *Shakespeare Studies.* 1967. 2: 174-91.

980

Seng, Peter J. "Songs, Time, and the Rejection of Falstaff." *Shakespeare Survey.* 1962. 15: 31-40.

981

Shaaber, M.A. "The Unity of *H4.*" *Joseph Quincy Adams Memorial Studies.* McManaway, James G., et al, eds. Washington, D.C.: Folger Shakespeare Library. 1948. 217-27.

982

Shaaber, M.A. 2H4: *A Bibliography to Supplement the New Variorum Edition of 1940.* New York: Modern Language Association. 1977.

983

Shaw, John. "The Staging of Parody and Parallels in *1H4.*" *Shakespeare Survey.* 1967. 20: 61-73.

984

Shirley, John W. "Falstaff, an Elizabethan Glutton." *Philological Quarterly.* 1938. 17: 271-87.

985

Shuchter, J.D. "Prince Hal and Francis: The Imitation of an Action." *Shakespeare Studies.* 1968. 3: 129-37.

986

Spivack, Bernard. "Falstaff and the Psychomachia." *SQ* . 1957. 8: 449-59.

987

Spivack, Bernard. *Shakespeare and the Allegory of Evil.* New York and London: Columbia University Press. 1958. 87-91, passim.

988

Sprague, Arthur C. "Gadshill Revisited." *SQ.* 1953. 4: 125-37.

989

Stewart, Douglas J. "Falstaff the Centaur." *SQ.* 1977. 28: 5-21.

990

Stoll, E.E. "Falstaff." *Shakespeare Studies, Historical and Comparative in Method.* New York: Macmillan. 1927. 403-90.

991

Sublette, Jack R. "Time's Fool: A Reading of *1H4.*" *Aligarh Journal of English Studies.* 1983. 8: 68-78.

992

Tave, Stuart M. "Notes on the Influence of Morgann's Essay on Falstaff."
Review of English Studies. 1952. N.S. 3: 371-5.

993

Toliver, Harold E. "Falstaff, the Prince, and the History Play." *SQ.* 1965.
16: 63-80.

994

Toliver, Harold E. "Workable Fictions in the Henry IV Plays." *University of
Toronto Quarterly.* 1983. 53: 53-71.

995

Wilson, J. Dover. *The Fortunes of Falstaff.* Cambridge: Cambridge University Press; New York: Macmillan. 1944.

996

Wilson, J. Dover. "The Political Background of Shakespeare's *R2* and *H4*."
Shakespeare-Jahrbuch. 1939. 75: 36-51.

997

Witt, Robert W. "Prince Hal and Castiglione." *Ball State University Forum.*
1983. 24: 73-9.

998

Zeeveld, W. Gordon. "'Food for Powder'--'Food for Worms'." *SQ.* 1952.
3: 249-53.

999

Zitner, S.P. "Staging the Occult in *1H4*." *Mirror Up to Shakespeare: Essays
in Honor of G.R. Hibbard.* Gray, J.C., ed. Toronto, Buffalo, and London:
University of Toronto Press. 1984. 138-48.

See also works listed under *History Plays*, especially by Blanpied, Malheim,
Ornstein, Prior, Reese, and Rossiter: and the work by Palmer under *General Studies*.

Henry V

1000

Altieri, Joanne. "Romance in *H5.*" *Studies in English Literature.* 1981. 21: 223-40.

1001

Barber, Charles L. "Prince Hal, Henry V, and the Tudor Monarchy." *The Morality of Art: Essays Presented to G. Wilson Knight.* Jefferson, D.W., ed. New York: Barnes and Noble; London: Routledge and Kegan Paul. 1969. 67-75.

1002

Barton, Anne. "The King Disguised: Shakespeare's *H5 and the Comical History.*" The Triple Bond. *Price, Joseph G., ed. University Park: University of Pennsylvania Press. 1975. 92-117.*

1003

Berman, Ronald S. "Shakespeare's Alexander: Henry V." *College English.* 1962. 23: 532-9.

1004

Boughner, Daniel C. "Pistol and the Roaring Boys." *Shakespeare Association Bulletin.* 1936. 11: 226-37.

1005

Braddy, Haldeen. "Shakespeare's *H5* and the French Nobility." *Texas Studies in Literature and Language.* 1961. 3: 189-96.

1006

Brennan, Anthony. "That Within Which Passes Show: The Function of the Chorus in *H5.*" *Philological Quarterly.* 1979. 58: 40-52.

1007

Candido, Joseph, and Forker, Charles R., comps. H5: *An Annotated Bibliography.* New York: Garland. 1983.

1008

Collins, David G. "On Re-interpreting *H5.*" *Upstart Crow.* 1982. 4: 18-34.

1009

Davison, Peter. H5 *in the Context of the Popular Dramatic Tradition.* Winchester: King Alfred's College. 1981.

1010

Dean, Paul. "Chronicle and Romance Modes in *H5*." *SQ*. 1981. 32: 18-27.

1011

Dollimore, Jonathan, and Sinfield, Alan. "History and Ideology: The Instance of *H5*." *Alternative Shakespeares*. Drakakis, John, ed. London & New York: Methuen. 1985. 206-27.

1012

Egan, Robert. "A Muse of Fire: *H5* in the Light of *Tamburlaine*." *Modern Language Quarterly*. 1968. 29:15-28.

1013

Fleissner, Robert F. "Falstaff's Green Sickness unto Death." *SQ*. 1961. 12: 47-55.

1014

Godshalk, W.L. "Henry V's Politics of Non-Responsibility." *Cahiers Elisabéthains*. 1980. 17: 11-20.

1015

Gurr, Andrew. "*H5* and the Bees' Commonwealth." *Shakespeare Survey*. 1977. 30: 61-72.

1016

Jorgensen, Paul A. "Accidental Judgments, Casual Slaughters, and Purposes Mistook: Critical Reactions to Shakespeare's *H5*." *Shakespeare Association Bulletin*. 1947. 22: 51-61.

1017

Jorgensen, Paul A. "The Courtship Scene in *H5*." *Modern Language Quarterly*. 1950. 11: 180-8.

1018

Lenz, Joseph M. "The Politics of Honor: The Oath in *H5*." *Journal of English and Germanic Philology*. 1981. 80: 1-12.

1019

Lever, J.W. "Shakespeare's French Fruits." *Shakespeare Survey*. 1953. 6: 79-90.

1020

Levin, Richard. "Hazlitt on *H5*, and the Appropriation of Shakespeare." *SQ*. 1984. 35: 134-41.

1021

Lewis, Marlo, Jr. "On War and Legitimacy in Shakespeare's *H5*." *Statesmanship: Essays in Honor of Sir Winston Spencer Churchill*. Jaffa, Harry

V., ed. Durham, N.C.: Carolina Academic Press. 1981. 41-61.

1022

Lynch, Amy. "Henry V: Majesty and the Man." *Upstart Crow*. 1982. 4: 35-40.

1023

Macdonald, Andrew, and Macdonald, Gina. "*H5*: A Shakespearean Defini-tion of Politic Reign." *Studies in the Humanities*. (Indiana, Pa.) 1982. 9: 32-9.

1024

MacIntyre, Jean. "Shakespeare and the Battlefield: Tradition and Innovation in Battle Scenes." *Theatre Survey*. 1982. 23: 31-44.

1025

Mendilow, A.A. "Falstaff's Death of a Sweat." *SQ*. 1958. 9: 479-83.

1026

Merchant, W. Moelwyn. "The Status and Person of Majesty." *Shakespeare-Jahrbuch*. 1954. 90: 285-9.

1027

Phialas, Peter G. "Shakespeare's Henry V and the Second Tetralogy." *Stud-ies in Philology*. 1965. 62: 155-75.

1028

Rabkin, Norman. "Rabbits, Ducks, and *H5*." *SQ* . 1977. 28: 279-96.

1029

Radoff, M.L. "Influence of the French Farce in *H5* and *Wiv*." *Modern Lan-guage Notes*. 1933. 48: 427-35.

1030

Richardson, W.M. "The Brave New World of Shakespeare's *H5* Revisited." *Allegorica*. 1981. 6: 149-54.

1031

Salomon, Brownell. "Thematic Contraries and the Dramaturgy of *H5*." *SQ*. 1980. 31: 343-56.

1032

Schwartz, Helen J. "The Comic Scenes in *H5*." *Hebrew University Studies in Literature*. 1976. 4: 18-26.

1033

Smith, Gordon Ross. "Shakespeare's *H5*: Another Part of the Critical Forest." *Journal of the History of Ideas*. 1976. 37: 3-26.

1034

Stribrný, Zdenek. "Henry V and History." *Shakespeare in a Changing World*. Kettle, Arnold, ed. London: Lawrence and Wishart. 1964. 84-101.

1035

Tolman, Albert H. "The Epic Character of Henry V." *Modern Language Notes*. 1919. 34: 7-16.

1036

Webber, Joan. "The Renewal of the King's Symbolic Role: From *R2* to *H5*." *Texas Studies in Literature and Language*. 1963. 4: 530-8.

1037

Williamson, Marilyn L. "The Episode with Williams in *H5*." *Studies in English Literature*. 1969. 9: 275-82.

1038

Wilson, J. Dover. "Martin Marprelate and Shakespeare's Fluellen." *Library*. 1912. 3, Series III: 113-51, 241-76.

See also works listed under *History Plays*, especially by Blanpied, Ornstein, Prior, Reese, and Rossiter: and the work by Alvis under *Henry IV, Parts 1 and 2*.

Henry VI, Parts 1, 2, and 3

1039

Beauchamp, Gorman. "The Dream of Cockaigne: Some Motives for the Utopias of Escape." *Centennial Review*. 1981. 25: 345-62.

1040

Berman, Ronald S. "Fathers and Sons in the *H6* Plays." *SQ*. 1962. 13: 487-97.

1041

Bevington, David M. "The Domineering Female in *1H6*." *Shakespeare Studies*. 1967. 2: 51-8.

1042

Boas, Frederick S. "Joan of Arc in Shakespeare, Schiller, and Shaw." *SQ*. 1951. 2: 35-45.

1043

Brockbank, J.P. "The Frame of Disorder: *H6*." *Early Shakespeare*. Brown, John Russell, and Harris, Bernard, eds. London: Arnold. 1961. 73-99.

Stratford-upon-Avon Studies 3.

1044

Burckhardt, Sigurd. "'I Am But Shadow of Myself': Ceremony and Design in *1H6.*" *Modern Language Quarterly.* 1967. 28: 139-58. Reprinted in Burckhardt's *Shakespearean Meanings.* Princeton: Princeton University Press, 1968.

1045

Calderwood, James L. "Shakespeare's Evolving Imagery: *2H6.*" *English Studies.* 1967. 48: 481-93.

1046

Candido, Joseph. "Getting Loose in the *H6* Plays." *SQ.* 1984. 35: 392-406.

1047

Clemen, Wolfgang. "Some Aspects of Style in the *H6* Plays." *Shakespeare's Styles: Essays in Honour of Kenneth Muir.* Edwards, Philip, et al, eds. Cambridge: Cambridge University Press. 1980. 9-24.

1048

French, A.L. "*H6* and the Ghost of Richard II." *English Studies.* 1969. Anglo-American Supp., 50: xxvii-xliii.

1049

French, A.L. "Joan of Arc and *H6.*" *English Studies.* 1968. 49: 425-9.

1050

French, A.L. "The Mills of God and Shakespeare's Early History Plays." *English Studies.* 1974. 55: 313-24.

1051

Greenblatt, Stephen. "Murdering Peasants: Status, Genre, and the Representation of Rebellion." *Representations.* February 1983. 1 (1): 1-29.

1052

Greer, Clayton A. "The Place of *1H6* in the York-Lancaster Tetralogy." *PMLA.* 1938. 53: 687-701.

1053

Griffiths, R.A. "The Sense of Dynasty in the Reign of Henry VI." *Patronage, Pedigree, and Power in Later Medieval England.* Ross, Charles, ed. Gloucester, England: Alan Sutton; Totowa, N.J.: Rowman and Littlefield. 1979. 13-36.

1054

Hinchcliffe, Judith, comp. H6 Parts 1,2, and 3: *An Annotated Bibliography.* New York: Garland. 1984.

1055

Kernan, Alvin B. "A Comparison of the Imagery in *3H6* and *The True Tra-gedie of Richard, Duke of York*." *Studies in Philology*. 1954. 51: 431-2.

1056

Leech, Clifford. "The Two-Part Play: Marlowe and the Early Shakespeare." *Shakespeare-Jahrbuch*. 1958. 94: 90-100.

1057

Manheim, Michael. "Silence in the Henry VI Plays." *Educational Theatre Journal*. March 1977. 29: 70-76.

1058

McNeal, Thomas H. "Margaret of Anjou: Romantic Princess and Troubled Queen." *SQ*. 1958. 9: 1-10.

1059

Mincoff, Marco. "The Composition of *1H6*." *SQ* . 1965. 16: 279-87.

1060

Mincoff, Marco. "*3H6* and *The True Tragedy*." *English Studies*. 1961. 42: 273-88.

1061

Norvell, Betty G. "The Dramatic Portrait of Margaret in Shakespeare's Henry VI Plays." *Bulletin of the West Virginia Association of College Eng-lish Teachers*. 1983. 8: 38-44.

1062

Pratt, Samuel M. "Shakespeare and Humphrey Duke of Gloucester: A Study in Myth." *SQ*. 1965. 16: 201-16.

1063

Price, Hereward T. *Construction in Shakespeare*. Ann Arbor: University of Michigan Press. 1951.

1064

Rackin, Phyllis. "Anti-Historians: Women's Roles in Shakespeare's Histo-ries." *Theatre Journal*. 1985. 37: 329-44.

1065

Ricks, Don. *Shakespeare's Emergent Form: A Study of the Structure of the "H6" Plays*. Logan: Utah State University Press. 1968.

1066

Swander, Homer. "The Rediscovery of *H6*." *SQ* . 1978. 19: 146-63.

1067

Swayne, Mattie. "Shakespeare's Henry VI as a Pacifist." *College English.* 1941. 3: 143-9.

1068

Utterback, Raymond V. "Public Men, Private Wills, and Kingship in *3H6.*" *Renaissance Papers 1978.* 1979. 47-54.

1069

Warren, Roger. "'Contrarieties Agree': An Aspect of Dramatic Technique in *H6.*" *Shakespeare Survey.* 1984. 37: 75-83.

1070

Wineke, Donald R. "The Relevance of Machiavelli to Shakespeare: A Discussion of *1H6.*" *Clio.* 1983. 13: 17-36.

1071

Zeeveld, W. Gordon. "The Influence of Hall on Shakespeare's English Historical Plays." *English Literary History.* 1936. 3: 317-53.

See also works listed under *History Plays*, especially by Berry, Blanpied, Boris, Clemen, Kelly, Manheim, Ornstein, Prior, Riggs, and Turner.

Henry VIII

1072

Auberlen, Eckhard. "*H8*: Shakespeare's Break with the 'Bluff-King-Harry' Tradition." *Anglia.* 1980. 98: 319-47.

1073

Berman, Ronald. "*H8*: History and Romance." *English Studies.* 1967. 48: 112-21.

1074

Berry, Edward I. "Henry VIII and the Dynamics of Spectacle." *Shakespeare Studies.* 1979. 12: 229-46.

1075

Bertram, Paul. "*H8:* The Conscience of the King." *In Defense of Reading.* Brower, Reuben A., and Poirier, Richard, eds. New York: Dutton; Toronto: Clarke Irwin. 1962. 153-73.

1076

Bliss, Lee. "The Wheel of Fortune and the Maiden Phoenix of Shakespeare's *H8.*" *English Literary History.* 1975. 42: 1-25.

1077

Candido, Joseph. "Katherine of Aragon and Female Greatness: Shakespeare's Debt to Dramatic Tradition." *Iowa State Journal of Research.* 1980. 54: 491-8.

1078

Cespedes, Frank V. "'We Are One in Fortunes': The Sense of History in *H8*." *English Literary Renaissance.* 1980. 10: 413-38.

1079

Clark, Cumberland. *A Study of Shakespeare's* H8. London: Golden Vista. 1931.

1080

Cutts, John P. "Shakespeare's Song and Masque Hand in *H8*." *Shakespeare-Jahrbuch.* 1963. 99: 184-95.

1081

Felperin, Howard. "Shakespeare's *H8*: History as Myth." *Studies in English Literature.* 1966. 6: 225-46.

1082

Harris, Bernard. "'What's Past is Prologue'*: Cym and H8*." *Later Shake-speare.* Brown, John Russell, and Harris, Bernard, eds. London: Arnold. 1966. 203-34. Stratford-upon-Avon Studies 8.

1083

Kermode, Frank. "What Is Shakespeare's *H8* About?" *Durham University Journal.* 1947. N.S. 8: 48-55.

1084

Kermode, Frank. "Holinshed and *H8*." *Texas Studies in English.* 1957. 36: 3-11.

1085

Leggatt, Alexander. "*H8* and the Ideal England." *Shakespeare Survey.* 1985. 38: 131-43.

1086

Micheli, Linda, comp. H8*: An Annotated Bibliography.* New York: Garland. 1986.

1087

Mincoff, Marco. "*H8* and Fletcher." *SQ.* 1961. 12: 239-60.

1088

Oman, C.W.C. "The Personality of Henry VIII." *Quarterly Review.* 1937. 269: 88-104.

1089

Richmond, H.M. "Shakespeare's *H8*: Romance Redeemed by History." *Shakespeare Studies.* 1969. 4: 334-49.

1090

Sahel, Pierre. "The Strangeness of a Dramatic Style: Rumour in *H8*." *Shakespeare Survey.* 1985. 38: 145-51.

1091

Tillyard, E.M.W. "Why Did Shakespeare Write *H8*?" *Critical Quarterly.* 1961. 3: 22-7.

1092

Waage, Frederick O., Jr. "*H8* and the Crisis of the English History Play." *Shakespeare Studies.* 1975. 8: 297-309.

1093

Wasson, John. "In Defense of *H8*." *Research Studies.* (Washington State University) 1964. 32: 261-76.

1094

Wickham, Glynne. "The Dramatic Structure of Shakespeare's *H8*: An Essay in Rehabilitation." *Proceedings of the British Academy.* 1984. 70: 149-66.

1095

Wiley, Paul L. "Renaissance Exploitation of Cavendish's *Life of Wolsey*." *Studies in Philology.* 1946. 43: 121-46.

Julius Caesar

1096

Anderson, Peter S. "Shakespeare's *Caesar*: The Language of Sacrifice." *Comparative Drama.* 1969. 3: 3-26.

1097

Anson, John S. "*JC*: The Politics of the Hardened Heart." *Shakespeare Studies.* 1967. 2: 11-33.

1098

Barton, Anne. "*JC and Cor:* Shakespeare's Roman World of Words." *Shakespeare's Craft: Eight Lectures.* Highfill, Philip H., Jr., ed. Carbon-dale and Edwardsville: Southern Illinois University Press for George Washington University. 1982. 24-47.

1099

Bellringer, A.W. "*JC*: Room Enough." *Critical Quarterly*. 1970. 12: 31-48.

1100

Berry, Ralph. "*JC*: A Roman Tragedy." *Dalhousie Review*. 1981. 61: 325-36.

1101

Bligh, John. "Cicero's Choric Comment in *JC*." *English Studies in Canada*. 1982. 8: 391-408.

1102

Blits, Jan H. "Caesarism and the End of Republican Rome: *JC* Act I, scene i." *Journal of Politics*. 1981. 43: 40-55.

1103

Bonjour, Adrien. *The Structure of* JC. Liverpool: Liverpool University Press. 1958.

1104

Bowden, William R. "The Mind of Brutus." *SQ*. 1966. 17: 57-67.

1105

Breyer, Bernard R. "A New Look at *JC*." *Essays in Honor of Walter Clyde Curry*. Nashville: Vanderbilt University Press. 1954. 161-80.

1106

Burke, Kenneth. "Antony in Behalf of the Play." *Southern Review*. 1935. 1: 308-19.

1107

Chang, Joseph S.M.J. "*JC* in the Light of Renaissance Historiography." *Journal of English and Germanic Philology*. 1970. 69: 63-71.

1108

Connolly, Thomas F. "Shakespeare and the Double Man." *SQ* . 1950. 1: 30-5.

1109

Coursen, Herbert R., Jr. "The Fall and Decline of *JC*." *Texas Studies in Literature and Language*. 1962. 4: 241-51.

1110

Dort, Bernard. "Sartre on Theatre: Politics and Imagination." *Canadian Theatre Review*. 1981. 32: 32-43.

1111

Feldman, Harold. "Unconscious Envy in Brutus." *American Imago*. 1952. 9: 307-35.

1112

Felheim, Marvin. "The Problem of Time in *JC.*" *Huntington Library Quarterly.* 1950. 13: 399-405.

1113

Foakes, R.A. "An Approach to *JC.*" *SQ.* 1954. 5: 259-70.

1114

Fortin, René E. "*JC*: An Experiment in Point of View." *SQ.* 1968. 19: 341-7.

1115

Giankaris, C.J., comp. JC: *An Annotated Bibliography.* New York: Garland. 1985.

1116

Greene, Gayle. "'The Power of Speech/To Stir Men's Blood': The Language of Tragedy in Shakespeare's *JC.*" *Renaissance Drama.* 1980; publ. 1981. N.S. 11: 67-93.

1117

Hall, Vernon, Jr. "*JC*: A Play without Political Bias." *Studies in the English Renaissance Drama in Memory of Karl Julius Holzknecht.* Bennett, Josephine W., et al, eds. New York: New York University Press. 1959. 106-24.

1118

Hapgood, Robert. "Speak Hands for Me: Gesture as Language in *JC.*" *Drama Survey.* (Minneapolis) 1966. 5: 162-70.

1119

Hartsock, Mildred E. "The Complexity of *JC.*" *PMLA.* 1966. 81: 56-62.

1120

Hatlen, Burton. "A World Without Absolutes: Dialectic in Shakespeare's *JC.*" *Proceedings of the P[atristic] M[ediaeval] and R[enaissance] Conference.* (Villanova University) 1978. 3: 167-82.

1121

Kaula, David. "'Let Us Be Sacrificers': Religious Motifs in *JC.*" *Shakespeare Studies.* 1981. 14: 197-214.

1122

Kayser, John R., and Lettieri, Ronald J. "'The Last of All the Romans': Shakespeare's Commentary on Classical Republicanism." *Clio.* 1980. 9: 197-227.

1123

Kirschbaum, Leo. "Shakespeare's Stage Blood and Its Critical Significance." *PMLA.* 1949. 64: 517-29.

1124

Klein, David. "Has Cassius Been Misinterpreted?" *Shakespeare Association Bulletin.* 1939. 14: 27-36.

1125

Knights, L.C. "Personality and Politics in *JC.*" *Anglica.* 1964. 5: 1-24.

1126

Knights, L.C. "Shakespeare and Political Wisdom: A Note on the Personalism of *JC* and *Cor.*" *Sewanee Review.* 1953. 61: 43-55.

1127

Levitsky, Ruth M. "'The Elements Were So Mix'd ...'." *PMLA.* 1973. 88: 240-5.

1128

Lloyd, Michael. "Antony and the Game of Chance." *Journal of English and Germanic Philology.* 1962. 61: 548-54.

1129

Lowenthal, David. "Shakespeare's Caesar's Plan." *Interpretation.* 1982. 10: 223-50.

1130

Markels, Julian, ed. *Shakespeare's* JC. New York: Scribner's. 1961.

1131

McAlindon, Thomas. "The Numbering of Men and Days: Symbolic Design in *JC.*" *Studies in Philology.* 1984. 81: 372-93.

1132

Miller, Anthony. "The Roman State in *JC* and *Sejanus.*" *Jonson and Shakespeare.* Donaldson, Ian, ed. London: Macmillan; Canberra: Australian National University; Atlantic Highlands, N.J.: Humanities Press. 1983. 179-201.

1133

Miola, Robert S. "*JC* and the Tyrannicide Debate." *Renaissance Quarterly.* 1985. 38: 271-89.

1134

Moore, Nancy. "The Stoicism of Brutus and the Structure of *JC.*" *Shakespeare and Renaissance Association of West Virginia: Selected Papers.* 1983. 8: 29-37.

1135

Ornstein, Robert. "Seneca and the Political Drama of *JC*." *Journal of English and Germanic Philology*. 1958. 57: 51-6.

1136

Paolucci, Anne. "The Tragic Hero in *JC*." *SQ* . 1960. 11: 329-33.

1137

Peterson, Douglas L. "'Wisdom Consumed in Confidence': An Examination of Shakespeare's *JC*." *SQ*. 1965. 16: 19-28.

1138

Pinciss, G.M. "Rhetoric as Character: The Forum Speeches in *JC*." *Upstart Crow*. 1982. 4: 113-21.

1139

Prior, Moody E. "The Search for a Hero in *JC*." *Renaissance Drama*. 1969. N.S. 2: 81-101.

1140

Rabkin, Norman. "Structure, Convention and Meaning in *JC*." *Journal of English and Germanic Philology*. 1964. 63: 240-54.

1141

Ribner, Irving. "Political Issues in *JC*." *Journal of English and Germanic Philology*. 1957. 56: 10-22.

1142

Rish, Shirley. "Shakespeare's and Plutarch's Brutus: Shakespeare's Dramatic Strategy to Undercut the Noble Image." *Journal of the Rocky Mountain Medieval and Renaissance Association*. 1982. 3: 191-7.

1143

Sanders, Norman. "The Shift of Power in *JC*." *Review of English Literature*. 1964. 5: 24-35.

1144

Schanzer, Ernest. "The Problem of *JC*." *SQ*. 1955. 6: 297-308.

1145

Schanzer, Ernest. "The Tragedy of Shakespeare's Brutus." *English Literary History*. 1955. 22: 1-15.

1146

Smith, Gordon Ross. "Brutus, Virtue, and Will." *SQ*. 1959. 10: 367-79.

1147

Stirling, Brents. "'Or Else This Were a Savage Spectacle'." *PMLA*. 1951. 66: 765-74.

1148

Toole, William B. "The Cobbler, the Disrobed Image and the Motif of Movement in *JC*." *Upstart Crow*. 1982. 4: 41-55.

1149

Vawter, Marvin L. "'After Their Fashion': Cicero and Brutus in *JC*." *Shakespeare Studies*. 1976. 9: 205-219.

1150

Vawter, Marvin L. "'Division 'tween Our Souls': Shakespeare's Stoic Brutus." *Shakespeare Studies*. 1974. 7: 173-95.

1151

Velz, John W. "Clemency, Will, and Just Cause in *JC*." *Shakespeare Survey*. 1969. 22: 109-18.

1152

Velz, John W. "'If I Were Brutus Now   .   .   .': Role-Playing in *JC*." *Shakespeare Studies*. 1969. 4: 149-59.

1153

Velz, John W. "*Orator* and *Imperator* in *JC*: Style and the Process of Roman History." *Shakespeare Studies*. 1982. 15: 55-75.

1154

Velz, John W. JC*: A Bibliography to Supplement the New Variorum Edition of 1913*. New York: Modern Language Association. 1977.

1155

Velz, John W. "Undular Structure in *JC*." *Modern Language Review*. 1971. 66: 21-30.

1156

Wilkinson, Andrew M. "A Psychological Approach to *JC*." *Review of English Literature*. 1966. 7: 65-78.

1157

Yoder, R.A. "History and the Histories in *JC*." *SQ* . 1973. 24: 309-27.

1158

Zandvoort, R.W. "Brutus's Forum Speech in *JC*." *Review of English Studies*. 1940. 16: 62-6.

See also works listed under *Tragedy*, especially by Brower, Charney, Knight, MacCallum, Phillips, Simmons, Traversi, and Velz: and by Rabkin (*Understanding*) listed under *General Studies*.

1159

Baldwin, Dean R. "Style in Shakespeare's *Jn.*" *Language and Style.* 1983. 16: 64-76.

1160

Battenhouse, Roy. "King John: Shakespeare's Perspective and Others." *Notre Dame English Journal.* 1982. 14: 191-215.

1161

Berman, Ronald. "Anarchy and Order in *R3* and *Jn.*" *Shakespeare Survey.* 1967. 20: 51-9.

1162

Bonjour, Adrien. "Bastinado for the Bastard?" *English Studies 45 Supplement.* 1964. 169-76.

1163

Bonjour, Adrien. "The Road to Swinstead Abbey: A Study of the Sense and Structure of *Jn.*" *English Literary History.* 1951. 18: 253-74.

1164

Burckhardt, Sigurd. "*Jn*: The Ordering of This Present Time." *English Literary History.* 1966. 33: 133-53. Reprinted in Burckhardt's *Shakespearean Meanings.* Princeton: Princeton University Press, 1968.

1165

Calderwood, James L. "Commodity and Honour in *Jn.*" *University of Toronto Quarterly.* 1960. 29: 341-56.

1166

Elliott, John R. "Shakespeare and the Double Image of King John." *Shakespeare Studies.* 1965. 1: 64-84.

1167

Elson, John. "Studies in the King John Plays." *Joseph Quincy Adams Memorial Studies.* McManaway, James G., et al, eds. Washington, D.C.: Folger Shakespeare Library. 1948. 183-97.

1168

Jones, Robert C. "Truth in *Jn.*" *Studies in English Literature.* 1985. 25: 397-417.

1169

Levin, Carole. "The Historical Evolution of the Death of King John in Three Renaissance Plays." *Journal of the Rocky Mountain Medieval and Renaissance Association.* 1982. 3: 85-106.

1170

Levin, Richard. "*Jn*'s Bastard." *Upstart Crow.* 1980. 3: 29-41.

1171

Matchett, William H. "Richard's Divided Heritage in *Jn.*" *Essays in Criticism.* 1962. 12: 231-53.

1172

Mattsson, May. *Five Plays about King John.* Studia Anglistica Upsaliensia 34. Stockholm: Almqvist and Wiksell; Atlantic Highlands, N.J.: Humanities Press. 1977.

1173

May, James E. "Imagery of Disorderly Motion in *Jn*: A Thematic Gloss." *Essays in Literature.* (Western Illinois University) 1983. 10: 17-28.

1174

Ortego, Philip D. "Shakespeare and the Doctrine of Monarchy in *Jn.*" *College Language Association Journal.* 1970. 13: 392-401.

1175

Pettet, E.C. "Hot Irons and Fever: A Note on Some of the Imagery of *Jn.*" *Essays in Criticism.* 1954. 4: 128-44.

1176

Rackin, Phyllis. "Anti-Historians: Women's Roles in Shakespeare's Histories." *Theatre Journal.* 1985. 37: 329-44.

1177

Salter, F.M. "The Problem of *Jn.*" *Transactions of the Royal Society of Canada.* 1949. 43: 115-36.

1178

Sibly, John. "The Anomalous Case of *Jn.*" *English Literary History.* 1966. 33: 415-21.

1179

Simmons, J.L. "Shakespeare's *Jn* and Its Source: Coherence, Pattern, and Vision." *Tulane Studies in English.* 1969. 17: 53-72.

1180

Stevick, Robert D. "'Repentant Ashes': The Matrix of 'Shakespearian' Poetic Language." *SQ.* 1962. 13: 366-70.

1181

Trace, Jacqueline. "Shakespeare's Bastard Faulconbridge: An Early Tudor Hero." *Shakespeare Studies*. 1980. 13: 59-69.

1182

Van de Water, Julia C. "The Bastard in *Jn.*" *SQ* . 1960. 11: 137-46.

1183

Vaughan, Virginia Mason. "Between Tetralogies: *Jn* as Transition." *SQ*. 1984. 35: 407-20.

1184

Waith, Eugene M. "*Jn* and the Drama of History." *SQ*. 1978. 29: 192-211.

See also works listed under *History Plays*, especially by Ornstein and Ribner.

King Lear

1185

Aers, David, and Kress, Gunther. "The Language of Social Order: Individual, Society and Historical Process in *Lr.*" *Literature, Language and Society in England, 1580-1680*. Aers, David, et al, eds. Dublin: Gill and Macmillan; Totowa, N.J.: Barnes and Noble. 1981. 75-99.

1186

Alpers, Paul J. "*Lr* and the Theory of the 'Sight Pattern'." *In Defense of Reading*. Brower, Reuben A., and Poirier, Richard, eds. New York: Dutton; Toronto: Clarke, Irwin. 1962. 133-52.

1187

Anshutz, H.L. "Cordelia and the Fool." *Research Studies*. (Washington State University) 1964. 32: 240-60.

1188

Archer, Paul T. "Lear's Incomplete Catharsis: A Misconception of Love." *Upstart Crow*. 1982. 4: 122-36.

1189

Bald, R.C. "'Thou Nature, Art My Goddess': Edmund and Renaissance Free-Thought." *Joseph Quincy Adams Memorial Studies*. McManaway, James G., et al, eds. Washington, D.C.: Folger Shakespeare Library. 1948. 337-49.

1190

Barish, Jonas A., and Waingrow, Marshall. "'Service' in *Lr*." *SQ*. 1958. 9: 347-55.

1191

Barnet, Sylvan. "Some Limitations of a Christian Approach to Shakespeare." *English Literary History*. 1955. 22: 81-92.

1192

Bauer, Robert J. "Despite of Mine Own Nature: Edmund and the Orders, Cosmic and Moral." *Texas Studies in Literature and Language*. 1968. 10: 359-66.

1193

Bennett, Josephine Waters. "The Storm Within: The Madness of Lear." *SQ*. 1962. 13: 137-55.

1194

Berger, Harry, Jr. "Text Against Performance: The Gloucester Family Romance." *Shakespeare's "Rough Magic": Renaissance Essays in Honor of C.L. Barber*. Erickson, Peter, and Kahn, Coppélia, eds. Newark: University of Delaware Press; London and Toronto: Associated University Presses. 1985. 210-29.

1195

Berry, Ralph. "Lear's System." *SQ*. 1984. 35: 421-9.

1196

Birenbaum, Harvey. "The Art of Our Necessities: The Softness of *Lr*." *Yale Review*. 1983. N.S. 72: 581-99.

1197

Black, James. "*Lr*: Art Upside-Down." *Shakespeare Survey*. 1980. 33: 35-42.

1198

Blayney, Peter W.M. *The Texts of* Lr *and Their Origins*. Cambridge, New York etc.: Cambridge University Press. 1982+.

1199

Bonheim, Helmut W., ed. *The* Lr *Perplex*. Belmont, California: Wadsworth. 1960.

1200

Booth, Stephen. Lr, Mac, *Indefinition, and Tragedy*. New Haven and London: Yale University Press. 1983.

1201

Brooke, Nicholas. "The Ending of *Lr.*" *Shakespeare 1564-1964*. Bloom, Edward A., ed. Providence, R.I.: Brown University Press. 1964. 71-87.

1202

Brooke, Nicholas. *Shakespeare:* Lr. London: Arnold. 1963.

1203

Burke, Kenneth. "*Lr*: Its Form and Psychosis." *Shenandoah*. 1969. 21: 3-18.

1204

Butler, Guy. "King Lear and Ancient Britain." *Theoria*. 1985. 65: 27-33.

1205

Campbell, Oscar James. "The Salvation of Lear." *English Literary History*. 1948. 15: 93-109.

1206

Cavell, Stanley. "The Avoidance of Love: A Reading of *Lr.*" *Must We Mean What We Say?: A Book of Essays*. Cambridge, New York, etc.: Cambridge University Press. 1976. 267-353.

1207

Champion, Larry S., comp. Lr: *An Annotated Bibliography*. New York: Garland. 1980. 2 vols.

1208

Chaplin, William H. "Form and Psychology in *Lr.*" *Literature and Psychology*. 1969. 19: 31-45.

1209

Cohen, Walter. "*Lr* and the Social Dimensions of Shakespearean Tragic Form, 1603-1608." *Shakespeare: Contemporary Critical Approaches*. Garvin, Harry R., ed. Lewisburg, Pa.: Bucknell University Press; London and Toronto: Associated University Presses. 1980. 106-18.

1210

Colie, Rosalie L., and Flahiff, F.T., eds. *Some Facets of* Lr: *Essays in Prismatic Criticism*. Toronto and Buffalo: University of Toronto Press. 1974.

1211

Coursen, H.R. "'Age is Unnecessary': A Jungian Approach to *Lr.*" *Upstart Crow*. 1984. 5: 75-92.

1212

Coursen, H.R. "The Death of Cordelia: A Jungian Approach." *Hebrew University Studies in Literature*. 1980. 8: 1-12.

1213

Craig, Hardin. "The Ethics of *Lr*." *Philological Quarterly.* 1925. 4: 97-109.

1214

Danby, John F. "*Lr* and Christian Patience: A Culmination." *Poets on Fortune's Hill.* London: Faber and Faber. 1952. Reprinted as *Elizabethan and Jacobean Poets*, 1964. 108-27.

1215

Danby, John F. *Shakespeare's Doctrine of Nature: A Study of* Lr. London: Faber and Faber. 1949.

1216

Danson, Lawrence. "*Lr* and the Two Abysses." *On* Lr. Danson, Lawrence, ed. Princeton and Guildford, Surrey: Princeton University Press. 1981. 119-35.

1217

Donnelly, John. "Incest, Ingratitude, and Insanity: Aspects of the Psycho-pathology of *Lr*." *Psychoanalytic Review.* 1953. 40: 149-55.

1218

Draper, John W. "The Old Age of King Lear." *Journal of English and Germanic Philology.* 1940. 39: 527-40.

1219

Dundes, Alan. "'To Love my Father All': A Psychoanalytic Study of the Folktake Source of *Lr*." *Southern Folklore Quarterly.* 1976. 40: 353-66.

1220

Elton, William R. Lr *and the Gods.* San Marino, California: Huntington Library Press. 1966.

1221

Empson, William. "Fool in *Lr*." *The Structure of Complex Words.* London: Chatto and Windus; Toronto: Clarke Irwin; New York: New Directions. 1951. 125-57.

1222

Everett, Barbara. "The New King Lear." *Critical Quarterly.* 1960. 2: 325-39.

1223

Feder, Lillian. *Madness in Literature.* Princeton and Guildford, Surrey: Princeton University Press. 1980. Chapter on *Lr*, 98-146.

1224

Felperin, Howard. *Shakespearean Representation.* Princeton: Princeton University Press. 1977.

1225

Felperin, Howard. *Shakespearean Romance.* Princeton: Princeton University Press. 1972.

1226

Ferris, David S. "Aristotle's *Poetics* and the Purgation of History." *History and Mimesis.* Massey, Irving, and Lee, Sung-Won, eds. Buffalo, N.Y.: Department of English, S.U.N.Y. at Buffalo. 1983. 6-16.

1227

Fly, Richard D. "Beyond Extremity: *Lr* and the Limits of Poetic Drama." *Shakespeare's Mediated World.* Amherst: University of Massachusetts Press. 1976. 85-115.

1228

Fraser, Russell A. *Shakespeare's Poetics in Relation to* Lr. London: Routledge and Kegan Paul. 1962.

1229

French, Carolyn S. "Shakespeare's 'Folly': *Lr.*" *SQ.* 1959. 10: 523-9.

1230

Freud, Sigmund. "The Theme of the Three Caskets." *Complete Psychological Works of Sigmund Freud,* 24 vols. Strachey, James, et al, eds. London: Hogarth; Toronto: Clarke Irwin. Vol. 12 (1911-13). 291-301.

1231

Frost, William. "Shakespeare's Rituals and the Opening of *Lr.*" *Hudson Review.* 1957-58. 10: 577-85.

1232

Frye, Dean. "The Context of Lear's Unbuttoning." *English Literary History.* 1965. 32: 17-31.

1233

Gardner, Helen. "*Lr*". London: Athlone; Toronto and New York: Oxford University Press. 1967.

1234

Goldberg, S.L. *An Essay on* Lr. London and New York: Cambridge University Press. 1974.

1235

Goldman, Michael. "*Lr:* Acting and Feeling." *On* Lr. Danson, Lawrence, ed. Princeton and Guildford, Surrey: Princeton University Press. 1981. 25-46.

1236

Greenblatt, Stephen. "Shakespeare and the Exorcists." *Shakespeare and the Question of Theory.* Parker, Patricia, and Hartman, Geoffrey, eds. New York and London: Methuen. 1985. 163-87.

1237

Greenblatt, Stephen. "The Cultivation of Anxiety: King Lear and His Heirs." *Raritan.* (Rutgers University) 1982. 2: 92-114.

1238

Hardison, O.B., Jr. "Myth and History in *Lr.*" *SQ* . 1975. 26: 227-42.

1239

Hargrove, Nancy D. "The Theme of Destruction and Rebuilding in *Lr.*" *Upstart Crow.* 1980. 3: 42-53.

1240

Heilman, Robert Bechtold. *This Great Stage: Image and Structure in* Lr. Baton Rouge: Louisiana State University Press. 1948. Second edition, Seattle: University of Washington Press, 1963.

1241

Henderson, W.B. Drayton. "Montaigne's *Apologie of Raymond Sebond,* and *Lr.*" *Shakespeare Association Bulletin.* 1939. 14: 209-25. 1940. 15: 40-54.

1242

Hibbard, G.R. "*Lr*: A Retrospect, 1939-79." *Shakespeare Survey.* 1980. 33: 1-12.

1243

Hinchliffe, Michael. "The Error of King Lear: A Reading of the Love Game in Act I, Scene 1." *L'Erreur dans la littérature et la pensée anglaises: Actes du Centre Aixois de Recherches Anglaises.* Aix-en-Provence: Publications Univ. de Provence. 1980. 27-51.

1244

Hockey, Dorothy C. "The Trial Pattern in *Lr.*" *SQ* . 1959. 10: 389-95.

1245

Hodge, R.I.V., and Kress, Gunther. "The Semiotics of Love and Power: *Lr* and a New Stylistics." *Southern Review.* 1982. (Australia) 15: 143-56.

1246

Hole, Sandra. "The Background of Divine Action in *Lr.*" *Studies in English Literature.* 1968. 8: 217-33.

1247

Holland, Norman N. "How Can Dr. Johnson's Remarks on Cordelia's Death Add to My Own Response?" *Psychoanalysis and the Question of the Text.* Hartman, Geoffrey H., ed. Baltimore and London: Johns Hopkins University Press. 1985. 18-44.

1248

Hoover, Claudette. "Goneril and Regan: 'So Horrid as in Woman'." *San Jose Studies.* 1984. 10: 49-65.

1249

Humphries, Jefferson. "Seeing Through Lear's Blindness: Blanchot, Freud, Saussure, and Derrida." *Mosaic.* 1983. 16: 29-43.

1250

Hyland, Peter. "Disguise and Renaissance Tragedy." *University of Toronto Quarterly.* 1985-86. 55:161-71.

1251

Isenberg, Arnold. "Cordelia Absent." *SQ.* 1951. 2: 185-94.

1252

Jackson, Esther Merle. "*Lr*: The Grammar of Tragedy." *SQ.* 1966. 17: 25-40.

1253

Jacobson, Howard. "Nomen Omen: Lear's Three Daughters." *Revue Belge de Philologie et d'Histoire.* 1980. 58: 595-603.

1254

Jaffa, Harry V. "The Limits of Politics: An Interpretation of *Lr*, Act I, Scene 1." *American Political Science Review.* 1957. 51: 405-27.

1255

James, D.G. *The Dream of Learning: An Essay on the Advancement of Learning,* Ham *and* Lr. Oxford: Clarendon. 1951.

1256

Jayne, Sears. "Charity in *Lr*." *SQ.* 1964. 15: 277-88.

1257

Jorgensen, Paul A. *Lear's Self-Discovery.* Berkeley and Los Angeles: University of California Press; London: Cambridge University Press. 1967.

1258

Kahn, Sholom J. "'Enter Lear Mad'." *SQ.* 1957. 8: 311-29.

1259

Kanzer, Mark. "Imagery in *Lr*." *American Imago.* 1965. 22: 3-13.

1260

Kaula, David. "Edgar on Dover Cliff: An Emblematic Reading." *English Studies in Canada.* 1979. 5: 377-87.

1261

Keast, W.R. "Imagery and Meaning in the Interpretation of *Lr*." *Modern Philology.* 1949. 47: 45-64.

1262

Kermode, Frank. "Why *Lr* Is the Cruellest Play." *The Listener.* 16 Sept. 1982. 108: 13-14.

1263

Kernan, Alvin B. "Formalism and Realism in Elizabethan Drama: The Miracles in *Lr*." *Renaissance Drama.* 1966. 9: 59-66.

1264

Kernan, Alvin B. "*Lr* and the Shakespearean Pageant of History." *On* Lr. Danson, Lawrence, ed. Princeton and Guildford, Surrey: Princeton University Press. 1981. 7-24.

1265

Kernodle, George R. "The Symphonic Form of *Lr*." *Elizabethan Studies and Other Essays in Honor of George F. Reynolds.* Boulder: University of Colorado Press. 1945. 185-91.

1266

Kestenbaum, Clarice J. "Fathers and Daughters: The Father's Contribution to Feminine Identification in Girls as Depicted in Fairy Tales and Myths." *American Journal of Psychoanalysis.* 1983. 43: 119-27.

1267

Kirschbaum, Leo. "Albany." *Shakespeare Survey.* 1960. 13: 20-29.

1268

Kirschbaum, Leo. "Banquo and Edgar: Character or Function?" *Essays in Criticism.* 1957. 7: 1-21.

1269

Knights, L.C. "*Lr* as Metaphor." *Further Explorations.* London: Chatto and Windus; Toronto: Clarke Irwin. 1965. 169-85.

1270

Knights, L.C. *Some Shakespearean Themes.* London: Chatto and Windus; Toronto: Clarke Irwin. 1959. 84-119.

1271

Langenfeld, Robert. "The Role of Suffering in *Lr.*" *Elizabethan Miscellany 3*. Hogg, James, ed. Salzburg: Inst. für Anglistik und Amerikanistik, Univ. Salzburg. 1981. 74-85.

1272

Law, Robert Adger. "Holinshed's Leir Story and Shakespeare's." *Studies in Philology*. 1950. 47: 42-50.

1273

Law, Robert Adger. "*King Leir* and *Lr:* An Examination of Two Plays." *Studies in Honor of T.W. Baldwin*. Allen, Don Cameron, ed. Urbana: University of Illinois Press. 1958.

1274

Lothian, John M. L*r: A Tragic Reading of Life*. Toronto: Clarke, Irwin. 1949.

1275

Lukes, Timothy J. "Marcuse and Lear: The Politics of Motley." *Midwest Quarterly*. 1980. 22: 32-45.

1276

McCombie, Frank. "Medium and Message in *AYL* and *Lr.*" *Shakespeare Survey*. 1980. 33: 67-80.

1277

McCullen, J.T. "Edgar: The Wise Bedlam." *Shakespeare in the Southwest*. Stafford, T.J., ed. El Paso: Texas Western Press of the University of Texas. 1969. 43-55.

1278

McFarland, Thomas. "The Image of the Family in *Lr.*" *On* Lr. Danson, Lawrence, ed. Princeton and Guildford, Surrey: Princeton University Press. 1981. 91-118.

1279

MacIntyre, Jean. "Truth, Lies, and Poesie in *Lr.*" *Renaissance and Reformation*. 1982. 6: 34-45.

1280

Maclean, Hugh. "Disguise in *Lr*: Kent and Edgar." *SQ*. 1960. 11: 49-54.

1281

McLuskie, Kathleen. "The Patriarchal Bard: Feminist Criticism and Shakespeare*: Lr* and *MM.*" *Political Shakespeare*. Dollimore, Jonathan, and Sinfield, Alan, eds. Manchester: Manchester University Press. 1985. 88-108.

117

1282

McNeir, Waldo F. "The Role of Edmund in *Lr*." *Studies in English Literature*. 1968. 8: 187-216.

1283

Markels, Julian. "Shakespeare's Confluence of Tragedy and Comedy: *TN* and *Lr*." *SQ*. 1964. 15: 75-88.

1284

Marks, Carol L. "'Speak What We Feel': The End of *Lr*." *English Language Notes*. 1968. 5: 163-71.

1285

Mason, H.A. "Can We Derive Wisdom about Old Age from *Lr*?" *Cambridge Quarterly*. 1975. 6: 203-13.

1286

Maxwell, J.C. "The Technique of Invocation in *Lr*." *Modern Language Review*. 1950. 45: 142-7.

1287

Merchant, W. Moelwyn. "Costume in *Lr*." *Shakespeare Survey*. 1960. 13: 72-80.

1288

Mooney, Michael E. "'Edgar I Nothing Am': *Figurenposition* in *Lr*." *Shakespeare Survey*. 1985. 38: 153-66.

1289

Mortenson, Peter. "The Role of Albany." *SQ*. 1965. 16: 217-25.

1290

Muir, Edwin. *The Politics of* Lr. Glasgow: Jackson. 1947.

1291

Muir, Kenneth. "Madness in *Lr*." *Shakespeare Survey*. 1960. 13: 30-40.

1292

Myrick, Kenneth. "Christian Pessimism in *Lr*." *Shakespeare 1564-1964*. Bloom, Edward A., ed. Providence, R.I.: Brown University Press. 1964. 56-70.

1293

Neel, Jasper. "Plot, Character, or Theme? *Lr* and the Teacher." *Writing and Reading Differently: Deconstruction and the Teaching of Composition and Literature*. Atkins, G. Douglas, and Johnson, Michael L., eds. Lawrence: University Press of Kansas. 1985. 185-205.

1294

Nowottny, Winifred M.T. "Lear's Questions." *Shakespeare Survey.* 1957.
10: 90-7.

1295

Nowottny, Winifred M.T. "Some Aspects of the Style of *Lr.*" *Shakespeare Survey.* 1960. 13: 49-57.

1296

Oates, Joyce Carol. "'Is This the Promised End?': The Tragedy of *Lr.*" *Contraries: Essays.* New York: Oxford University Press. 1981. 51-81.

1297

Orwell, George. "Lear, Tolstoy, and the Fool." *Shooting an Elephant and Other Essays.* London: Secker and Warburg; New York: Harcourt, Brace and World. 1950. 33-56.

1298

Peat, Derek. "'And That's True Too': *Lr* and the Tension of Uncertainty." *Shakespeare Survey.* 1980. 33: 43-53.

1299

Peck, Russell A. "Edgar's Pilgrimage: High Comedy in *Lr.*" *Studies in English Literature.* 1967. 7: 219-37.

1300

Perry, T. Anthony. "Withdrawal or Service: The Paradox of *Lr.*" *Erotic Spirituality: The Integrative Tradition from Leone Ebreo to John Donne.* University, Ala.: University of Alabama Press. 1980. 99-115.

1301

Pirie, David. "Lear as King." *Critical Quarterly.* 1980. 22: 5-20.

1302

Presson, Robert K. "Boethius, King Lear, and 'Maystresse Philosophie'." *Journal of English and Germanic Philology.* 1965. 64: 406-24.

1303

Reibetanz, John. *The Lear World: A Study of Lr in Its Dramatic Context.* Toronto and Buffalo: University of Toronto Press. 1977.

1304

Reid, S.W. "The Texts of *Lr*: A Review Essay." *Shakespeare Studies.* 1982.
15: 327-39.

1305

Robinson, James E. "*Lr* and the Space Between." *Notre Dame English Journal.* 1979. 12: 27-54.

1306

Roche, Thomas P., Jr. "'Nothing Almost Sees Miracles': Tragic Knowledge in *Lr*." *On* Lr. Danson, Lawrence, ed. Princeton and Guildford, Surrey: Princeton University Press. 1981. 136-62.

1307

Rosenberg, Marvin. *The Masks of* Lr. Berkeley, Los Angeles, and London: University of California Press. 1972.

1308

Rosinger, Lawrence. "Gloucester and Lear: Men Who Act Like Gods." *English Literary History*. 1968. 35: 491-504.

1309

Rusche, Harry. "Edmund's Conception and Nativity in *Lr*." *SQ*. 1969. 20: 161-4.

1310

Schaum, Melita. "The Social Dynamic: Liminality and Reaggregation in *Lr*." *Aligarh Journal of English Studies*. 1984. 9: 148-54.

1311

Schell, Edgar. *Strangers and Pilgrims: From* The Castle of Perseverance *to* Lr. Chicago and London: University of Chicago Press. 1983.

1312

Schoff, Francis G. "King Lear: Moral Example or Tragic Protagonist?" *SQ*. 1962. 13: 157-72.

1313

Sell, Roger D. "Two Types of Style Contrast in *Lr*: A Literary-Critical Appraisal." *Style and Text: Studies Presented to Nils Erik Enkvist*. Ringbom, Hakan, et al, eds. Stockholm: Sprakförlaget Skriptor AB and Abo Akademi. 1975. 158-71.

1314

Serpieri, Alessandro. "The Breakdown of Medieval Hierarchy in *Lr*." *A Semiotic Landscape: Proceedings of the First Congress of the International Association for Semiotic Studies, Milan, June 1974*. Chatman, Seymour, et al, eds. The Hague, Paris, and New York: Mouton. 1979. 1067-72.

1315

Sewall, Richard B. *The Vision of Tragedy*. New Haven: Yale University Press. 1959. New enlarged edition, New Haven and London: Yale University Press, 1980. 68-79.

1316

Shakespeare Survey 13. 1960. 9 essays on *Lr*.

1317

Siegel, Paul N. "Adversity and the Miracle of Love in *Lr*." *SQ*. 1955. 6: 325-36.

1318

Skulsky, Harold. "*Lr* and the Meaning of Chaos." *SQ*. 1966. 17: 3-17.

1319

Smith, Robert M. "A Good Word for Oswald." *A Tribute to George Coffin Taylor*. Williams, Arnold, ed. Chapel Hill: University of North Carolina Press. 1952. 62-6.

1320

Snyder, Susan. "*Lr* and the Prodigal Son." *SQ* . 1966. 17: 361-9.

1321

Snyder, Susan. "*Lr* and the Psychology of Dying." *SQ*. 1982. 33: 449-60.

1322

Stampfer, J. "The Catharsis of *Lr*." *Shakespeare Survey*. 1960. 13: 1-10.

1323

States, Bert O. "Standing on the Extreme Verge in *Lr* and Other High Places." *Georgia Review*. 1982. 36: 417-25.

1324

Stetner, S.C.V, and Goodman, Oscar B. "Lear's Darker Purpose." *Literature and Psychology*. 1968. 18: 82-90.

1325

Stevenson, Warren. "Albany as Archetype in *Lr*." *Modern Language Quarterly*. 1965. 26: 257-63.

1326

Stewart, J.I.M. "The Blinding of Gloster." *Review of English Studies*. 1945. 21: 264-70.

1327

Stockholder, Katherine. "The Multiple Genres of *Lr*: Breaking the Archetypes." *Bucknell Review*. 1968. 16: 40-63.

1328

Stockholder, Katherine. "Sex and Authority in *Ham*, *Lr*, and *Per*." *Mosaic*. 1985. 18: 17-29.

1329

Stoll, Elmer Edgar. *Art and Artifice in Shakespeare*. Cambridge: Cambridge
  University Press; New York: Macmillan. 1933. Reprinted 1962.

1330

Stone, George Winchester. "Garrick's Production of *Lr*: A Study in the
  Temper of the Eighteenth-Century Mind." *Studies in Philology*. 1948. 45:
  89-103.

1331

Stone, P.W.K. *The Textual History of* Lr. London: Scolar Press. 1980.

1332

Summers, Joseph H. "'Look there, look there!': The Ending of *Lr*." *English
  Renaissance Studies Presented to Dame Helen Gardner in Honour of Her
  Seventieth Birthday*. Carey, John, ed. Oxford: Clarendon Press. 1980.
  74-93.

1333

Swinburne, Algernon Charles. "*Lr*." *Three Plays of Shakespeare*. New
  York: Harper. 1909.

1334

Szyfman, Arnold. "*Lr* on the Stage: A Producer's Reflections." *Shakespeare
  Survey*. 1960. 13: 69-71.

1335

Talbert, Ernest William. "Lear the King: A Preface to a Study of
  Shakespeare's Tragedy." *Medieval and Renaissance Studies*. Hardison,
  O.B., ed. Chapel Hill: University of North Carolina Press. 1966. 83-114.
  (Medieval and Renaissance Series, 1.)

1336

Taylor, Gary. "The War in *Lr*." *Shakespeare Survey*. 1980. 33: 27-34.

1337

Taylor, Gary, and Warren, Michael, eds. *The Division of the Kingdoms:
  Shakespeare's Two Versions of* Lr. Oxford: Clarendon Press. 1983.

1338

Traversi, D.A. "*Lr*." *Scrutiny*. 1952-53. 19: 43-64, 126-42, 206-30.

1339

Traversi, D.A. "'Unaccommodated Man' in *Lr*." *The Literary Imagination:
  Studies in Dante, Chaucer, and Shakespeare*. Newark: University of Delaware Press; London and Toronto: Associated University Presses. 1982.
  145-96.

122

1340

Urkowitz, Steven. *Shakespeare's Revision of* Lr. Princeton and Guildford,
  Surrey: Princeton University Press. 1980.

1341

Vickers, Brian. "*Lr* and Renaissance Paradoxes." *Modern Language Review*.
  1968. 63: 305-14.

1342

Walton, J.K. "Lear's Last Speech." *Shakespeare Survey*. 1960. 13: 11-19.

1343

Weidhorn, Manfred. "Lear's Schoolmasters." *SQ*. 1962. 13: 305-16.

1344

Weiss, Theodore. "As the Wind Sits: The Poetics of *Lr.*" *On* Lr. Danson,
  Lawrence, ed. Princeton and Guildford, Surrey: Princeton University
  Press. 1981. 61-90.

1345

Williamson, C.F. "The Hanging of Cordelia." *Review of English Studies*.
  1983. N.S. 34: 414-18.

1346

Wittreich, Joseph. "*Image of that Horror*": *History, Prophecy, and Apoc-
  alypse in* Lr. San Marino: Huntington Library Press. 1984.

1347

Young, David. "The Natural Fool of Fortune: *Lr.*" *The Heart's Forest: A
  Study of Shakespeare's Pastoral Plays*. New Haven and London: Yale
  University Press. 1972. 73-103.

1348

Zelicovici, Dvora. "Madness: A Good or Evil Dispensation for King Lear?"
  English Record. 1982. 33: 10-14.

See also works listed under *Tragedy*, especially by Bradley, Brower, Cunningham, Holloway, R. G. Hunter, Rosen, Speaight, and Wilson.

1349

Agnew, Gates K. "Berowne and the Progress of *LLL*." *Shakespeare Studies.* 1969. 4: 40-72.

1350

Beiner, G. "Endgame in *LLL*." *Anglia.* 1985. 103: 48-70.

1351

Berek, Peter. "Artifice and Realism in Lyly, Nashe, and *LLL*." *Studies in English Literature.* 1983. 23: 207-21.

1352

Berry, Ralph. "The Words of Mercury." *Shakespeare Survey.* 1969. 22: 69-77.

1353

Boughner, Daniel C. "Don Armado and the *Commedia dell'Arte*." *Studies in Philology.* 1940. 37: 201-24.

1354

Boughner, Daniel C. "Don Armado as a Gallant." *Revue Anglo-Américaine.* 1935. 13: 18-28.

1355

Bradbrook, M.C. "Shakespeare, the School and Nashe." *The School of Night: A Study in the Literary Relationships of Sir Walter Raleigh.* Cambridge: Cambridge University Press. 1936. 151-78.

1356

Calderwood, James L. "*LLL*: A Wantoning with Words." *Studies in English Literature.* 1965. 5: 317-32.

1357

Calderwood, James L. "*LLL*: A Dalliance with Language." *Shakespearean Metadrama.* Minneapolis: University of Minnesota Press. 1971. 52-84.

1358

Carroll, William C. *The Great Feast of Language in* LLL. Princeton and Guildford, Surrey: Princeton University Press. 1976.

1359

Coursen, Herbert R., Jr. "*LLL* and the Comic Truth." *Papers on Language and Literature.* 1970. 6: 316-22.

124

1360

Draper, John W. "Tempo in *LLL*." *English Studies*. 1948. 29: 129-37.

1361

Elam, Keir. "The Words of Mercury and the Songs of Apollo: The Status of the Linguistic Sign in *LLL* and Other Shakespearean Comedies. Part 1." *Anglistica*. 1981. 24: 7-43.

1362

Erickson, Peter B. "The Failure of Relationship Between Men and Women in *LLL*." *Women's Studies*. 1981. 9: 65-81.

1363

Evans, Malcolm. "Mercury Versus Apollo: A Reading of *LLL*." *SQ*. 1975. 26: 113-27.

1364

Godshalk, William Leigh. "Pattern in *LLL*." *Renaissance Papers 1968*. 1969. 41-8.

1365

Goldstien, Neal L. "*LLL* and the Renaissance Vision of Love." *SQ*. 1974. 25: 335-50.

1366

Greene, Thomas M. "*LLL*: The Grace of Society." *SQ*. 1971. 22: 315-28.

1367

Harbage, Alfred. "*LLL* and the Early Shakespeare." *Philological Quarterly*. 1962. 41: 18-36.

1368

Harvey, Nancy Lenz, and Carey, Anna Kirwan, comps. LLL: *An Annotated Bibliography*. New York and London: Garland. 1984.

1369

Heninger, S.K., Jr. "The Pattern of *LLL*." *Shakespeare Studies*. 1974. 7: 25-53.

1370

Hoy, Cyrus. "*LLL* and the Nature of Comedy." *SQ*. 1962. 13: 31-40.

1371

Hunter, G.K. "Poem and Context in *LLL*." *Shakespeare's Styles: Essays in Honour of Kenneth Muir*. Edwards, Philip, et al, eds. Cambridge, New York etc.: Cambridge University Press. 1980. 25-38.

1372

Hunter, Robert G. "The Function of the Songs at the End of *LLL*." *Shakespeare Studies*. 1974. 7: 55-64.

1373

Lamb, Mary Ellen. "The Nature of Topicality in *LLL*." *Shakespeare Survey*. 1985. 38: 49-59.

1374

Levin, Harry. "Sitting in the Sky *(LLL* 4.3*)*." *Shakespeare's "Rough Magic": Renaissance Essays in Honor of C.L. Barber*. Erickson, Peter, and Kahn, Coppélia, eds. Newark: University of Delaware Press; London and Toronto: Associated University Presses. 1985. 113-30.

1375

McLay, Catherine M. "The Dialogues of Spring and Winter: A Key to the Unity of *LLL*." *SQ*. 1967. 18: 119-27.

1376

Montrose, Louis Adrian. *"Curious-Knotted Garden": The Form, Themes, and Contexts of Shakespeare's* LLL. Salzburg: Institut für Englische Sprache und Literatur, Univ., Salzburg. 1977.

1377

Parsons, Philip. "Shakespeare and the Mask." *Shakespeare Survey*. 1963. 16: 121-31.

1378

Perryman, Judith C. "A Tradition Transformed in *LLL*." *Etudes Anglaises*. 1984. 37: 156-62.

1379

Roesen, Bobbyann. *"LLL*." *SQ*. 1953. 4: 411-26.

1380

Shulman, Jeff. "At the Crossroads of Myth: The Hermeneutics of Hercules from Ovid to Shakespeare." *English Literary History*. 1983. 50: 83-105.

1381

Vyvyan, John. *Shakespeare and the Rose of Love*. London: Chatto and Windus; Toronto: Clarke Irwin; New York: Barnes and Noble. 1960. 23-67.

1382

Westlund, Joseph. "Fancy and Achievement in *LLL*." *SQ*. 1967. 18: 37-46.

Yates, Frances A. *A Study of* LLL. Cambridge: Cambridge University Press. 1936.

See also works listed under *Comedy: General Studies*, especially by Barber, Berry, Charlton, Evans, R. G. Hunter, McFarland, Stevenson, Tillyard, and Traversi; under *Comedy: The Early Comedies*, especially by Cody; and the work by Mahood under *General Studies*.

Macbeth

1384

Anderson, Ruth L. "The Pattern of Behavior Culminating in *Mac.*" *Studies in English Literature*. 1963. 3: 151-73.

1385

Arthos, John. "The Naîve Imagination and the Destruction of Macbeth." *English Literary History*. 1947. 14: 114-26.

1386

Asp, Carolyn. "'Be Bloody, Bold and Resolute': Tragic Action and Sexual Stereotyping in *Mac.*" *Studies in Philology*. 1981. 78: 153-69.

1387

Auden, W.H. "The Dyer's Hand." *The Listener*. 53 (16 June 1955): 1063-6.

1388

Bartholomeusz, Dennis. Mac *and the Players*. Cambridge and London: Cambridge University Press. 1969.

1389

Berger, Harry, Jr. "The Early Scenes of *Mac:* Preface to a New Interpretation." *English Literary History*. 1980. 47: 1-31.

1390

Berger, Harry, Jr. "Text Against Performance in Shakespeare: The Example of *Mac.*" *Genre*. 1982. 15: 49-79.

1391

Bernad, Miguel A. "The Five Tragedies in *Mac.*" *SQ* . 1962. 13: 49-61.

1392

Birenbaum, Harvey. "Consciousness and Responsibility in *Mac.*" *Mosaic*. 1982. 15: 17-32.

1393

Black, Michael. "Myth, Folklore and Character in Shakespeare and Racine." *The Equilibrium of Wit: Essays for Odette de Mourgues.* Bayley, Peter, and Coleman, Dorothy Gabe, eds. Lexington, Ky.: French Forum. 1982. 166-75.

1394

Blissett, William. "The Secret'st Man of Blood: A Study of Dramatic Irony in *Mac.*" *SQ.* 1959. 10: 397-408.

1395

Booth, Stephen. Lr, Mac, *Indefinition, and Tragedy.* New Haven and London: Yale University Press. 1983.

1396

Booth, Wayne C. "Macbeth as Tragic Hero." *Journal of General Education.* 1951. 6: 17-25. Revised version, "Shakespeare's Tragic Villain", in *Shakespeare's Tragedies: A Selection of Modern Criticism.* Lerner, Laurence, ed. Harmondsworth: Penguin, 1963. Rpt. as *Shakespeare's Tragedies: An Anthology of Modern Criticism,* 1963. 180-90.

1397

Brashear, Lucy. "'My Dearest Partner in Greatness': A Reappraisal of Lady Macbeth." *Shakespeare and Renaissance Association of West Virginia: Selected Papers.* 1980. 5: 14-24.

1398

Brooks, Cleanth. "The Naked Babe and the Cloak of Manliness." *The Well Wrought Urn.* New York: Harcourt, Brace. 1947. 21-46.

1399

Calderwood, James L. "*Mac*: Counter-*Hamlet.*" *Shakespeare Studies.* 1985. 17: 103-21.

1400

Calderwood, James L. "'More Than What You Were': Augmentation and Increase in *Mac.*" *English Literary Renaissance.* 1984. 14: 70-82.

1401

Collmer, Robert G. "An Existentialist Approach to *Mac.*" *Person.* 1960. 41: 484-91.

1402

Coursen, Herbert R., Jr. "In Deepest Consequence: *Mac.*" *SQ.* 1967. 18: 375-88.

1403

Coursen, Herbert R., Jr. "A Jungian Approach to Characterization: *Mac.*" *Shakespeare's "Rough Magic": Renaissance Essays in Honor of C.L. Barber.* Erickson, Peter, and Kahn, Coppélia, eds. Newark: University of Delaware Press; London and Toronto: Associated University Presses. 1985. 230-44.

1404

Cunningham, Dolora G. "*Mac*: The Tragedy of the Hardened Heart." *SQ.* 1963. 14: 39-47.

1405

Curry, Walter Clyde. "The Demonic Metaphysics of *Mac.*" *Studies in Philology.* 1933. 30: 395-426. Reprinted, Curry's *Shakespeare's Philosophical Patterns.* Baton Rouge: Louisiana State University Press, 1937. 53-93.

1406

Curry, Walter Clyde. "Macbeth's Changing Character." *Journal of English and Germanic Philology.* 1935. 34: 311-38. Reprinted in *Shakespeare's Philosophical Patterns.* Baton Rouge: Louisiana State University Press, 1937. Second edition, 1959.

1407

Davis, Derek Russell. "Hurt Minds." *Focus on* Mac. Brown, John Russell, ed. London, Boston, and Henley: Routledge and Kegan Paul. 1982. 210-28.

1408

Diehl, Huston. "Horrid Image, Sorry Sight, Fatal Vision: The Visual Rhetoric of *Mac.*" *Shakespeare Studies.* 1983. 16: 191-203.

1409

Doebler, Bettie Anne. "'Rooted Sorrow': Verbal and Visual Survivals of an *Ars* Commonplace (1590-1620)." *Texas Studies in Literature and Language.* 1980. 22: 358-68.

1410

Donohue, Joseph W., Jr. "Kemble and Mrs. Siddons in *Mac*: The Romantic Approach to Tragic Character." *Theatre Notebook.* 1967-68. 22: 65-86.

1411

Doran, Madeleine. "The *Mac* Music." *Shakespeare Studies.* 1983. 16: 153-73.

1412

Doran, Madeleine. "That Undiscovered Country: A Problem Concerning the Use of the Supernatural in *Ham* and *Mac*." *Philological Quarterly.* 1941. 20: 413-27.

1413

Duthie, G.I. "Antithesis in *Mac*." *Shakespeare Survey.* 1966. 19: 25-33.

1414

Dyson, J.P. "The Structural Function of the Banquet Scene in *Mac*." *SQ*. 1963. 14: 369-78.

1415

Elliott, G. R. *Dramatic Providence in* Mac. Princeton: Princeton University Press. 1958.

1416

Empson, William. "Dover Wilson on *Mac*." *Kenyon Review.* 1952. 14: 84-102.

1417

Fergusson, Francis. "*Mac* as the Imitation of an Action." *The Human Image in Dramatic Literature.* Garden City, N. Y.: Doubleday, 1957; London: Mayflower Press, 1958. 115-25.

1418

Ferrucci, Franco. "*Mac* and the Imitation of Evil." *The Poetics of Disguise: The Autobiography of the Work in Homer, Dante, and Shakespeare.* Dunnigan, Ann, trans. Ithaca and London: Cornell University Press. 1980. 125-58.

1419

Foakes, R. A. "Images of Death: Ambition in *Mac*." *Focus on* Mac. Brown, John Russell, ed. London, Boston, and Henley: Routledge and Kegan Paul. 1982. 7-29.

1420

Freud, Sigmund. "Those Wrecked by Success." *Complete Psychological Works of Sigmund Freud.* Strachey, James, et al, eds. London: Hogarth; Toronto: Clarke Irwin. 1953 +. 24 Vols. Vol. 14 (1914-1916). 316-31.

1421

Frye, Roland M. "*Mac* and the Powers of Darkness." *Emory University Quarterly.* 1952. 8: 164-74.

1422

Gardner, Helen. "Interpretation." *The Business of Criticism.* Oxford: Clarendon. 1959. 52-75.

1423

Gent, Lucy. "The Self-Cozening Eye." *Review of English Studies.* 1983. N.S. 34: 419-28.

1424

Goldman, Michael. "Language and Action in *Mac.*" *Focus on* Mac. Brown, John Russell, ed. London, Boston, and Henley: Routledge and Kegan Paul. 1982. 140-52.

1425

Greene, James L. "Macbeth: Masculinity as Murder." *American Imago.* 1984. 41: 155-80.

1426

Grove, Robin. "Multiplying Villainies of Nature." *Focus on* Mac. Brown, John Russell, ed. London, Boston, Henley: Routledge and Kegan Paul. 1982. 113-39.

1427

Halio, Jay L. *Approaches to* Mac. Belmont, California: Wadsworth. 1966.

1428

Harding, D. W. "Women's Fantasy of Manhood: A Shakespearian Theme." *SQ.* 1969. 20: 245-53.

1429

Hawkins, Michael. "History, Politics, and *Mac.*" *Focus on* Mac. Brown, John Russell, ed. London, Boston, and Henley: Routledge and Kegan Paul. 1982. 155-88.

1430

Heilman, Robert B. "The Criminal as Tragic Hero: Dramatic Methods." *Shakespeare Survey.* 1966. 19: 12-24.

1431

Hunter, G. K. "*Mac* in the Twentieth Century." *Shakespeare Survey.* 1966. 19: 1-11.

1432

Jaarsma, Richard J. "The Tragedy of Banquo." *Literature and Psychology.* 1967. 17: 87-94.

131

1433

Jack, Jane H. "*Mac*, King James, and the Bible." *English Literary History*. 1955. 22: 173-93.

1434

Jaech, Sharon L. Jansen. "Political Prophecy and Macbeth's 'Sweet Bodements'." *SQ*. 1983. 34: 290-97.

1435

Jorgensen, Paul A. *Our Naked Frailties: Sensational Art and Meaning in* Mac. Berkeley, Los Angeles, and London: University of California Press. 1971.

1436

Jorgensen, Paul A. "Shakespeare's Dark Vocabulary." *The Drama of the Renaissance: Essays for Leicester Bradner*. Blistein, Elmer M., ed. Providence, R.I.: Brown University Press. 1970. 108-22.

1437

Kantak, V. Y. "An Approach to Shakespearian Tragedy: The 'Actor' Image in *Mac*." *Shakespeare Survey*. 1963. 16: 42-52.

1438

Kimbrough, Robert. "Macbeth: The Prisoner of Gender." *Shakespeare Studies*. 1983. 16: 175-90.

1439

Kirsch, Arthur. "Macbeth's Suicide." *ELH* . 1984. 51: 269-96.

1440

Kirschbaum, Leo. "Banquo and Edgar: Character or Function?" *Essays in Criticism*. 1957. 7: 1-21.

1441

Klein, Joan Larsen. "Lady Macbeth: 'Infirm of Purpose'." *The Woman's Part*. Lenz, Carolyn Ruth Swift, et al, eds. Urbana, Chicago, and London: University of Illinois Press. 1980. 240-55.

1442

Knights, L.C. "On the Background of Shakespeare's Use of Nature in *Mac*." *Sewanee Review*. 1956. 64: 207-17.

1443

Knights, L. C. *Some Shakespearean Themes*. London: Chatto and Windus; Toronto: Clarke Irwin. 1959. 120-42.

1444

Lawlor, John. "Mind and Hand: Some Reflections on the Study of Shakespeare's Imagery." *SQ.* 1957. 8: 179-93.

1445

Leech, Clifford. "The Dark Side of *Mac.*" *Literary Half-Yearly.* 1967. 8: 27-34.

1446

Lordi, Robert J. "Macbeth and His 'Dearest Partner of Greatness,' Lady Macbeth." *Upstart Crow.* 1982. 4: 94-106.

1447

Marsh, Derick. "*Mac*: Easy Questions, Difficult Answers." *Sydney Studies in English.* 1982-3. 8: 3-15.

1448

Melchiori, Barbara Arnett. "A Note on the Murdered Duncan and the Drowned Ophelia." *English Miscellany.* 1977-8. 26-27: 155-61.

1449

Mellamphy, Ninian. "The Ironic Catastrophe in *Mac.*" *Ariel: A Review of International English Literature.* 1980. 11: 3-19.

1450

Merchant, W. Moelwyn. "'His Fiend-like Queen'." *Shakespeare Survey.* 1966. 19: 75-81.

1451

Morris, Brian. "The Kingdom, the Power and the Glory in *Mac.*" *Focus on Mac.* Brown, John Russell, ed. London, Boston, and Henley: Routledge and Kegan Paul. 1982. 30-53.

1452

Muir, Kenneth. "Image and Symbol in *Mac.*" *Shakespeare Survey.* 1966. 19: 45-54.

1453

Murray, W. A. "Why Was Duncan's Blood Golden?" *Shakespeare Survey.* 1966. 19: 34-44.

1454

Neill, Michael. "Remembrance and Revenge: *Ham, Mac, Tmp.*" *Jonson and Shakespeare.* Donaldson, Ian, ed. Canberra: Australian National University; Atlantic Highlands, N. J.: Humanities Press. 1983. 35-56.

1455

Nielsen, Elizabeth. "*Mac*: The Nemesis of the Post-Shakespearian Actor." *SQ*. 1965. 16: 193-99.

1456

Pack, Robert. "*Mac*: The Anatomy of Loss." *Yale Review*. 1956. 45: 533-48.

1457

Palmer, D. J. "'A new Gorgon': Visual Effects in *Mac.*" *Focus on* Mac. Brown, John Russell, ed. London, Boston, and Henley: Routledge and Kegan Paul. 1982. 54-69.

1458

Paris, Bernard J. "Bargains with Fate: The Case of *Mac.*" *American Journal of Psychoanalysis*. 1982. 42: 7-20.

1459

Paul, Henry N. *The Royal Play of* Mac. New York: Macmillan. 1950.

1460

Pearlman, E. "Malcolm and Macduff." *Studies in the Humanities*. (Indiana, Pa.) 1981. 9: 5-10.

1461

Reid, B. L. "*Mac* and the Play of Absolutes." *Sewanee Review*. 1965. 73: 19-46.

1462

Ribner, Irving. "Political Doctrine in *Mac.*" *SQ* . 1953. 4: 202-5.

1463

Rosenberg, Marvin. *The Masks of* Mac. Berkeley, Los Angeles, and London: University of California Press. 1978.

1463A

Shakespeare Survey 19. Nine articles on *Mac*. 1966.

1464

Smidt, Kristian. "Two Aspects of Ambition in Elizabethan Tragedy: *Doctor Faustus* and *Mac.*" *English Studies*. 1969. 50: 235-48.

1465

Spargo, John Webster. "The Knocking at the Gate in *Mac:* An Essay in Interpretation." *Joseph Quincy Adams Memorial Studies*. McManaway, James G., et al, eds. Washington, D.C.: Folger Shakespeare Library. 1948. 269-78.

1466

Spender, Stephen. "Time, Violence, and *Mac.*" *Penguin New Writing.*
1940-41. 3: 115-26.

1467

Stallybrass, Peter. "*Mac* and Witchcraft." *Focus on* Mac. Brown, John Russell, ed. London, Boston, and Henley: Routledge and Kegan Paul. 1982.
189-209.

1468

States, Bert O. "The Horses of *Mac.*" *Kenyon Review.* 1985. 7: 52-66.

1469

Stein, Arnold. "*Mac* and Word-Magic." *Sewanee Review.* 1951. 59: 271-84.

1470

Stirling, Brents. "The Unity of *Mac.*" *SQ.* 1953. 4: 385-94.

1471

Stoll, Elmer Edgar. "Source and Motive in *Mac* and *Oth.*" *Review of English
Studies.* 1943. 19: 25-32.

1472

Veszy-Wagner, L. "*Mac*: 'Fair Is Foul and Foul Is Fair'." *American Imago.*
1968. 25: 242-57.

1473

Wentersdorf, Karl P. "Witchcraft and Politics in *Mac.*" *Folklore Studies in
the Twentieth Century: Proceedings of the Centenary Conference of the
Folklore Society.* Newall, Venetia, ed. London: D. S. Brewer; Totowa, N.
J.: Rowman and Littlefield. 1980. 431-37.

1474

Wickham, Glynne. "Hell-Castle and Its Door-Keeper." *Shakespeare Survey.*
1966. 19: 68-74.

1475

Williams, Raymond. "Monologue in *Mac.*" *Teaching the Text.* Kappeler,
Susanne, and Bryson, Norman, eds. London, Boston, Melbourne, and
Henley: Routledge and Kegan Paul. 1983. 180-202.

1476

Zender, Karl F. "The Death of Young Siward: Providential Order and
Tragic Loss in *Mac.*" *Texas Studies in Literature and Language.* 1975. 17:
415-25.

See also works listed under *Tragedy*, especially by Bradley, Farnham,

Holloway, R. G. Hunter, Lawlor, Mack, Rosen, Speaight, and Wilson.

Measure for Measure

1477

Aers, David, and Kress, Gunther. "The Politics of Style: Discourses of Law and Authority in *MM*." *Style*. 1982. 16: 22-37.

1478

Bache, William B. MM *as Dialectical Art*. Lafayette: Purdue University Press. 1969.

1479

Battenhouse, Roy W. "*MM* and Christian Doctrine of the Atonement." *PMLA*. 1946. 61: 1029-59.

1480

Bawcutt, N. W. "'He Who the Sword of Heaven Will Bear': The Duke versus Angelo in *MM*." *Shakespeare Survey*. 1984. 37: 89-97.

1481

Bennett, Josephine W. MM *as Royal Entertainment*. New York: Columbia University Press. 1966.

1482

Berman, Ronald. "Shakespeare and the Law." *SQ*. 1967. 18: 141-50.

1483

Birje-Patil, J. "Marriage Contracts in *MM*." *Shakespeare Studies*. 1970. 5: 106-11.

1484

Boni, John. "From Medieval to Renaissance: Paradigm Shifts and Artistic Problems in English Renaissance Drama." *Journal of the Rocky Mountain Medieval and Renaissance Association*. 1983. 3: 45-63.

1485

Bradbrook, M. C. "Authority, Truth, and Justice in *MM*." *Review of English Studies*. 1941. 17: 385-99.

1486

Bradbrook, M. C. "The Balance and the Sword in *MM*." *Poetry and Drama in the English Renaissance--In Honour of Professor Jiro Ozu*. Tokyo: Kinokuniya. 1980. 21-32. English section.

136

1487

Caputi, Anthony. "Scenic Design in *MM.*" *Journal of English and Germanic Philology.* 1961. 60: 423-34.

1488

Chambers, R. W. *The Jacobean Shakespeare and* MM. Oxford: Oxford University Press. 1937. Reprinted in *Man's Unconquerable Mind.* London· Cape, 1939.

1489

Coghill, Nevill. "Comic Form in *MM.*" *Shakespeare Survey.* 1955. 8: 14-27.

1490

Cole, Howard C. "The 'Christian' Context of *MM.*" *Journal of English and Germanic Philology.* 1965. 64: 425-51.

1491

Cook, Ann Jennalie. "Wooing and Wedding: Shakespeare's Dramatic Distortion of the Customs of His Time." *Shakespeare's Art From a Comparative Perspective.* Aycock, Wendell M., ed. Lubbock: Texas Tech. Press. 1981. 83-100.

1492

Cox, John D. "The Medieval Background of *MM.*" *Modern Philology.* 1983-84. 81: 1-13.

1493

Dickinson, John W. "Renaissance Equity and *MM.*" *SQ.* 1962. 13: 287-97.

1494

Dodge, Dennis. "Life and Death in *MM.*" *Recovering Literature: Journal of Contextualist Criticism.* (Alpine, California). 1975. 4: 43-58.

1495

Dollimore, Jonathan. "Transgression and Surveillance in *MM.*" *Political Shakespeare.* Dollimore, Jonathan, and Sinfield, Alan, eds. Manchester: Manchester University Press. 1985. 72-87.

1496

Dunkel, Wilbur. "Law and Equity in *MM.*" *SQ.* 1962. 13: 275-85.

1497

Durham, W. H. "*MM* as Measure for Critics." *Essays in Criticism,* First Series. Durham, W. H., et al, eds. Berkeley and London: University of California Press. 1929. 113-32.

1498

Durham, W. H. "'What Art Thou, Angelo?'." *Studies in the Comic.* Bronson, B. H., et al, eds. Berkeley and Los Angeles: University of California Press; London: Cambridge University Press. 1941. 155-74.

1499

Empson, William. "Sense in *MM.*" *The Structure of Complex Words.* London: Chatto and Windus; New York: New Directions; Toronto: Clarke Irwin. 1951. 270-88.

1500

Fairchild, Hoxie N. "The Two Angelo's." *Shakespeare Association Bulletin.* 1931. 6: 53-9.

1501

Fitz, L. T. "Humanism Questioned: A Study of Four Renaissance Characters." *English Studies in Canada.* 1979. 5: 388-405.

1502

Fly, Richard. *Shakespeare's Mediated World.* Amherst: University of Massachusetts Press. 1976.

1503

Gless, Darryl J. MM, *the Law, and the Convent.* Princeton: Princeton University Press. 1979.

1504

Harding, Davis P. "Elizabethan Betrothals and *MM.*" *Journal of English and Germanic Philology.* 1950. 49: 139-58.

1505

Harrison, John L. "The Convention of 'Heart and Tongue' and the Meaning of *MM.*" *SQ.* 1954. 5: 1-10.

1506

Hawkins, Harriett. "'They that have power to hurt and will do none': Tragic Facts and Comic Fictions in *MM.*" *Likenesses of Truth in Elizabethan and Restoration Drama.* Oxford: Clarendon. 1972. 51-78.

1507

Howard, Jean E. "*MM* and the Restraints of Convention." *Essays in Literature.* (Western Illinois University) 1983. 10: 149-58.

1508

Hyman, Lawrence W., et al. "Exchange on *MM.*" *PMLA.* 1982. 97: 875-8.

1509

Jaffa, Harry V. "Chastity as a Political Principle: An Interpretation of Shakespeare's *MM*." *Shakespeare as Political Thinker*. Alvis, John, and West, Thomas G., eds. Durham, N. C.: Carolina Academic Press. 1981. 181-213.

1510

Kaufmann, R. J. "Bond Slaves and Counterfeits: Shakespeare's *MM*." *Shakespeare Studies*. 1968. 3: 85-97.

1511

Kirsch, Arthur C. "The Integrity of *MM*." *Shakespeare Survey*. 1975. 28: 89-105.

1512

Klene, Jean, C. S. C. "The Fool, Folly and the World Upside-Down in *MM*." *Upstart Crow*. 1980. 3: 1-10.

1513

Kliman, Bernice W. "Isabella in *MM*." *Shakespeare Studies*. 1982. 15: 137-48.

1514

Knights, L. C. "The Ambiguity of *MM*." *Scrutiny*. 1941-42. 10: 222-33.

1515

Krieger, Murray. "*MM* and Elizabethan Comedy." *PMLA*. 1951. 66: 775-84.

1516

Lascelles, Mary. *Shakespeare's* MM. London: Athlone. 1953.

1517

Lawrence, William W. "*MM* and Lucio." *SQ*. 1958. 9: 443-53.

1518

Lawry, J. S. "Imitations and Creation in *MM*." *Shakespeare and the Arts*. Cary, Cecile Williamson, and Limouze, Henry S., eds. Washington, D. C.: University Press of America. 1982. 217-29.

1519

Leavis, F. R. "The Greatness of *MM*." *Scrutiny*. 1941-42. 10: 234-47.

1520

Leech, Clifford. "The 'Meaning' of *MM*." *Shakespeare Survey*. 1950. 3: 66-73.

1521

Levin, Richard A. "Duke Vincentio and Angelo: Would 'A Feather Turn the Scale'?" *Studies in English Literature*. 1982. 22: 257-70.

1522

Lewis, Cynthia. "'Dark Deeds Darkly Answered': Duke Vincentio and
    Judgement in *MM*." *SQ*. 1983. 34: 271-89.

1523

Mansell, Darrel, Jr. "'Seemers' in *MM*." *Modern Language Quarterly*. 1966.
    27: 270-84.

1524

Marsh, D. R. C. "The Mood of *MM*." *SQ*. 1963. 14: 31-8.

1525

Martz, William J. *The Place of* MM *in Shakespeare's Universe of Comedy*.
    Lawrence, Kansas: Coronado Press. 1982.

1526

Maxwell, J. C. "*MM*: A Footnote to Recent Criticism." *Downside Review*.
    1947. 65: 45-59.

1527

McGuire, Philip C. "Silence and Genre: The Example of *MM*." *Iowa State
    Journal of Research*. 1985. 59: 241-51.

1528

McLuskie, Kathleen. "The Patriarchal Bard: Feminist Criticism and Shake-
    speare: *Lr* and *MM*." *Political Shakespeare*. Dollimore, Jonathan, and
    Sinfield, Alan, eds. Manchester: Manchester University Press. 1985.
    88-108.

1529

Merchant, William Moelwyn. "*MM:* An Essay in Visual Interpretation."
    Shakespeare and the Artist. Oxford: Oxford University Press. 1959.

1530

Miles, Rosalind. *The Problem of* MM: *A Historical Investigation*. New York:
    Barnes and Noble; London: Vision Press. 1976.

1531

Mills, Paul. "Brothers and Enemies in *MM*." *Self and Society in
    Shakespeare's* Tro *and* MM. Jowitt, J. A., and Taylor, R. K. S, eds. Brad-
    ford: University of Leeds Centre for Adult Education. 1982. 96-109.

1532

Mincoff, Marco. "*MM*: A Question of Approach." *Shakespeare Studies*.
    1967. 2: 141-52.

1533

Moore, Susan. "Virtue and Power in *MM*." *English Studies*. 1982. 63: 308-17.

1534

Nagarajan, S. "*MM* and Elizabethan Betrothals." *SQ* . 1963. 14: 115-19.

1535

Nowottny, W. M. T. "The Character of Angelo in *MM*." *Modern Language Review*. 1946. 41: 246-55.

1536

Nuttall, A. D. "*MM*: Quid pro Quo?" *Shakespeare Studies*. 1969. 4: 231-51.

1537

Ornstein, Robert T. "The Human Comedy: *MM*." *University Review*. 1957. 24: 15-22.

1538

Paris, Bernard J. "The Inner Conflicts of *MM*: A Psychological Approach." *Centennial Review*. 1981. 25: 266-76.

1539

Pope, Elizabeth Marie. "The Renaissance Background of *MM*." *Shakespeare Survey*. 1949. 2: 66-82.

1540

Potts, Abbie Findlay. "*MM* and the Book of Justice." *Shakespeare and* The Faerie Queene. Ithaca: Cornell University Press. 1958. 150-73.

1541

Price, Jonathan R. "*MM* and the Critics: Towards a New Approach." *SQ*. 1969. 20: 179-204.

1542

Rico, Barbara Roche. "From 'Speechless Dialect' to 'Prosperous Art': Shakespeare's Recasting of the Pygmalion Image." *Huntington Library Quarterly*. 1985. 48: 285-95.

1543

Riefer, Marcia. "'Instruments of Some More Mightier Member': The Construction of Female Power in *MM*." *SQ*. 1984. 35: 157-69.

1544

Roscelli, William J. "Isabella, Sin, and Civil Law." *University Review*. 1961-62. 28: 215-27.

1545

Rose, Jacqueline. "Sexuality in the Reading of Shakespeare: *Ham* and *MM*."
   Alternative Shakespeares. Drakakis, John, ed. London and New York:
   Methuen. 1985. 95-118.

1546

Rosenheim, Judith. "The Stoic Meaning of the Friar in *MM*." *Shakespeare
   Studies.* 1982. 15: 171-215.

1547

Sacks, Elizabeth. *Shakespeare's Images of Pregnancy.* New York: St.
   Martin's Press. 1980.

1548

Sale, Roger. "The Comic Mode of *MM*." *SQ.* 1968. 19: 55-61.

1549

Schanzer, Ernest. "The Marriage-Contracts in *MM*." *Shakespeare Survey.*
   1960. 13: 81-9.

1550

Schleiner, Louise. "Providential Improvisation in *MM*." *PMLA.* 1982. 97:
   227-36.

1551

Scott, Margaret. "'Our City's Institutions': Some Further Reflections on the
   Marriage Contracts in *MM*." *English Literary History.* 1982. 49: 790-804.

1552

Scouten, Arthur H. "An Historical Approach to *MM*." *Philological Quarterly.* 1975. 54: 68-84.

1553

Siegel, Paul N. "*MM*: The Significance of the Title." *SQ.* 1953. 4: 317-20.

1554

Skulsky, Harold. "Pain, Law, and Conscience in *MM*." *Journal of the History of Ideas.* 1964. 25: 147-68.

1555

Smith, Don. "Truth and Seeming Truth: The Language of *MM* and *Tro*."
   Self and Society in Shakespeare's Tro *and* MM. Jowitt, J. A., and Taylor,
   R. K. S., eds. Bradford: University of Leeds Centre for Adult Education.
   1982. 45-60.

1556

Smith, Gordon Ross. "Isabella and Elbow in Varying Contexts of Interpretation." *Journal of General Education.* 1965. 17: 63-78.

1557

Snyder, Karl E. "The Harrowing of Vienna." *Proceedings of the Conference of College Teachers of English of Texas.* 1981. 46: 10-16.

1558

Southall, Raymond. "*MM* and the Protestant Ethic." *Essays in Criticism.* 1961. 11: 10-33.

1559

Stead, C. K., ed. *Shakespeare's* MM: *A Casebook.* London: Macmillan. 1971.

1560

Stevenson, David Lloyd. *The Achievement of Shakespeare's* MM. Ithaca: Cornell University Press. 1966.

1561

Sundelson, David. "Misogyny and Rule in *MM*." *Women's Studies.* 1981. 9: 83-91.

1562

Sypher, Wylie. "Shakespeare as Casuist: *MM*." *Sewanee Review.* 1950. 58: 262-80.

1563

Tennenhouse, Leonard. "Representing Power: *MM* in Its Time." *Genre.* 1982. 15: 139-56.

1564

Traversi, D. A. "*MM*." *Scrutiny.* 1942-43. 11: 40-58.

1565

Van Tassel, David E. "Clarence, Claudio, and Hamlet: 'The Dread of Something After Death'." *Renaissance and Reformation.* 1983. 7: 48-62.

1566

Wasson, John. "*MM*: A Play of Incontinence." *English Literary History.* 1960. 27: 262-75.

1567

Welsh, Alexander. "The Loss of Men and Getting of Children: *AWW* and *MM*." *Modern Language Review.* 1978. 73: 17-28.

1568

Whitlow, Roger. "*MM*: Shakespearean Morality and the Christian Epic." *Encounter.* (Indianapolis) 1978. 39: 165-73.

1569

Wilson, Harold S. "Action and Symbol in *MM* and *Tmp*." *SQ*. 1953. 4: 375-84.

1570

Winston, Mathew. "'Craft Against Vice': Morality Play Elements in *MM*." *Shakespeare Studies*. 1981. 14: 229-48.

See also works listed under *Comedy: General Studies* and *Comedy: The Problem Comedies*, especially by Schanzer.

The Merchant of Venice

1571

Anderson, Douglas. "The Old Testament Presence in *MV*." *English Literary History*. 1985. 52: 119-32.

1572

Andrews, Mark E. *Law versus Equity in* MV. Boulder: University of Colorado Press. 1965.

1573

Bady, David. "The Sum of Something: Arithmetic in *MV*." *SQ*. 1985. 36: 10-30.

1574

Barnet, Sylvan. "Prodigality and Time in *MV*." *PMLA*. 1972. 87: 26-30.

1575

Berger, Harry, Jr. "Marriage and Mercifixion in *MV*: The Casket Scene Revisited." *SQ*. 1981. 32: 155-62.

1576

Bloom, Allan. "Shakespeare on Jew and Christian: An Interpretation of *MV*." *Social Research*. 1963. 30: 1-22.

1577

Bronstein, Herbert. "Shakespeare, the Jews, and *MV*." *SQ*. 1969. 20: 3-10.

1578

Brown, Beatrice D. "Mediaeval Prototypes of Lorenzo and Jessica." *Modern Language Notes*. 1929. 44: 227-32.

1579

Bruyn, Lucy de. *Woman and the Devil in Sixteenth-Century Literature*. Tisbury, Wiltshire: Compton Press. 1979.

1580

Burckhardt, Sigurd. "*MV*: The Gentle Bond." *English Literary History*. 1962. 29: 239-62. Reprinted in Burkhardt's *Shakespearean Meanings*. Princeton: Princeton University Press, 1968.

1581

Carnovsky, Morris. "Mirror of Shylock." *Tulane Drama Review*. 1959. 3: 35-45.

1582

Charney, Maurice. "Jessica's Turquoise Ring and Abigail's Poisoned Porridge: Shakespeare and Marlowe as Rivals and Imitators." *Renaissance Drama*. 1979. 10: 33-44.

1583

Cohen, D. M. "The Jew and Shylock." *SQ*. 1980. 31: 53-63.

1584

Cohen, D. M. "The Rage of Shylock." *Forum for Modern Language Studies*. 1982. 18: 193-200.

1585

Cohen, Walter. "*MV* and the Possibilities of Historical Criticism." *English Literary History*. 1982. 49: 765-89.

1586

Colley, John Scott. "Launcelot, Jacob, and Esau: Old and New Law in *MV*." *Yearbook of English Studies*. 1980. 10: 181-89.

1587

Crocker, Lester G. "*MV* and Christian Conscience." *Diogenes*. 1982. 118: 77-102.

1588

Danson, Lawrence. *The Harmonies of* MV. New Haven and London: Yale University Press. 1978.

1589

Donow, Herbert S. "Shakespeare's Caskets: Unity in *MV*." *Shakespeare Studies*. 1969. 4: 86-93.

1590

Draper, John W. "Shakespeare's Antonio and the Queen's Finance." *Neophilologus*. 1967. 51: 178-85.

1591

Erlich, Bruce. "Queenly Shadows: On Mediation in Two Comedies." *Shakespeare Survey*. 1982. 35: 65-77.

145

1592

Fodor, A. "Shakespeare's Portia." *American Imago*. 1959. 16: 49-64.

1593

Freud, Sigmund. "The Theme of the Three Caskets." *Complete Psychological Works of Sigmund Freud*. Strachey, James, ed. London: Hogarth. 1953+. Vol. 12 (1911-1913). 291-301.

1594

Fujimura, Thomas H. "Mode and Structure in *MV*." *PMLA*. 1966. 81: 499-511.

1595

Garner, Shirley Nelson. "Shylock: 'His Stones, his Daughter, and his Ducats'." *Upstart Crow*. 1984. 5: 35-49.

1596

Geary, Keith. "The Nature of Portia's Victory: Turning to Men in *MV*." *Shakespeare Survey*. 1984. 37: 55-68.

1597

Girard, René. "'To Entrap the Wisest': A Reading of *MV*." *Literature and Society: Selected Papers from the English Institute, 1978*. Said, Edward W., ed. Baltimore and London: Johns Hopkins University Press. 1980.

1598

Gollancz, Israel. *Allegory and Mysticism in Shakespeare: A Medievalist on MV*. London: Jones. 1931.

1599

Graham, Cary B. "Standards of Value in *MV*." *SQ* . 1953. 4: 145-51.

1600

Grebanier, Bernard D. *The Truth about Shylock*. New York: Random House. 1962.

1601

Hapgood, Robert. "Portia and the Merchant of Venice: The Gentle Bond." *Modern Language Quarterly*. 1967. 28: 19-32.

1602

Hatlen, Burton. "Feudal and Bourgeois Concepts of Value in *MV*." *Shakespeare: Contemporary Critical Approaches*. Garvin, Harry R., ed. Lewisburg, Pa.: Bucknell University Press; London and Toronto: Associated University Presses. 1980. 91-105.

1603

Heifetz, Jeanne. *Love Calls Us to the Things of This World: The Return to Belmont in* MV. Cambridge, Massachusetts and London: Harvard University Press. 1981.

1604

Heinzelman, Kurt. *The Economics of the Imagination.* Amherst: University of Massachusetts Press. 1980.

1605

Holaday, Allan. "Antonio and the Allegory of Salvation." *Shakespeare Studies.* 1969. 4: 109-18.

1606

Holmer, Joan Ozark. "The Education of the Merchant of Venice." *Studies in English Literature.* 1985. 25: 307-35.

1607

Jordan, William Chester. "Approaches to the Court Scene in the Bond Story: Equity and Mercy or Reason and Nature." *SQ.* 1982. 33: 49-59.

1608

Kahn, Coppélia. "The Cuckoo's Note: Male Friendship and Cuckoldry in *MV.*" *Shakespeare's "Rough Magic": Renaissance Essays in Honor of C. L. Barber.* Erickson, Peter, and Kahn, Coppélia, eds. Newark: University of Delaware Press; London and Toronto: Associated University Presses. 1985. 104-12.

1609

Kleinberg, Seymour. "*MV*: The Homosexual as Anti-Semite in Nascent Capitalism." *Journal of Homosexuality.* 1983. 8: 113-26.

1610

Kozikowski, Stanley J. "The Allegory of Love and Fortune: The Lottery in *MV.*" *Renascence.* 1979-80. 32: 105-15.

1611

Lelyveld, Toby. *Shylock on the Stage.* Cleveland: Press of Western Reserve University. 1960.

1612

Lever, J. W. "Shylock, Portia, and the Values of Shakespearian Comedy." *SQ.* 1952. 3: 383-6. Rejoinder by Norman Nathan, *SQ.* 1952. 3: 386-8.

1613

Levitsky, Ruth M. "Shylock as Unregenerate Man." *SQ* . 1977. 28: 58-64.

147

1614

Lewalski, Barbara K. "Biblical Allusion and Allegory in *MV*." *SQ*. 1962. 13: 327-43.

1615

MacKay, Maxine. "*MV*: A Reflection of the Early Conflict Between Courts of Law and Courts of Equity." *SQ*. 1964. 15: 371-5.

1616

McTague, Michael J. *The Businessman in Literature: Dante to Melville.* New York: Philosophical Library. 1979. Chapter 3, especially pp. 37-49.

1617

McVeagh, John. *Tradefull Merchants: The Portrayal of the Capitalist in Literature.* London, Boston, and Henley: Routledge and Kegan Paul. 1981. 16-19.

1618

Midgley, Graham. "*MV*: A Reconsideration." *Essays in Criticism.* 1960. 10: 119-33.

1619

Mitchell, Charles. "The Conscience of Venice: Shakespeare's Merchant." *Journal of English and Germanic Philology.* 1964. 63: 215-25.

1620

Novy, Marianne L. "Giving, Taking, and the Role of Portia in *MV*." *Philological Quarterly.* 1979. 58: 137-54.

1621

Parten, Anne. "Re-Establishing Sexual Order: The Ring Episode in *MV*." *Shakespeare and Renaissance Association of West Virginia: Selected Papers.* 1981. 6: 27-34. Reprinted, *Women's Studies.* 1982. 9: 145-155.

1622

Pettet, Ernest C. "*MV* and the Problem of Usury." *Essays and Studies by Members of the English Association.* 1945. 31: 19-33.

1623

Plowman, Max. "Money and *The Merchant*." *The Adelphi.* 1931. 2: 508-13.

1624

Poznar, Walter. "Shylock and the Social Order." *Centennial Review.* 1982. 26: 302-11.

1625

Prior, Moody E. "Which Is the Jew That Shakespeare Drew? Shylock Among the Critics." *American Scholar.* 1980-81. 50: 479-98.

1626

Rabkin, Norman. *Shakespeare and the Problem of Meaning.* Chicago: University of Chicago Press. 1981. 1-32.

1627

Shell, Marc. *Money, Language, and Thought: Literary and Philosophical Economies from the Medieval to the Modern Era.* Berkeley, Los Angeles, and London: University of California Press. 1982. 47-83.

1628

Slights, Camille. "In Defense of Jessica: The Runaway Daughter in *MV*." *SQ*. 1980. 31: 357-68.

1629

Smith, John Hazel. "Shylock: 'Devil Incarnation' or 'Poor Man... Wronged'?" *Journal of English and Germanic Philology*. 1961. 60: 1-21.

1630

Stoll, Elmer Edgar. "Shylock." *Shakespeare Studies, Historical and Comparative in Method.* New York: Macmillan. 1927. 255-336.

1631

Stonex, Arthur Birens. "The Usurer in Elizabethan Drama." *PMLA*. 1916. 31: 190-210.

1632

Tennenhouse, Leonard. "The Counterfeit Order of *MV*." *Representing Shakespeare*. Schwartz, Murray M., and Kahn, Coppélia, eds. Baltimore and London: Johns Hopkins University Press. 1980. 54-69.

1633

Tovey, Barbara. "The Golden Casket: An Interpretation of *MV*." *Shakespeare as Political Thinker*. Alvis, John, and West, Thomas G., eds. Durham, N. C.: Carolina Academic Press. 1981. 215-37.

1634

Wheeler, Thomas, comp. MV: *An Annotated Bibliography*. New York: Garland. 1985.

1635

Whigham, Frank. "Ideology and Class Conduct in *MV*." *Renaissance Drama*. 1979. 10: 93-115. See also works listed under *Comedy: General Studies*, especially by Barber and Brown, and under *Comedy: The Middle and Romantic Comedies*, especially by Kermode and Leggatt.

1636

Barton, Anne. "Falstaff and the Comic Community." *Shakespeare's "Rough Magic": Renaissance Essays in Honor of C. L. Barber*. Erickson, Peter, and Kahn, Coppélia, eds. Newark: University of Delaware Press; London and Toronto: Associated University Presses. 1985. 131-48.

1637

Boughner, Daniel C. "Traditional Elements in Falstaff." *Journal of English and Germanic Philology*. 1944. 43: 417-28.

1638

Bryant, J. A., Jr. "Falstaff and the Renewal of Windsor." *PMLA*. 1974. 89: 296-301.

1639

Carroll, William. "'A Received Belief': Imagination in *Wiv*." *Studies in Philology*. 1977. 74: 186-215.

1640

Felheim, Marvin, and Traci, Philip. "Realism in *Wiv*." *Ball State University Forum*. 1981. 22: 52-9.

1641

Fleissner, Robert F. "The Malleable Knight and the Unfettered Friar: *Wiv* and Boccaccio." *Shakespeare Studies*. 1978. 11: 77-93.

1642

Freedman, Barbara. "Falstaff's Punishment: Buffoonery as Defensive Posture in *Wiv*." *Shakespeare Studies*. 1981. 14: 163-74.

1643

Gallenca, Christiane. "Ritual and Folk Custom in *Wiv*." *Cahiers Elisabéthains*. 1985. 27: 27-41.

1644

Green, William. *Shakespeare's Wiv*. Princeton: Princeton University Press. 1962.

1645

Grindon, Rosa L. *In Praise of Shakespeare's Wiv*. Manchester: Sherratt and Hughes. 1902.

1646

Hapgood, Robert. "Falstaff's Vocation." *SQ*. 1965. 16: 91-8.

1647

Hardin, Richard F. "Honor Revenged: Falstaff's Fortunes and *Wiv.*"
Essays in Literature. (Western Illinois University) 1978. 5: 143-51.

1648

Hemingway, Samuel B. "On Behalf of That Falstaff." *SQ* . 1952. 3: 307-11.

1649

Hinely, Jan Lawson. "Comic Scapegoats and the Falstaff of *Wiv.*" *Shakespeare Studies.* 1982. 15: 37-54.

1650

Hotson, Leslie. *Shakespeare versus Shallow.* Boston: Little, Brown; London: Nonesuch. 1931.

1651

Huebert, Ronald. "Levels of Parody in *Wiv.*" *English Studies in Canada.* 1977. 3: 136-52.

1652

Huntley, Frank Livingstone. "The Whole Comic Plot of Falstaff." *Essays in Persuasion: On Seventeenth-Century English Literature.* Chicago and London: University of Chicago Press. 1981. 12-21.

1653

Leggatt, Alexander. *Citizen Comedy in the Age of Shakespeare.* Toronto and Buffalo: University of Toronto Press. 1973.

1654

Parten, Anne. "Falstaff's Horns: Masculine Inadequacy and Feminine Mirth in *Wiv.*" *Studies in Philology.* 1985. 82: 184-99.

1655

Radoff, M. L. "Influence of the French Farce in *H5* and *Wiv.*" *Modern Language Notes.* 1933. 48: 427-35.

1656

Reik, Theodor. "Comedy of Intrigue." *The Secret Self.* New York: Farrar, Straus, and Young. 1953.

1657

Roberts, Jeanne Addison. *Shakespeare's English Comedy:* Wiv *in Context.* Lincoln: University of Nebraska Press. 1979.

1658

Roberts, Jeanne Addison. "*Wiv*: Suitably Shallow, but neither Simple nor Slender." *Shakespeare Studies.* 1972. 6: 109-23.

151

1659

Shirley, John W. "Falstaff, an Elizabethan Glutton." *Philological Quarterly.*
1938. 17: 271-87.

1660

Slights, Camille Wells. "Pastoral and Parody in *Wiv.*" *English Studies in Canada.* 1985. 11: 12-25.

1661

Steadman, John M. "*Wiv*: Falstaff as Actaeon: A Dramatic Emblem." *SQ.*
1963. 14: 230-44. Reprinted in Steadman's *Nature into Myth: Medieval and Renaissance Moral Symbols.* Pittsburgh: Duquesne University Press; Atlantic Highlands, N. J.: Humanities Press, 1979. 117-130.

1662

West, E. J. "On Master Slender." *College English.* 1946-47. 8: 228-30.

See also works listed under *Comedy: General Studies*, especially by Charlton.

1663

Allen, John A. "Bottom and Titania." *SQ.* 1967. 18: 107-17.

1664

Berry, Ralph. "No Exit from Arden." *Modern Language Review.* 1971. 66: 11-20.

1665

Bethurum, Dorothy. "Shakespeare's Comment on Mediaeval Romance in *MND.*" *Modern Language Notes.* 1945. 60: 85-94.

1666

Black, James. "The Monster in Shakespeare's Landscape." *The Elizabethan Theatre VII.* Hibbard, G. R., ed. Hamden, Conn.: Archon Books, 1980; London: Macmillan, 1981. 51-68.

1667

Briggs, K. M. *The Anatomy of Puck: An Examination of Fairy Beliefs Among Shakespeare's Contemporaries and Successors.* London: Routledge and Kegan Paul. 1959.

1668

Calderwood, James L. "*MND*: The Illusion of Drama." *Modern Language Quarterly.* 1965. 26: 506-22.

1669

Carroll, D. Allen, and Williams, Gary Jay, comps. MND*: An Annotated Bibliography.* New York: Garland. 1986.

1671

Comtois, M. E. "The Hardiness of *MND.*" *Theatre Journal (Columbia, Mo.).* 1980. 32: 305-11.

1672

Cox, Richard H. "Shakespeare: Poetic Understanding and Comic Action (A Weaver's Dream)." *The Artist and Political Vision.* Barber, Benjamin R., and McGrath, Michael J. Gargas, eds. New Brunswick, N. J. and London: Transaction Books. 1982. 165-92.

1673

Dent, R. W. "Imagination in *MND.*" *SQ.* 1964. 15: 115-29.

153

1674

Doran, Madeleine. "Pyramus and Thisbe Once More." *Essays on Shakespeare and Elizabethan Drama in Honor of Hardin Craig.* Hosley, Richard, ed. Columbia: University of Missouri Press. 1962. 149-61.

1675

Falk, Florence. "Dream and Ritual Process in *MND.*" *Comparative Drama.* 1980-81. 14: 263-79.

1676

Fender, Stephen. *Shakespeare:* MND. London: Arnold. 1968.

1677

Finch, G. J. "Shakespeare and the Nature of Metaphor." *Ariel: A Review of International English Literature.* 1981. 12: 3-19.

1678

Franke, Wolfgang. "The Logic of *Double Entendre* in *MND.*" *Philological Quarterly.* 1979. 58: 282-97.

1679

Garber, Marjorie B. *Dream in Shakespeare: From Metaphor to Metamorphosis.* New Haven and London: Yale University Press. 1974.

1680

Garner, Shirley Nelson. "*MND*: 'Jack shall have Jill;/ Nought shall go ill'." *Women's Studies.* 1981. 9: 47-63.

1681

Girard, René. "Myth and Ritual in Shakespeare: *MND.*" *Textual Strategies: Perspectives in Post-Structuralist Criticism.* Harari, Josué V., ed. Ithaca: Cornell University Press. 1979. 189-212.

1682

Girard, René. "Shakespeare's Theory of Mythology." *Classical Mythology in Twentieth-Century Thought and Literature.* Aycock, Wendell M., and Klein, Theodore M., eds. Lubbock: Texas Tech. Press. 1980. 107-24.

1683

Green, Roger Lancelyn. "Shakespeare and the Fairies." *Folklore.* 1962. 73: 89-103.

1684

Greenfield, Thelma N. "*MND* and *The Praise of Folly.*" *Comparative Literature.* 1968. 20: 236-44.

154

1685

Greer, Germaine. "Love and the Law." *Politics, Power, and Shakespeare.*
Leonard, Frances McNeely, ed. Arlington, Texas: Texas Humanities
Resource Center, University of Texas at Arlington Library. 1981. 29-45.

1686

Hawkes, Terence. "Comedy, Orality, and Duplicity: *MND* and *TN.*" *New
York Literary Forum.* 1978. 5-6: 155-63.

1687

Holland, Norman N. "Hermia's Dream." *Representing Shakespeare.*
Schwartz, Murray M., and Kahn, Coppélia, eds. Baltimore and London:
Johns Hopkins University Press. 1980. 1-20.

1688

Homan, Sidney R. "The Single World of *MND.*" *Bucknell Review.* 1969. 17:
72-84.

1689

Keightley, Thomas. *The World Guide to Gnomes, Fairies, Elves, and Other
Little People.* New York: Avenel Books. 1978. 38-42, 314-47. First
published 1878.

1690

Kott, Jan. "The Bottom Translation." *Assays: Critical Approaches to Medieval and Renaissance Texts.* Knapp, Peggy A., and Stugrin, Michael A., eds.
Pittsburgh: University of Pittsburgh Press. 1981. Vol. I. 117-49.

1691

Latham, Minor White. *The Elizabethan Fairies: The Fairies of Folklore and
the Fairies of Shakespeare.* New York: Columbia University Press. 1930.

1692

Lindblad, Ishrat. "The Autotelic Function of *MND.*" *Papers from the First
Nordic Conference for English Studies, Oslo, 17-19 September 1980.*
Johansson, Stig, and Tysdahl, Bjorn, eds. Oslo: Inst. of English Studies,
University of Oslo. 1981. 134-47.

1693

Longo, Joseph A. "Myth in *MND.*" *Cahiers Elisabéthains.* 1980. 18: 17-27.

1694

Marcus, Mordecai. "*MND*: The Dialectic of Eros-Thanatos." *American
Imago.* 1981. 38: 269-78.

1695

Marshall, David. "Exchanging Visions: Reading *MND*." *English Literary History*. 1982. 49: 543-75.

1696

Mebane, John S. "Structure, Source, and Meaning in *MND*." *Texas Studies in Literature and Language*. 1982. 24: 255-70.

1697

Montrose, Louis Adrian. "'Shaping Fantasies': Figurations of Gender and Power in Elizabethan Culture." *Representations*. 1983. 1: 61-94.

1698

Muir, Kenneth. "Pyramus and Thisbe: A Study in Shakespeare's Method." *SQ*. 1954. 5: 141-53.

1699

Nemerov, Howard. "The Marriage of Theseus and Hippolyta." *Kenyon Review*. 1956. 18: 633-41.

1700

Olson, Paul A. "*MND* and the Meaning of Court Marriage." *English Literary History*. 1957. 24: 95-119.

1701

Priestley, J. B. *The English Comic Characters*. London: Bodley Head. 1925.

1702

Riffaterre, Michael. *Semiotics of Poetry*. Bloomington and London: Indiana University Press. 1978. 99-105.

1703

Robinson, James E. "The Ritual and Rhetoric of *MND*." *PMLA*. 1968. 83: 380-91.

1704

Schanzer, Ernest. "The Central Theme of *MND*." *University of Toronto Quarterly*. 1950-51. 20: 233-8.

1705

Schanzer, Ernest. "The Moon and the Fairies in *MND*." *University of Toronto Quarterly*. 1955. 24: 234-46.

1706

Sewell, Elizabeth. *The Orphic Voice: Poetry and Natural History*. New Haven: Yale University Press. 1960. 53-168.

1707

Siegel, Paul N. "*MND* and the Wedding Guests." *SQ* . 1953. 4: 139-44.

1708

Stansbury, Joan. "Characterization of the Four Young Lovers in *MND.*"
Shakespeare Survey. 1982. 35: 57-63.

1709

Taylor, Michael. "The Darker Purpose of *MND.*" *Studies in English Literature.* 1969. 9: 259-73.

1710

Weil, Herbert S., Jr. "Comic Structure and Tonal Manipulation in Shakespeare and Some Modern Plays." *Shakespeare Survey.* 1969. 22: 27-33.

1711

Weller, Barry. "Identity Dis-Figured: *MND.*" *Kenyon Review.* 1985. 7:
66-78.

1712

Young, David P. *Something of Great Constancy: The Art of* MND. New
Haven and London: Yale University Press. 1966.

1713

Zitner, Sheldon P. "The Worlds of *MND.*" *South Atlantic Quarterly.* 1960.
59: 397-403.

See also works listed under *Comedy: General Studies*, especially by Barber,
and under *Comedy: The Middle and Romantic Comedies*, especially by Kermode and Leggatt.

Much Ado About Nothing

1714

Barish, Jonas A. "Pattern and Purpose in the Prose of *Ado.*" *Rice University
Studies.* 1974. 60: 19-30.

1715

Berger, Harry, Jr. "Against the Sink-a-Pace: Sexual and Family Politics in
Ado." *SQ.* 1982. 33: 302-13.

1716

Cook, David. "'The Very Temple of Delight': The Twin Plots of *Ado.*"
Poetry and Drama, 1570-1700: Essays in Honour of Harold F. Brooks.
Coleman, Antony, and Hammond, Antony, eds. London and New York:

Methuen. 1982. 32-46.

1717

Craik, T. W. "*Ado*." *Scrutiny*. 1952-53. 19: 297-316.

1718

Dawson, Anthony B. "Much Ado about Signifying." *Studies in English Literature*. 1982. 22: 211-21.

1719

Everett, Barbara. "*Ado*." *Critical Quarterly*. 1961. 3: 319-35.

1720

Hartley, Lodwick. "Claudio and the Unmerry War." *College English*. 1964-65. 26: 609-14.

1721

Hays, Janice. "Those 'soft and delicate desires': *Ado* and the Distrust of Women." *The Woman's Part*. Lenz, Carolyn Ruth Swift, et al, eds. Urbana, Chicago, and London: University of Illinois Press. 1980. 79-99.

1722

Jorgensen, Paul A. "Much Ado about *Nothing*." *SQ* . 1954. 5: 287-95.

1723

King, Walter N. "Much Ado about *Something*." *SQ* . 1964. 15: 143-55.

1724

Lewalski, B. K. "Love, Appearance and Reality: Much Ado about Something." *Studies in English Literature*. 1968. 8: 235-51.

1725

Mares, F. H. "Comic Procedures in Shakespeare and Jonson: *Ado* and *The Alchemist*." *Jonson and Shakespeare*. Donaldson, Ian, ed. Canberra: Australian National University; Atlantic Highlands, N. J.: Humanities Press. 1983. 101-18.

1726

McCollom, William G. "The Role of Wit in *Ado*." *SQ* . 1968. 19: 165-74.

1727

Mueschke, Paul, and Mueschke, Miriam. "Illusion and Metamorphosis in *Ado*." *SQ*. 1967. 18: 53-65.

1728

Neill, J. Kerby. "More Ado about Claudio: An Acquittal for the Slandered Groom." *SQ*. 1952. 3: 91-107.

1729

Page, Nadine. "Beatrice: My Lady Disdain." *Modern Language Notes*. 1935. 50: 494-9.

1730

Page, Nadine. "The Public Repudiation of Hero." *PMLA*. 1935. 50: 739-44.

1731

Rose, Steven. "Love and Self-Love in *Ado*." *Essays in Criticism*. 1970. 20: 143-50.

1732

Smith, James C. "*Ado*." *Scrutiny*. 1945-46. 13: 242-57.

1733

Storey, Graham. "The Success of *Ado*." *More Talking of Shakespeare*. Garrett, John, ed. New York: Theatre Arts Books; London: Longmans, Green. 1959. 128-43.

1734

Sypher, Wylie. "Nietzsche and Socrates in Messina." *Partisan Review*. 1949. 16: 702-13.

1735

Taylor, Michael. "*Ado*: The Individual in Society." *Essays in Criticism*. 1973. 23: 146-53.

1736

Traci, Philip. "'Come, 'tis no matter./ Do not you meddle': Too Much Ado in Shakespeare's Comedy." *Upstart Crow*. 1982. 4: 107-12.

1737

Traugott, John. "Creating a Rational Rinaldo: A Study in the Mixture of the Genres of Comedy and Romance in *Ado*." *Genre*. 1982. 15: 157-81.

1738

Wain, John. "The Shakespearean Lie-Detector: Thoughts on *Ado*." *Critical Quarterly*. 1967. 9: 27-42.

1739

West, E. J. "Much Ado About An Unpleasant Play." *Shakespeare Association Bulletin*. 1947. 22: 30-4.

1740

Wey, James J. "'To Grace Harmony': Musical Design in *Ado*." *Boston University Studies in English*. 1960. 4: 181-8.

1741

Williams, Mary C. "Much Ado About Chastity in *Ado.*" *Renaissance Papers.* 1984. 37-45.

1742

Woodbridge, Linda. *Women and the English Renaissance.* Urbana and Chicago: University of Illinois Press; Brighton: Harvester. 1984. 279-89, passim.

See also works listed under *Comedy: General Studies*, especially by Brown, Gordon, R. G. Hunter, Salingar, and Stevenson.

Othello

1743

Adamson, Jane. Oth *as Tragedy.* New York and Cambridge: Cambridge University Press. 1980.

1744

Adamson, W. D. "Unpinned or Undone?: Desdemona's Critics and the Problem of Sexual Innocence." *Shakespeare Studies.* 1980. 13: 169-86.

1745

Adler, Doris. "Imaginary Toads in Real Gardens." *English Literary Renaissance.* 1981. 11: 235-60.

1746

Altieri, Charles. "Criticism as the Situating of Performances: Or What Wallace Stevens Has to Tell Us About *Oth.*" *American Critics at Work: Examinations of Contemporary Literary Theories.* Kramer, Victor A., ed. Troy, N. Y.: Whitston. 1984. 265-95.

1747

Arthos, John. "The Fall of Othello." *SQ.* 1958. 9: 93-104.

1748

Bethell, S. L. "Shakespeare's Imagery: The Diabolic Images in *Oth.*" *Shakespeare Survey.* 1952. 5: 62-80.

1749

Bodkin, Maud. *Archetypal Patterns in Poetry.* Oxford: Oxford University Press. 1934. 211-18.

1750

Bonnard, Georges A. "Are Othello and Desdemona Innocent or Guilty?"
English Studies. 1949. 30: 175-84.

1751

Burke, Kenneth. "*Oth*: An Essay to Illustrate a Method." *Hudson Review.*
1951. 4: 165-203.

1752

Camden, Carroll C. "Iago on Women." *Journal of English and Germanic
Philology.* 1949. 48: 57-71.

1753

Charney, Maurice. "Comic Villainy in Shakespeare and Middleton." *Shakespearean Comedy.* Charney, Maurice, ed. New York: New York Literary
Forum. 1980. 165-73.

1754

Cook, Ann Jennalie. "The Design of Desdemona: Doubt Raised and
Resolved." *Shakespeare Studies.* 1980. 13: 187-96.

1755

Cowhig, Ruth. "Blacks in English Renaissance Drama and the Role of
Shakespeare's Othello." *The Black Presence in English Literature.* Dabydeen, David, ed. Manchester: Manchester University Press. 1985. 1-25.

1756

Dean, Leonard F., ed. *A Casebook on* Oth. New York: Crowell. 1961.

1757

Dickey, Franklin. *Not Wisely But Too Well: Shakespeare's Love Tragedies.*
San Marino, California: Huntington Library Press. 1957.

1758

Doran, Madeleine. "Good Name in *Oth.*" *Studies in English Literature.*
1967. 7: 195-217.

1759

Elliott, G. R. *Flaming Minister: A Study of* Oth *as Tragedy of Love and
Hate.* Durham, N. C.: Duke University Press. 1953.

1760

Empson, William. "Honest in *Oth.*" *The Structure of Complex Words.*
London: Chatto and Windus; New York: New Directions. 1951. 218-49.

1761

Evans, K. W. "The Racial Factor in *Oth.*" *Shakespeare Studies.* 1970. 5:
124-40.

161

1762

Everett, Barbara. "Reflections on the Sentimentalist's *Oth.*" *Critical Quarterly.* 1961. 3: 127-39.

1763

Gardner, Helen. *The Noble Moor.* London: Oxford University Press. 1955.

1764

Gardner, Helen. "*Oth*: A Retrospect, 1900-67." *Shakespeare Survey.* 1968. 21: 1-11.

1765

Gelven, Michael. "Heidegger and Tragedy." *Boundary 2.* 1976. 4: 555-68.

1766

Gérard, Albert S. "'Egregiously an Ass': The Dark Side of the Moor, a View of Othello's Mind." *Shakespeare Survey.* 1957. 10: 98-106.

1767

Gérard, Albert S. "The Loving Killers: The Rationale of Righteousness in Baroque Tragedy." *Comparative Literature Studies.* 1965. 2: 209-32.

1768

Gohlke, Madelon. "'All That Is Spoke Is Marred': Language and Consciousness in *Oth.*" *Women's Studies.* 1982. 9: 157-76.

1769

Green, André. "*Oth:* A Tragedy of Conversion, Black Magic and White Magic." *The Tragic Effect: The Oedipus Complex in Tragedy.* Sheridan, Alan, trans. New York, London, and Cambridge: Cambridge University Press. 1979. 88-136.

1770

Greenblatt, Stephen J. "Improvisation and Power." *Literature and Society.* Said, Edward W., ed. Baltimore and London: Johns Hopkins University Press. 1980. 57-99.

1771

Greene, Gayle. "'But Words Are Words': Shakespeare's Sense of Language in *Oth.*" *Etudes Anglaises.* 1981. 34: 270-81.

1772

Hallstead, R. N. "Idolatrous Love: A New Approach to *Oth.*" *SQ.* 1968. 19: 107-24.

1773

Halstead, William L. "Artifice and Artistry in *R2* and *Oth.*" *Sweet Smoke of Rhetoric: A Collection of Renaissance Essays.* Lawrence, Natalie G., and

Reynolds, Jack A., eds. Coral Gables, Florida: University of Miami Press. 1964. 19-51.

1774

Hapgood, Robert. "The Trial of Othello." *Pacific Coast Studies in Shakespeare.* McNeir, Waldo F., and Greenfield, Thelma N., eds. Eugene: University of Oregon Press. 1966. 134-47.

1775

Hawkes, Terence. "Iago's Use of Reason." *Studies in Philology.* 1961. 58: 160-9.

1776

Hawkins, Harriett. "'The Victim's Side': Webster's *Duchess of Malfi* and Chaucer's *Clerk's Tale." Poetic Freedom and Poetic Truth.* Oxford: Clarendon. 1976. 26-54.

1777

Heilman, Robert B. *Magic in the Web.* Lexington: University of Kentucky Press. 1956.

1778

Hibbard, George R. "*Oth* and the Pattern of Shakespearian Tragedy." *Shakespeare Survey.* 1968. 21: 39-46.

1779

Homan, Sidney R. "Iago's Aesthetics: *Oth* and Shakespeare's Portrait of an Artist." *Shakespeare Studies.* 1970. 5: 141-8.

1780

Hubler, Edward L. "The Damnation of Othello: Some Limitations on the Christian View of the Play." *SQ.* 1958. 9: 295-300.

1781

Hunter, G. K. "Othello and Colour Prejudice." *Proceedings of the British Academy.* 1967. 53: 139-63.

1782

Hyman, Stanley E. *Iago: Some Approaches to the Illusion of His Motivation.* New York: Atheneum. 1970.

1783

Jones, Eldred D. *Othello's Countrymen: The African in English Renaissance Drama.* London: Oxford University Press. 1965.

1784

Jordan, Hoover H. "Dramatic Illusion in *Oth." SQ* . 1950. 1: 146-52.

1785

Jorgensen, Paul A. "*Honesty* in *Oth.*" *Studies in Philology.* 1950. 47: 557-67.

1786

Jorgensen, Paul A. "'Perplex'd in the Extreme': The Role of Thought in *Oth.*" *SQ.* 1964. 15: 265-75.

1787

Josipovici, Gabriel. *Writing and the Body.* Princeton: Princeton University Press. 1982. 34-63.

1788

Kaula, David. "Othello Possessed: Notes on Shakespeare's Use of Magic and Witchcraft." *Shakespeare Studies.* 1967. 2: 112-32.

1789

Kay, Carol McGinnis. "Othello's Need for Mirrors." *SQ* . 1983. 34: 261-70.

1790

Kirschbaum, Leo. "The Modern Othello." *English Literary History.* 1944. 11: 283-96.

1791

Leavis, Frank R. "Diabolic Intellect and the Noble Hero: or The Sentimentalist's Othello." *The Common Pursuit.* London: Chatto and Windus. 1952. 136-59.

1792

Lerner, Laurence. "The Machiavel and the Moor." *Essays in Criticism.* 1959. 9: 339-60.

1793

Levin, Harry. "*Oth* and the Motive-Hunters." *Centennial Review.* 1964. 8: 1-16.

1794

Linfield, Nicholas. "*You* and *Thou* in Shakespeare: *Oth* as an Example." *Iowa State Journal of Research.* 1982. 57: 163-78.

1795

McCullen, Joseph T. "Iago's Use of Proverbs for Persuasion." *Studies in English Literature.* 1964. 4: 247-62.

1796

McGee, Arthur R. "Othello's Motive for Murder." *SQ.* 1964. 15: 45-54.

1797

Matthews, G. M. "*Oth* and the Dignity of Man." *Shakespeare in a Changing World.* Kettle, Arnold, ed. London: Lawrence and Wishart. 1964.

123-45.

1798

Melchiori, Giorgio. "The Rhetoric of Character Construction: *Oth.*" *Shakespeare Survey.* 1981. 34: 61-72.

1799

Mendonca, Barbara Heliodora C. de. "*Oth*: A Tragedy Built on a Comic Structure." *Shakespeare Survey.* 1968. 21: 31-8.

1800

Mercer, Peter. "*Oth* and the Form of Heroic Tragedy." *Critical Quarterly.* 1969. 11: 45-61.

1801

Money, John. "Othello's 'It Is the Cause. . .': An Analysis." *Shakespeare Survey.* 1953. 6: 94-105.

1802

Moore, John R. "Othello, Iago, and Cassio as Soldiers." *Philological Quarterly.* 1952. 31: 189-94.

1803

Muir, Kenneth. "The Jealousy of Iago." *English Miscellany.* 1951. 2: 65-83.

1804

Neely, Carol Thomas. "Women and Men in *Oth*: 'What Should Such a Fool/ Do with So Good a Woman'?" *Shakespeare Studies.* 1977. 10: 133-58. Revised version, *The Woman's Part.* Lenz, Carolyn Ruth Swift, eds. et al. Urbana, Chicago, and London: University of Illinois Press. 1980. 211-39.

1805

Neill, Michael. "Changing Places in *Oth.*" *Shakespeare Survey.* 1984. 37: 115-31.

1806

Nelson, Timothy G. A., and Haines, Charles. "Othello's Unconsummated Marriage." *Essays in Criticism.* 1983. 33: 1-18.

1807

Nowottny, Winifred M. T. "Justice and Love in *Oth.*" *University of Toronto Quarterly.* 1951-52. 21: 330-44.

1808

Paris, Bernard J. "'His Scorn I Approve': The Self-Effacing Desdemona." *American Journal of Psychoanalysis.* 1984. 44: 413-24.

1809

Parker, Patricia. "Shakespeare and Rhetoric: 'Dilation' and 'Delation' in *Oth.*" *Shakespeare and the Question of Theory.* Parker, Patricia, and Hartman, Geoffrey, eds. New York and London: Methuen. 1985. 54-74.

1810

Prior, Moody E. "Character in Relation to Action in *Oth.*" *Modern Philology.* 1947. 44: 225-37.

1811

Ranald, Margaret Loftus. "The Indiscretions of Desdemona." *SQ.* 1963. 14: 127-39.

1812

Rogers, Robert. "Endopsychic Drama in *Oth.*" *SQ* . 1969. 20: 205-15.

1813

Rose, Mark. "Othello's Occupation: Shakespeare and the Romance of Chivalry." *English Literary Renaissance.* 1985. 15: 293-311.

1814

Rosenberg, Marvin. *The Masks of Othello: The Search for the Identity of Othello, Iago, and Desdemona by Three Centuries of Actors and Critics.* Berkeley and Los Angeles: University of California Press. 1961.

1815

Russell, G. W., and Lambert, W. B. "Sherlock Holmes Meets Othello: An MDS [i.e., Multidimensional Scaling] Analysis of Literary Characters." *British Journal of Educational Psychology.* 1980. 50: 277-88.

1816

Schwartz, Elias. "Stylistic 'Impurity' and the Meaning of *Oth.*" *Studies in English Literature.* 1970. 10: 297-313.

1817

Scragg, Leah. "Iago -- Vice or Devil?" *Shakespeare Survey.* 1968. 21: 53-65.

1818

Seltzer, Daniel. "Elizabethan Acting in *Oth.*" *SQ* . 1959. 10: 201-10.

1819

Shapiro, Stephen A. "Othello's Desdemona." *Literature and Psychology.* 1964. 14: 56-61.

1820

Shaw, Catherine M. "'Dangerous Conceits Are in Their Natures Poisons': The Language of *Oth.*" *University of Toronto Quarterly.* 1980. 49: 304-19.

1821

Siegel, Paul N. "The Damnation of Othello." *PMLA*. 1953. 68: 1068-78.

1822

Snow, Edward A. "Sexual Anxiety and the Male Order of Things in *Oth*." *English Literary Renaissance*. 1980. 10: 384-412.

1823

Snyder, Susan. "*Oth* and the Conventions of Romantic Comedy." *Renaissance Drama*. 1972. n.s. 5: 123-41.

1824

Spencer, Theodore. "The Elizabethan Malcontent." *Joseph Quincy Adams Memorial Studies*. McManaway, James G., et al, eds. Washington, D. C.: Folger Shakespeare Library. 1948. 523-35.

1825

Spivack, Bernard. *Shakespeare and the Allegory of Evil*. New York and London: Columbia University Press. 1958. 3-59, passim.

1826

Splitter, Randolph. "Language, Sexual Conflict and 'Symbiosis Anxiety' in *Oth*." *Mosiac*. 1982. 15.3: 17-26.

1827

Sproat, Kezia Vanmeter. "Rereading *Oth* II.i." *Kenyon Review*. 1985. 7: 44-51.

1828

Stanislavsky (Alekseev, Konstantin S.). *Stanislavsky Produces* Oth. Nowak, Helen, trans. London: Geoffrey Bles. 1948.

1829

Stewart, William F. "Does Iago Die?: The Problem of His Motivation in The Light of Elias Canetti's Theory of Survival." *Jahrbuch der Deutschen - Shakespeare Gesellschaft West*. 1985. 78-93.

1830

Stirling, Brents. "Psychology in *Oth*." *Shakespeare Association Bulletin*. 1944. 19: 135-44.

1831

Stoll, E. E. "Iago Not a 'Malcontent'." *Journal of English and Germanic Philology*. 1952. 51: 163-7.

1832

Stoll, E. E. Oth*: An Historical and Comparative Study*. Minneapolis: University of Minnesota Press. 1915.

1833

Stoll, E. E. "Slander in Drama." *SQ.* 1953. 4: 433-50.

1834

Swinburne, Algernon Charles. *"Oth." Three Plays of Shakespeare.* New York and London: Harper. 1909.

1835

Teodorescu-Brinzeu, Pia. "A Systemic Approach to the Theatre." *Poetics.* 1977. 6: 351-74.

1836

Walton, James K. "'Strength's Abundance': A View of *Oth.*" *Review of English Studies.* 1960. n.s. 11: 8-17.

1837

Webb, Henry J. "The Military Background in *Oth.*" *Philological Quarterly.* 1951. 30: 40-52.

1838

West, Robert H. "The Christianness of *Oth.*" *SQ.* 1964. 15: 333-43.

1839

Widdowson, H. G. "Othello in Person." *Language and Literature: An Introductory Reader in Stylistics.* Carter, Ronald, ed. London, Boston and Sydney: Allen and Unwin. 1982. 41-52.

1840

Willson, Robert F., Jr. "Symbol and Character: The Function of Othello's Candle (V.ii.1-22)." *Literatur in Wissenschaft und Unterricht.* 1981. 14: 29-35.

See also works listed under *Tragedy*, especially by Bradley, Hawkes, Holloway, Speaight, Spivack, and Wilson.

1841

Arthos, John. "*Per*: A Study in the Dramatic Use of Romantic Narrative." *SQ*. 1953. 4: 257-70.

1842

Barber, C. L. "'Thou That Beget'st Him That Did Thee Beget': Transformation in *Per* and *WT*." *Shakespeare Survey*. 1969. 22: 59-67.

1843

Barker, Gerard A. "Themes and Variations in Shakespeare's *Per*." *English Studies*. 1963. 44: 401-14.

1844

Bates, Paul A. "Elements of Folk Literature and Humanism in *Per*." *Shakespeare-Jahrbuch*. (Weimar) 1983. 119: 112-14.

1845

Berry, Francis. "Word and Picture in the Final Plays." *Later Shakespeare*. Brown, John Russell, and Harris, Bernard, eds. Stratford-upon-Avon Studies 8. London: Arnold. 1966. 81-101.

1846

Brockbank, J. Philip. "*Per* and the Dream of Immortality." *Shakespeare Survey*. 1971. 24: 105-16.

1847

Comito, Terry. "Exile and Return in the Greek Romances." *Arion*. 1975. n.s. 2: 58-80.

1848

Cutts, John P. "Pericles' 'Downright Violence'." *Shakespeare Studies*. 1969. 4: 275-93.

1849

Dunbar, Mary Judith. "'To the Judgement of Your Eyes': Iconography and the Theatrical Art of *Per*." *Shakespeare, Man of the Theater*. Muir, Kenneth, et al, eds. Newark: University of Delaware Press; London and Toronto: Associated University Presses. 1983. 86-97.

1850

Edwards, Philip. "An Approach to the Problem of *Per*." *Shakespeare Survey*. 1952. 5: 25-49.

1851

Ewbank, Inga-Stina. "'My Name is Marina': The Language of Recognition." *Shakespeare's Styles: Essays in Honour of Kenneth Muir*. Edwards, Philip, et al, eds. Cambridge, London, and New York: Cambridge University Press. 1980. 111-30.

1852

Ewbank, Inga-Stina. "The Word in the Theater." *Shakespeare, Man of the Theater*. Muir, Kenneth, et al, eds. Newark: University of Delaware Press; London and Toronto: Associated University Presses. 1983. 55-75.

1853

Felperin, Howard. "Shakespeare's Miracle Play." *SQ*. 1967. 18: 363-74.

1854

Fienberg, Nona. "Marina in *Per*: Exchange Values and the Art of Moral Discourse." *Iowa State Journal of Research*. 1982. 57: 153-61.

1855

Greenfield, Thelma N. "A Re-Examination of the 'Patient' Pericles." *Shakespeare Studies*. 1968. 3: 51-61.

1856

Hillman, Richard. "Shakespeare's Gower and Gower's Shakespeare: The Larger Debt of *Per*." *SQ*. 1985. 36: 427-37.

1857

Hoeniger, F. D. "Gower and Shakespeare in *Per*." *SQ*. 1982. 33: 461-79.

1858

Hunt, Maurice. "'Opening the Book of Monarchs' Faults': *Per* and Redemptive Speech." *Essays in Literature*. 1985. 12: 155-70.

1859

Kaul, Mythili. "References to Food and Feeding in *Per*." *Notes and Queries*. 1982. n.s. 29: 124-6.

1860

Knowles, Richard Paul. "'Wishes Fall Out as They're Will'd': Artist, Audience, and *Per*'s Gower." *English Studies in Canada*. 1983. 9: 14-24.

1861

Meszaros, Patricia K. "*Per:* Shakespeare's Divine Musical Comedy." *Shakespeare and the Arts*. Cary, Cecile Williamson, and Limouze, Henry S., eds. Washington, D. C.: University Press of America. 1982. 3-20.

1862

Michael, Nancy, comp. Per: *An Annotated Bibliography*. New York: Garland. 1986.

1863

Muir, Kenneth. "The Problem of *Per*." *English Studies*. 1949. 30: 65-83.

1864

Peterson, Douglas L. *Time, Tide, and Tempest: A Study of Shakespeare's Romances*. San Marino, California: Huntington Library Press. 1973.

1865

Stockholder, Kay. "Sex and Authority in *Ham*, *Lr*, and *Per*." *Mosaic*. 1985. 18: 17-29.

1866

Taylor, Michael. "'Here Is a Thing Too Young for Such a Place': Innocence in *Per*." *Ariel: A Review of International English Literature*. 1982. 13.3: 3-19.

1867

Tompkins, J. M. S. "Why *Per*?" *Review of English Studies*. 1952. 3: 315-24.

See also works listed under *Comedy: The Late Romances*.

The Phoenix and the Turtle

1868

Garber, Marjorie. "Two Birds with One Stone: Lapidary Re-Inscription in *PhT*." *Upstart Crow*. 1984. 5: 5-19.

1869

Hammond, Gerald, ed. *Elizabethan Poetry: Lyrical and Narrative*. London: Macmillan. 1984.

1870

Knight, G. Wilson. *The Mutual Flame: On Shakespeare's* Son *and* PhT. London: Methuen. 1955.

Poetry

1871

Robbin, Robin. ". . . And the Counter-Argument." *Times Literary Supplement*. 1985. Dec. 20, 4316: 1449-50.

1872

Taylor, Gary. "A New Shakespeare Poem? The Evidence." *Times Literary Supplement*. 1985. Dec. 20, 4316: 1447-48.

The Rape of Lucrece

1873

Allen, Don Cameron. "Some Observations on *Luc*." *Shakespeare Survey*. 1962. 15: 89-98.

1874

Bowers, A. Robin. "Iconography and Rhetoric in Shakespeare's *Luc*." *Shakespeare Studies*. 1981. 14: 1-21.

1875

Bromley, Laura G. "Lucrece's Re-Creation." *SQ*. 1983. 34: 200-11.

1876

Donaldson, Ian. *The Rapes of Lucretia: A Myth and Its Transformations*. Oxford: Clarendon. 1982.

1877

Dundas, Judith. "Mocking the Mind: The Role of Art in Shakespeare's *Luc*." *Sixteenth Century Journal*. 1983. 14: 13-22.

1878

French, Tita. "A 'Badge of Fame': Shakespeare's Rhetorical Lucrece." *Explorations in Renaissance Culture*. 1984. 10: 97-106.

1879

Hulse, S. Clark. "'A Piece of Skilful Painting' in Shakespeare's *Luc*." *Shakespeare Survey*. 1978. 31: 13-22.

1880

Hulse, S. Clark. *Metamorphic Verse: The Elizabethan Minor Epic*. Princeton: Princeton University Press. 1981. 141-94.

1881

Kahn, Coppélia. "The Rape in Shakespeare's *Luc*." *Shakespeare Studies*. 1976. 9: 45-72.

1882

Langham, Michael. "*Err* and *Luc.*" *Kenyon Review*. 1964. 26: 556-9.

1883

Lanham, Richard A. "The Politics of *Luc.*" *Hebrew University Studies in Literature*. 1980. 8: 66-76.

1884

Lever, J. W. "Shakespeare's Narrative Poems." *A New Companion to Shakespeare Studies*. Muir, Kenneth, and Schoenbaum, Samuel, eds. Cambridge: Cambridge University Press. 1971. 116-26.

1885

Levin, Richard. "The Ironic Reading of *Luc* and the Problem of External Evidence." *Shakespeare Survey*. 1981. 34: 85-92.

1886

Majors, G. W. "Shakespeare's First Brutus: His Role in *Luc.*" *Modern Language Quarterly*. 1974. 35: 339-51.

1887

Montgomery, Robert L. "Shakespeare's Gaudy: The Method of *Luc.*" *Studies in Honor of DeWitt T. Starnes*. Harrison, Thomas P., et al, eds. Austin: University of Texas Press. 1967. 25-36.

1888

Muir, Kenneth. "*Luc.*" *Angelica*. 1964. 5: 25-40.

1889

Prince, F. T. *William Shakespeare: The Poems*. London: Longmans, Green. 1963. 12-17.

1890

Rosand, David. "'Troyes Painted Woes': Shakespeare and the Pictorial Imagination." *Hebrew University Studies in Literature*. 1980. 8: 77-97.

1891

Stimpson, Catharine R. "Shakespeare and the Soil of Rape." *The Woman's Part*. Lenz, Carolyn Ruth Swift, et al, eds. Urbana, Chicago, and London: University of Illinois Press. 1980. 56-64.

1892

Sylvester, Bickford. "Natural Mutability and Human Responsibility: Form in Shakespeare's *Luc.*" *College English*. 1965. 26: 505-11.

1893

Truax, Elizabeth. "Lucrece! What Hath Your Conceited Painter Wrought?" *Shakespeare: Contemporary Critical Approaches*. Garvin, Harry R., ed.

Lewisburg, Pa.: Bucknell University Press; London and Toronto: Associated University Presses. 1980. 13-30.

1894

Vickers, Nancy. "'The Blazon of Sweet Beauty's Best': Shakespeare's *Luc.*" *Shakespeare and the Question of Theory.* Parker, Patricia, and Hartman, Geoffrey, eds. New York and London: Methuen. 1985. 95-115.

1895

Walley, Harold R. "*Luc* and Shakespearean Tragedy." *PMLA.* 1961. 76: 480-7.

Richard II

1896

Altick, Richard D. "Symphonic Imagery in *R2.*" *PMLA.* 1947. 62: 339-65.

1897

Baines, Barbara J. "Kingship of the Silent King: A Study of Shakespeare's Bolingbroke." *English Studies.* 1980. 61: 24-36.

1898

Barton, Anne. "Shakespeare and the Limits of Language." *Shakespeare Survey.* 1971. 24: 19-30.

1899

Baxter, John. *Shakespeare's Poetic Styles: Verse into Drama.* London, Boston, and Henley: Routledge and Kegan Paul. 1980.

1900

Berger, Harry, Jr. "Psychoanalyzing the Shakespeare Text: The First Three Scenes of the *Henriad.*" *Shakespeare and the Question of Theory.* Parker, Patricia, and Hartman, Geoffrey, eds. New York and London: Methuen. 1985. 210-29.

1901

Black, James. "The Interlude of the Beggar and the King in *R2.*" *Pageantry in the Shakespearean Theater.* Bergeron, David M., ed. Athens: University of Georgia Press. 1985. 104-13.

1902

Black, Matthew W., and Metz, G. Harold, comps. R2: *A Bibliography to Supplement the New Variorum Edition of 1955.* New York: Modern Language Association. 1977.

1903

Bloom, Alan. "*R2.*" *Shakespeare as Political Thinker.* Alvis, John, and West, Thomas G., eds. Durham, N. C.: Carolina Academic Press. 1981. 51-61.

1904

Bogard, Travis. "Shakespeare's Second Richard." *PMLA.* 1955. 70: 192-209.

1905

Bonnard, Georges A. "The Actor in *R2.*" *Shakespeare-Jahrbuch.* 1951-52. 87/88: 87-101.

1906

Brockbank, Philip. "*R2* and the Music of Men's Lives." *Leeds Studies in English.* 1983. 14: 57-73.

1907

Bryant, J. A. "The Linked Analogies of *R2.*" *Sewanee Review.* 1957. 65: 420-33.

1908

Calderwood, James L. *Shakespearean Metadrama.* Minneapolis: University of Minnesota Press. 1971.

1909

Cowan, Louise. "God Will Save the King: Shakespeare's *R2.*" *Shakespeare as Political Thinker.* Alvis, John, and West, Thomas G., eds. Durham, N. C.: Carolina Academic Press. 1981. 63-81.

1910

Dean, Leonard F. "*R2*: The State and the Image of the Theater." *PMLA.* 1952. 67: 211-18.

1911

Dodson, Sarah. "The Northumberland of Shakespeare and Holinshed." *University of Texas Studies in English.* 1939. 19: 74-85.

1912

Dorius, Raymond J. "A Little More Than a Little: Prudence and Excess in *R2* and the Histories." *SQ.* 1960. 11: 13-26.

1913

Douglas, D. L. "'After Such Knowledge, What Forgiveness?': A Critical Interpretation of *R2.*" *Parergon.* 1977. 18: 27-36.

1914

Elliott, John R. "History and Tragedy in *R2.*" *Studies in English Literature.* 1968. 8: 253-71.

175

1915

Elliott, John R. "*R2* and the Medieval." *Renaissance Papers 1965*. 1966. 25-34.

1916

French, A. L. "Who Desposed Richard II?" *Essays in Criticism*. 1967. 17: 411-33.

1917

Gardner, C. O. "The Great Deepening: An Essay on *R2*." *Generous Converse: English Essays in Memory of Edward Davis*. Cape Town: Oxford University Press. 1980. 37-43.

1918

Gaudet, Paul. "Northumberland's 'Persuasion': Reflections on *R2*, II.i.224-300." *Upstart Crow*. 1982. 4: 73-85.

1919

Gaudet, Paul. "The 'Parasitical' Counselors in Shakespeare's *R2*: A Problem in Dramatic Interpretation." *SQ*. 1982. 33: 142-54.

1920

Halstead, William L. "Artifice and Artistry in *R2* and *Oth*." *Sweet Smoke of Rhetoric: A Collection of Renaissance Essays*. Lawrence, Natalie Grimes, and Reynolds, J. A., eds. Coral Gables, Florida: University of Miami Press. 1964. 19-51.

1921

Hapgood, Robert. "Three Eras in *R2*." *SQ*. 1963. 14: 281-3.

1922

Heninger, Simeon K. "The Sun-King Analogy in *R2*." *SQ*. 1960. 11: 319-27.

1923

Hexter, J. H. "Property, Monopoly, and Shakespeare's *R2*." *Culture and Politics: From Puritanism to the Enlightenment*. Zagorin, Perez, ed. Berkeley, Los Angeles and London: University of California Press. 1980. 1-24.

1924

Hockey, Dorothy. "A World of Rhetoric in *R2*." *SQ* . 1964. 15: 179-91.

1925

Humphreys, Arthur R. *Shakespeare:* R2. London: Arnold. 1967.

1926

Jeffares, A. Norman. "In One Person Many People*: R2*." *The Morality of Art: Essays Presented to G. Wilson Knight*. Jefferson, Douglas W., ed. New York: Barnes and Noble; London: Routledge and Kegan Paul. 1969.

50-66.

1927

Jorgensen, Paul A. "Vertical Patterns in *R2.*" *Shakespeare Association Bulletin.* 1948. 23: 119-34.

1928

Kantorowicz, Ernst H. "Shakespeare*: R2.*" *The King's Two Bodies: A Study in Mediaeval Political Theology.* Princeton: Princeton University Press. 1957. 24-41.

1929

Kipling, Gordon. "Richard II's 'Sumptuous Pageants' and the Idea of the Civic Triumph." *Pageantry in the Shakespearean Theater.* Bergeron, David M., ed. Athens: University of Georgia Press. 1985. 83-103.

1930

Kliger, Samuel. "The Sun Imagery in *R2.*" *Studies in Philology.* 1948. 45: 196-202.

1931

Law, Robert A. "Deviations from Holinshed in *R2.*" *Texas Studies in English.* 1950. 29: 91-101.

1932

Law, Robert A. "Links Between Shakespeare's History Plays." *Studies in Philology.* 1953. 50: 168-87.

1933

MacDonald, Ronald R. "Uneasy Lies: Language and History in Shakespeare's Lancastrian Tetralogy." *SQ.* 1984. 35: 22-39.

1934

McMillin, Scott. "Shakespeare's *R2*: Eyes of Sorrow, Eyes of Desire." *SQ.* 1984. 35: 40-52.

1935

Montgomery, Robert L. "The Dimensions of Time in *R2.*" *Shakespeare Studies.* 1969. 4: 73-85.

1936

Petronella, Vincent F. "Regal Duality and Everyman: Dante to Shakespeare." *Humanities Association Review.* 1979. 30: 131-46.

1937

Phialas, Peter G. "The Medieval in *R2.*" *SQ.* 1961. 12: 305-10.

1938

Phialas, Peter G. "*R2* and Shakespeare's Tragic Mode." *Texas Studies in Literature and Language.* 1963. 5: 344-55.

1939

Provost, Foster. "On Justice and the Music in *R2* and *Lr.*" *Annuale Mediaevale.* 1961. 2: 55-71.

1940

Quinn, Michael. "'The King Is Not Himself': The Personal Tragedy of Richard II." *Studies in Philology.* 1959. 56: 169-86.

1941

Rackin, Phyllis. "The Role of the Audience in Shakespeare's *R2.*" *SQ.* 1985. 36: 262-81.

1942

Reed, Robert R. R2: *From Mask to Prophet.* University Park: Pennsylvania State University Press. 1968.

1943

Reiman, Donald H. "Appearance, Reality, and Moral Order in *R2.*" *Modern Language Quarterly.* 1964. 25: 34-45.

1944

Reynolds, James A. "The King as Judge in *R2.*" *Repentance and Retribution in Early English Drama.* Salzburg: Inst. für Anglistik und Amerikanistik, University of Salzburg. 1982. 43-52.

1945

Ribner, Irving. "The Political Problem in Shakespeare's Lancastrian Tetralogy." *Studies in Philology.* 1952. 49: 171-84.

1946

Ross, Gordon N. "Shakespeare's Poetic Gesture: Metaphor and Mimesis in *R2.*" *Shakespeare and Renaissance Association of West Virginia: Selected Papers.* 1978. 2: 30-7.

1947

Sanders, Wilbur. "Shakespeare's Political Agnosticism: *R2.*" *The Dramatist and the Received Idea: Studies in the Plays of Marlowe and Shakespeare.* Cambridge: Cambridge University Press. 1968. 158-93.

1948

Schoenbaum, Samuel. "*R2* and the Realities of Power." *Shakespeare Survey.* 1975. 28: 1-13.

1949

Stirling, Brents. "Bolingbroke's 'Decision'." *SQ*. 1951. 2: 27-34.

1950

Sublette, Jack R. "Order and Power in *R2*." *Ball State University Forum*. 1981. 22: 42-51.

1951

Suzman, Arthur. "Imagery and Symbolism in *R2*." *SQ* . 1956. 7: 355-70.

1952

Swinburne, Algernon C. "*R2*." *Three Plays of Shakespeare*. New York and London: Harper. 1909.

1953

Thompson, Karl F. "Richard II, Martyr." *SQ*. 1957. 8: 159-66.

1954

Trafton, Dain A. "Shakespeare's Henry IV: A New Prince in a New Principality." *Shakespeare as Political Thinker*. Alvis, John, and West, Thomas G., eds. Durham, N. C.: Carolina Academic Press. 1981. 83-94.

1955

Trousdale, Marion. "Reality and Illusion in the Theatre." *Critical Quarterly*. 1969. 11: 347-59.

1956

Ure, Peter. "The Looking-Glass of Richard II." *Philological Quarterly*. 1955. 34: 219-24.

1957

Wentersdorf, Karl P. "Shakespeare's *R2*: Gaunt's Part in Woodstock's Blood." *English Language Notes*. 1980. 18: 99-104.

1958

Wilson, J. Dover. "The Political Background of Shakespeare's *R2* and *H4*." *Shakespeare-Jahrbuch*. 1939. 75: 36-51.

1959

Yeats, W. B. "At Stratford-upon-Avon." *Ideas of Good and Evil,* collected in *Essays and Introductions*. London and New York: Macmillan. 1961. 96-110.

1960

Zitner, Sheldon P. "Aumerle's Conspiracy." *Studies in English Literature*. 1974. 14: 239-57.

See also works listed under *History Plays*, especially by Calderwood,

Forker, Ornstein, and Reese; the works by Burckhardt, Mahood, and Palmer listed under *General Studies*, and the work by Mack (*Killing the King*) listed under *Tragedy*.

Richard III

1961

Arnold, Aerol. "The Recapitulation Dream in *R3* and *Mac*." *SQ*. 1955. 6: 51-62.

1962

Berry, Ralph. "*R3:* Bonding the Audience." *Mirror up to Shakespeare: Essays in Honour of G. R. Hibbard*. Gray, J. C., ed. Toronto, Buffalo, and London: University of Toronto Press. 1984. 114-27.

1963

Bevington, David. "'Why Should Calamity Be Full of Words?': The Efficacy of Cursing in *R3*." *Iowa State Journal of Research*. 1981. 56: 9-21.

1964

Boyer, Clarence Valentine. *The Villain as Hero in Elizabethan Tragedy*. London: Routledge; New York: Dutton. 1914. 60-98.

1965

Brooke, Nicholas. "Reflecting Gems and Dead Bones: Tragedy versus History in *R3*." *Critical Quarterly*. 1965. 7: 123-34.

1966

Brooks, Harold F. "*R3*, Unhistorical Amplifications: The Women's Scenes and Seneca." *Modern Language Review*. 1980. 75: 721-37.

1967

Burton, Dolores M. "Discourse and Decorum in the First Act of *R3*." *Shakespeare Studies*. 1981. 14: 55-84.

1968

Champion, Larry S. "Myth and Counter-Myth: The Many Faces of *R3*." *A Fair Day in the Affections: Literary Essays in Honor of Robert B. White, Jr*. Durant, Jack M., and Hester, M. Thomas, eds. Raleigh, N. C.: Winston Press. 1980. 37-53.

1969

Clemen, Wolfgang H. *A Commentary on Shakespeare's* R3. Bonheim, Jean, trans. London: Methuen. 1968.

1970

Clemen, Wolfgang H. "Tradition and Originality in Shakespeare's *R3*." *SQ*. 1954. 5: 247-57.

1971

French, A. L. "The World of *R3*." *Shakespeare Studies*. 1969. 4: 25-39.

1972

Goll, August. "Criminal Types in Shakespeare." Moritzen, J., trans. *Journal of Criminal Law, Criminology and Police Science*. 1939. 30: 22-51.

1973

Hanham, Alison. *Richard III and His Early Historians: 1483-1535*. London: Oxford University Press. 1975.

1974

Hassel, R. Chris, Jr. "Military Oratory in *R3*." *SQ*. 1984. 35: 53-61.

1975

Hassel, R. Chris, Jr. "Richard versus Richmond: Aesthetic Warfare in *R3*." *Jahrbuch der Deutschen Shakespeare-Gesellschaft West*. 1985. 106-16.

1976

Heilman, Robert B. "Satiety and Conscience: Aspects of *R3*." *Antioch Review*. 1964. 24: 57-73.

1977

Hugenberg, Lawrence W., Sr., and Schaefermeyer, Mark J. "Soliloquy as Self-Discourse." *Quarterly Journal of Speech*. 1983. 69: 180-7.

1978

Krieger, Murray. "The Dark Generations of *R3*." *Criticism*. 1959. 1: 32-48.

1979

Mallett, Phillip. "Shakespeare's Trickster-Kings: Richard III and Henry V." *The Fool and the Trickster: Studies in Honor of Enid Welsford*. Williams, Paul V. A., ed. Cambridge: D. S. Brewer; Totowa, N. J.: Rowman and Littlefield. 1979. 64-82.

1980

Miner, Madonne M. "'Neither Mother, Wife, nor England's Queen': The Roles of Women in *R3*." *The Woman's Part*. Urbana, Chicago, and London: University of Illinois Press. 1980. 35-55.

1981

Moore, James A., comp. R3: *An Annotated Bibliography*. New York: Garland. 1986.

1982

Müller, Wolfgang G. "The Villain as Rhetorician in Shakespeare's *R3*." *Anglia.* 1984. 102: 37-59.

1983

Paris, Bernard J. "Richard III: Shakespeare's First Great Mimetic Character." *Aligarh Journal of English Studies.* 1983. 8: 40-67.

1984

Richmond, Hugh. "*R3* and the Reformation." *JEGP.* 1984. 83: 509-21.

1985

Rossiter, A. P. "The Structure of *R3*." *Durham University Journal.* 1938. 31: 44-75.

1986

Sanders, Wilbur. "Providence and Policy in *R3*." *The Dramatist and the Received Idea: Studies in the Plays of Marlowe and Shakespeare.* Cambridge: Cambridge University Press. 1968. 72-109.

1987

Sheriff, William E. "The Grotesque Comedy of *R3*." *Studies in the Literary Imagination.* 1972. 5: 51-64.

1988

Smith, Fred M. "The Relationship of *Mac* to *R3*." *PMLA.* 1945. 60: 1003-20.

1989

Stoll, E. E. "The Criminals." *Shakespeare Studies.* New York: Macmillan. 1927. 337-402.

1990

Tey, Josephine. *The Daughter of Time.* London: P. Davies. 1951.

1991

Thomas, Sidney. *The Antic Hamlet and Richard III.* New York: King's Crown. 1943.

1992

Wheeler, Richard P. "History, Character, and Conscience in *R3*." *Comparative Drama.* 1971-72. 5: 301-21.

1993

Williams, Philip. "*R3:* The Battle Orations." *English Studies in Honor of James S. Wilson.* University of Virginia Studies 4. Charlottesville: University of Virginia Press. 1951. 125-30.

Wood, Alice I. P. *The Stage History of Shakespeare's* R3. New York: Columbia University Press; Oxford: Oxford University Press. 1909.

See also works listed under *History Plays*, especially by Berry, Boris, Kelly, and Prior.

Romeo and Juliet

1995

Adams, Barry B. "The Prudence of Prince Escalus." *English Literary History*. 1968. 35: 32-50.

1996

Adams, John C. "*Rom*: As Played on Shakespeare's Stage." *Theatre Arts Monthly*. 1936. 20: 896-904.

1997

Black, James. "The Visual Artistry of *Rom*." *Studies in English Literature*. 1975. 15: 245-56.

1998

Bond, Ronald B. "Love and Lust in *Rom*." *Wascana Review*. 1980. 15.2: 22-31.

1999

Brenner, Gerry. "Shakespeare's Politically Ambitious Friar." *Shakespeare Studies*. 1980. 13: 47-58.

2000

Bryant, James C. "The Problematic Friar in *Rom*." *English Studies*. (Amsterdam) 1974. 55: 340-50.

2001

Carroll, William C. "'We Were Born to Die': *Rom*." *Comparative Drama*. 1981. 15: 54-71.

2002

Chang, Joseph S. M. J. "The Language of Paradox in *Rom*." *Shakespeare Studies*. 1968. 3: 22-42.

2003

Cribb, T. J. "The Unity of *Rom*." *Shakespeare Survey*. 1981. 34: 93-104.

2004

Dickey, Franklin M. *Not Wisely But Too Well: Shakespeare's Love Tragedies*. San Marino, California: Huntington Library Press. 1957.

2005

Estrin, Barbara L. "Romeo, Juliet and the Art of Naming Love." *Ariel: A Review of International English Literature*. 1981. 12.2: 31-49.

2006

Evans, Bertrand. "The Brevity of Friar Laurence." *PMLA*. 1950. 65: 841-65.

2007

Evans, Robert O. *The Osier Cage: Rhetorical Devices in* Rom. Lexington: Kentucky University Press. 1966.

2008

Everett, Barbara. "*Rom*: The Nurse's Story." *Critical Quarterly*. 1972. 14: 129-39.

2009

Greer, Germaine. "Juliet's Wedding." *The Listener*. 100 (7 Dec. 1978): 750-1.

2010

Harcourt, John B. "'Children of Divers Kind': A Reading of *Rom*." *Upstart Crow*. 1980. 3: 67-80.

2011

Harrison, Thomas P. "*Rom*, *MND*: Companion Plays." *Texas Studies in Literature and Language*. 1971-72. 13: 209-13.

2012

Hill, R. F. "Shakespeare's Early Tragic Mode." *SQ*. 1958. 9: 455-69.

2013

Holland, Norman. "Mercutio, Mine Own Son the Dentist." *Essays on Shakespeare*. Smith, Gordon Ross, ed. University Park and London: Pennsylvania State University Press. 1965. 3-14.

2014

Hosley, Richard. "The Use of the Upper Stage in *Rom*." *SQ*. 1954. 5: 371-9.

2015

Kahn, Coppélia. "Coming of Age in Verona." *Modern Language Studies*. 1977-78. 8: 5-22. Reprinted, *The Woman's Part*. Lenz, Carolyn Ruth Swift, et al, eds. Urbana, Chicago, and London: University of Illinois Press. 1980. 171-193.

2016

Kernberg, Otto F. "Adolescent Sexuality in the Light of Group Processes." *Psychoanalytic Quarterly*. 1980. 49: 27-47.

2017

Leech, Clifford. "The Moral Tragedy of *Rom.*" *English Renaissance Drama: Essays in Honor of Madeleine Doran and Mark Eccles*. Henning, Standish, et al, eds. Carbondale and Edwardsville: Southern Illinois University Press; London and Amsterdam: Feffer and Simons. 1976. 59-75.

2018

Levenson, Jill L. "The Definition of Love: Shakespeare's Phrasing in *Rom.*" *Shakespeare Studies*. 1982. 15: 21-36.

2019

Levenson, Jill L. "Romeo and Juliet before Shakespeare." *Studies in Philology*. 1984. 81: 325-47.

2020

Levin, Harry. "Form and Formality in *Rom.*" *SQ* . 1960. 11: 3-11.

2021

McGuire, Philip C. "On the Dancing in *Rom.*" *Renaissance and Reformation*. 1981. N. S. 5: 87-97.

2022

Moisan, Thomas E. "Rhetoric and the Rehearsal of Death: The 'Lamentations' Scene in *Rom.*" *SQ*. 1983. 34: 389-404.

2023

Moore, Olin H. *The Legend of Romeo and Juliet*. Columbus: Ohio State University Press. 1950.

2024

Nevo, Ruth. "Tragic Form in *Rom.*" *Studies in English Literature*. 1969. 9: 241-58.

2025

Newman, Paula, and Williams, George Walton. "Paris: The Mirror of Romeo." *Renaissance Papers 1981*. 1982. 13-19.

2026

Nosworthy, James M. "The Two Angry Families of Verona." *SQ*. 1952. 3: 219-26.

2027

Parker, Douglas H. "Light and Dark Imagery in *Rom.*" *Queen's Quarterly*. 1968. 75: 663-74.

2028

Peterson, Douglas L. "*Rom* and the Art of Moral Navigation." *Pacific Coast Studies in Shakespeare.* McNeir, Waldo F., and Greenfield, Thelma N., eds. Eugene: University of Oregon Press. 1966. 33-46.

2029

Pettet, Ernest C. "The Imagery of *Rom.*" *English.* 1950. 8: 121-6.

2030

Rozett, Martha Tuck. "The Comic Structures of Tragic Endings: The Suicide Scenes in *Rom* and *Ant.*" *SQ.* 1985. 36: 152-64.

2031

Siegel, Paul N. "Christianity and the Religion of Love in *Rom.*" *SQ.* 1961. 12: 371-92. Reprinted, Siegel's *Shakespeare in His Time and Ours.* Notre Dame and London: University of Notre Dame Press, 1968. 69-107.

2032

Smith, Gordon Ross. "The Balance of Themes in *Rom.*" *Essays on Shakespeare.* Smith, Gordon Ross, ed. University Park and London: Pennsylvania State University Press. 1965. 15-66.

2033

Snow, Edward. "Language and Sexual Difference in *Rom.*" *Shakespeare's "Rough Magic": Renaissance Essays in Honor of C. L. Barber.* Erickson, Peter, and Kahn, Coppélia, eds. Newark: University of Delaware Press; London and Toronto: Associated University Presses. 1985. 168-92.

2034

Snyder, Susan. "*Rom*: Comedy into Tragedy." *Essays in Criticism.* 1970. 20: 391-402.

2035

Strauch, Edward H. "Implications of Jung's Archetypal Approach for Literary Study." *Aligarh Journal of English Studies.* 1982. 7: 1-17.

2036

Sypher, Wylie. "Romeo and Juliet are Dead: Melodrama of the Clinical." *New York Literary Forum.* 1980. 7: 179-86.

2037

Tanselle, G. Thomas. "Time in *Rom.*" *SQ.* 1964. 15: 349-61.

2038

Toole, William B. "The Nurse's 'Vast Irrelevance': Thematic Foreshadowing in *Rom.*" *South Atlantic Bulletin.* 1980. 45: 21-30.

2039

Utterback, Raymond V. "The Death of Mercutio." *SQ*. 1973. 24: 105-16.

2040

Warmbrod, Nancy Compton. "A Psychological Profile of Shakespeare's Juliet: Or Was It Merely Hormones?" *English Journal*. 1980. 69.9: 29.

2041

Wells, Stanley. "Juliet's Nurse: The Uses of Inconsequentiality." *Shakespeare's Styles: Essays in Honour of Kenneth Muir*. Edwards, Philip, et al, eds. Cambridge: Cambridge University Press. 1980. 51-66.

2042

Williamson, Marilyn L. "Romeo and Death." *Shakespeare Studies*. 1981. 14: 129-37.

See also works listed under *Tragedy*, especially by Charlton and Lawlor.

The Sonnets

2043

Allen, Michael J. B. "Shakespeare's Man Descending a Staircase: Sonnets 126 to 154." *Shakespeare Survey*. 1978. 31: 127-38.

2044

Andrews, Michael Cameron. "Power to Hurt: Sonnets 109-10 and 117-20." *Upstart Crow*. 1984. 5: 146-51.

2045

Andrews, Michael Cameron. "Sincerity and Subterfuge in Three Shakespearean Sonnet Groups." *SQ*. 1982. 33: 314-27.

2046

Baldwin, Thomas W. *On the Literary Genetics of Shakespeare's Poems and Sonnets*. *Urbana: University of Illinois Press. 1950*.

2047

Barry, Jackson G. "'Had, Having, and In Quest to Have, Extreme': Shakespeare's Rhetoric of Time in Sonnet 129." *Language and Style*. 1981. 14: 1-12.

2048

Bates, Paul A. "Shakespeare's *Son* and Pastoral Poetry." *Shakespeare Jahrbuch*. (Weimar) 1967. 103: 81-96.

2049

Booth, Stephen. *An Essay on Shakespeare's* Son. New Haven and London: Yale University Press. 1969.

2050

Brinton, Laurel J. "The Iconic Role of Aspect in Shakespeare's Sonnet 129." *Poetics Today*. 1985. 6: 447-59.

2051

Colie, Rosalie. "*Mel* and *Sal:* Some Problems in Sonnet Theory." *Shakespeare's Living Art*. Princeton: Princeton University Press. 1974. 68-134.

2052

Cook, Elizabeth. "The Bravery of Shakespeare's Sonnets." *Proceedings of the British Academy*. 1983. 69: 189-207.

2053

Cruttwell, M. J. Patrick. "A Reading of the *Son.*" *Hudson Review*. 1953. 5: 554-70.

2054

Devereux, James A., S. J. "The Last Temptation of Shakespeare: The Sonnets and Despair." *Renaissance Papers 1979*. 1980. 29-38.

2055

Dubrow, Heather. "Shakespeare's Undramatic Monologues: Toward a Reading of *Son.*" *SQ*. 1981. 32: 55-68.

2056

Empson, William. "They That Have Power." *Some Versions of Pastoral*. London: Chatto and Windus. 1950. 89-115.

2057

Ferry, Anne. *The "Inward" Language: Sonnets of Wyatt, Sidney, Shakespeare, Donne*. Chicago and London: University of Chicago Press. 1983.

2058

Fineman, Joel. *Shakespeare's Perjured Eye: The Invention of Poetic Subjectivity in the Sonnets*. Berkeley, Los Angeles, and London: University of California Press. 1986.

2059

Gardiner, Judith Kegan. "The Marriage of Male Minds in Shakespeare's Sonnets." *Journal of English and Germanic Philology*. 1985. 84: 328-47.

2060

Gilbert, A. J. "Spenser and Shakespeare." *Literary Language from Chaucer to Johnson.* London: Macmillan. 1979. 63-88.

2061

Goldsmith, Ulrich K. "Words Out of a Hat? Alliteration and Assonance in Shakespeare's *Son.*" *Journal of English and Germanic Philology.* 1950. 49: 33-48.

2062

Greene, Thomas M. "Pitiful Thrivers: Failed Husbandry in *Son.*" *Shakespeare and the Question of Theory.* Parker, Patricia, and Hartman, Geoffrey, eds. New York and London: Methuen. 1985. 230-44.

2063

Grundy, Joan. "Shakespeare's *Son* and the Elizabethan Sonneteers." *Shakespeare Survey.* 1962. 15: 41-9.

2064

Hancher, Michael. "Understanding Poetic Speech Acts." *College English.* 1975. 36: 632-9. Reprinted in *Linguistic Perspectives on Literature.* Ching, Marvin K. L., et al, eds. London, Boston, and Henley: Routledge and Kegan Paul. 1980. 295-304.

2065

Herbert, T. Walter. "Dramatic Personae in Shakespeare's Sonnets." *Shakespeare's "More Than Words Can Witness": Essays on Visual and Nonverbal Enactment in the Plays.* Homan, Sidney, ed. Lewisburg, Pa.: Bucknell University Press; London: Associated University Presses. 1980. 77-91.

2066

Herrnstein, Barbara, ed. *Discussions of Shakespeare's* Son. Boston: Heath. 1964.

2067

Hobday, C. H. "Shakespeare's Venus and Adonis Sonnets." *Shakespeare Survey.* 1973. 26: 103-9.

2068

Hubler, Edward, et al. *The Riddle of Shakespeare's* Son: *The Text of* Son, *with Interpretive Essays* . . . . New York: Basic Books. 1962.

2069

Jones, Peter, ed. *Shakespeare,* Son: *A Casebook.* London: Macmillan. 1977.

189

2070

Kaula, David. "'In War with Time': Temporal Perspectives in Shakespeare's *Son.*" *Studies in English Literature.* 1963. 3: 45-57.

2071

Klause, John. "Shakespeare's *Son*: Age in Love and the Goring of Thoughts." *Studies in Philology.* 1983. 80: 300-24.

2072

Knight, G. Wilson. *The Mutual Flame: On Shakespeare's* Son *and* The Phoenix and the Turtle. London: Methuen. 1955.

2073

Krieger, Murray. "The Innocent Insinuations of Wit: The Strategy of Language in Shakespeare's *Son.*" *The Play and Place of Criticism.* Baltimore: Johns Hopkins University Press. 1967. 19-36.

2074

Krieger, Murray. *A Window to Criticism: Shakespeare's* Son *and Modern Poetics.* Princeton: Princeton University Press. 1964.

2075

Landry, Hilton. *Interpretations in Shakespeare's* Son. Berkeley and Los Angeles: University of California Press. 1963.

2076

Leishman, James B. *Themes and Variations in Shakespeare's* Son. New York: Hillary House; London: Hutchinson. 1961.

2077

Lever, J. W. *The Elizabethan Love Sonnet.* London: Methuen. 1956.

2078

Melchiori, Giorgio. *Shakespeare's Dramatic Meditations: An Experiment in Criticism.* Oxford: Clarendon. 1976.

2079

Mizener, Arthur. "The Structure of Figurative Language in Shakespeare's *Son.*" *Southern Review.* 1939-40. 5: 730-47.

2080

Muir, Kenneth. "Biographical Red Herrings and Shakespeare's *Son.*" *Literary Half-Yearly.* 1965. 6: 61-9.

2081

Nowottny, Winifred M. T. "Formal Elements in Shakespeare's *Son*: Sonnets I-VI." *Essays in Criticism.* 1952. 2: 76-84.

2082

Oliver, Raymond. "Yvor Winters and the English Renaissance." *Southern Review*. 1981. N.S. 17: 758-80.

2083

Pequigney, Joseph. *Such Is My Love: A Study of Shakespeare's Sonnets*. Chicago and London: University of Chicago Press. 1985.

2084

Peterson, Douglas L. "Shakespeare's *Son*." *The English Lyric from Wyatt to Donne*. Princeton: Princeton University Press. 1967. 212-51.

2085

Piper, William Bowman. *Evaluating Shakespeare's Sonnets*. Houston, Texas: William Marsh Rice University. 1979.

2086

Platt, Michael. "Shakespearean Wisdom?" *Shakespeare as Political Thinker*. Alvis, John, and West, Thomas G., eds. Durham, N. C.: Carolina Academic Press. 1981. 257-76.

2087

Ramsey, Paul. "Of Truth: Self-Reflexiveness in Shakespeare's Sonnets and Plays." *Upstart Crow*. 1982. 4: 1-4, 6.

2088

Ransom, John Crowe. "A Postscript on Shakespeare's *Son*." *Kenyon Review*. 1968. 30: 523-31.

2089

Ransom, John Crowe. "Shakespeare at Sonnets." *Southern Review*. 1937-38. 3: 531-53.

2090

Regan, Mariann Sanders. *Love Words: The Self and the Text in Medieval and Renaissance Poetry*. Ithaca and London: Cornell University Press. 1982.

2091

Roche, Thomas P., Jr. "How Petrarchan Is Shakespeare?" *Shakespeare's Art from a Comparative Perspective*. Aycock, Wendell M., ed. Lubbock: Texas Tech. Press. 1981. 147-64.

2092

Roessner, Jane. "The Coherence and the Context of Shakespeare's Sonnet 116." *Journal of English and Germanic Philology*. 1982. 81: 331-46.

2093

Rosmarin, Adena. "Hermeneutics versus Erotics: Shakespeare's *Son* and Interpretive History." *PMLA.* 1985. 100: 20-37. Response by Margreta de Grazia, rejoinder by Rosmarin, *PMLA* 100 (1985): 810-12.

2094

Rutelli, Romana. "Connotative Systems and Their Functions in Shakespeare's Sonnet 87." *A Semiotic Landscape.* Chatman, Seymour, et al, eds. The Hague, Paris and New York: Mouton. 1979. 702-8.

2095

Schoenbaum, Samuel. "Shakespeare's Dark Lady: A Question of Identity." *Shakespeare's Styles: Essays in Honour of Kenneth Muir.* Edwards, Philip, et al, eds. Cambridge: Cambridge University Press. 1980. 221-39.

2096

Smith, Hallett. *The Tension of the Lyre: Poetry in Shakespeare's Sonnets.* San Marino, California: Huntington Library Press. 1981.

2097

Snow, Edward A. "Loves of Comfort and Despair: A Reading of Shakespeare's Sonnet 138." *English Literary History.* 1980. 47: 462-83.

2098

Stirling, Brents. *The Shakespeare Sonnet Order.* Berkeley and Los Angeles: University of California Press. 1968.

2099

Wells, Stanley. "New Readings in Shakespeare's Sonnets." *Elizabethan and Modern Studies.* Vander Motten, J. P., ed. Ghent: Seminarie voor Eng. and Amer. Lit., Rijkuniversiteit Gent. 1985. 317-22.

2100

Willen, Gerald, and Reed, Victor B., eds. *A Casebook on Shakespeare's* Son. New York: Crowell. 1964.

2101

Winny, James. *The Master-Mistress: A Study of Shakespeare's* Son. London: Chatto and Windus; New York: Barnes and Noble. 1968.

2102

Young, H. McClure. *The* Son *of Shakespeare: A Psycho-Sexual Analysis.* Menasha, Wis.: G. Banta. 1937.

2103

Bean, John C. "Comic Structure and the Humanizing of Kate in *Shr.*" *The Woman's Part.* Lenz, Carolyn Ruth Swift, et al, eds. Urbana, Chicago, and London: University of Illinois Press. 1984. 65-78.

2104

Bergeron, David M. "The Wife of Bath and Shakespeare's *Shr.*" *University Review.* 1969. 35: 279-86.

2105

Brunvand, Jan H. "The Folktale Origin of *Shr.*" *SQ* . 1966. 17: 345-59.

2106

Burt, Richard A. "Charisma, Coercion, and Comic Form in *Shr.*" *Criticism.* 1984. 26: 295-311.

2107

Cooper, Marilyn M. "Implicature, Convention, and *Shr.*" *Poetics.* 1981. 10: 1-14.

2108

Craig, Terry Ann. "Petruchio as Exorcist: Shakespeare and Elizabethan Demonology." *Shakespeare and Renaissance Association of West Virginia: Selected Papers.* 1978. 3: 1-7.

2109

Farley-Hills, David. "Paradoxes and Problems: Shakespeare's Sceptical Comedy in *Shr.*" *The Comic in Renaissance Comedy.* Totowa, N. J.: Barnes and Noble; London: Macmillan. 1981. 160-78.

2110

Felheim, Marvin, and Traci, Philip. "Realism in *Shr.*" *Interpretations.* 1980. 12: 100-13.

2111

Fineman, Joel. "The Turn of the Shrew." *Shakespeare and the Question of Theory.* Parker, Patricia, and Hartman, Geoffrey, eds. New York and London: Methuen. 1985. 138-59.

2112

Greenfield, Thelma N. "The Transformation of Christopher Sly." *Philological Quarterly.* 1954. 33: 34-42.

2113

Greer, Germaine. *The Female Eunuch*. London: MacGibbon and Kee, 1970; New York: McGraw-Hill, 1971. 206-10.

2114

Heilman, Robert B. "The *Taming* Untamed, or, The Return of the Shrew." *Modern Language Quarterly*. 1966. 27: 147-61.

2115

Hosley, Richard. "Was There a 'Dramatic Epilogue' to *Shr?*." *Studies in English Literature*. 1961. 1: 17-34.

2116

Huston, J. Dennis. "'To Make a Puppet': Play and Play-Making in *Shr*." *Shakespeare Studies*. 1976. 9: 73-87.

2117

Jayne, Sears. "The Dreaming of *Shr*." *SQ*. 1966. 17: 41-56.

2118

Kahn, Coppélia. "*Shr:* Shakespeare's Mirror of Marriage." *Modern Language Studies*. 1975. 5: 88-102. Reprinted, *The Authority of Experience: Essays in Feminist Criticism*. Diamond, Arlyn, and Edwards, Lee R., eds. Amherst: University of Massachusetts Press, 1977. 84-100.

2119

McLuskie, Kathleen. "Feminist Deconstruction: The Example of Shakespeare's *Shr*." *Red Letters*. 1982. 12: 33-40.

2120

Perret, Marion. "Of Sows' Ears and Silk Purses: Transformation Images in *Shr*." *Iowa State Journal of Research*. 1980. 54: 431-9.

2121

Rico, Barbara Roche. "From 'Speechless Dialect' to 'Prosperous Art': Shakespeare's Recasting of the Pygmalion Image." *Huntington Library Quarterly*. 1985. 48: 285-95.

2122

Roberts, Jeanne Addison. "Horses and Hermaphrodites: Metamorphoses in *Shr*." *SQ*. 1983. 34: 159-71.

2123

Saccio, Peter. "Shrewd and Kindly Farce." *Shakespeare Survey*. 1984. 37: 33-40.

194

2124

Shurgot, Michael W. "From Fiction to Reality: Character and Stagecraft in *Shr.*" *Theatre Journal.* 1981. 33: 327-40.

2125

Thom, Martha Andresen. "Shrew-taming and Other Rituals of Aggression: Baiting and Bonding on the Stage and in the Wild." *Women's Studies.* 1982. 9: 121-43.

2126

Thorne, W. B. "Folk Elements in *Shr.*" *Queen's Quarterly.* 1968. 75: 482-96.

2127

Tillyard, E. M. W. "The Fairy-Tale Element in *Shr.*" *Shakespeare 1564-1964.* Bloom, E. A., ed. Providence, R. I.: Brown University Press. 1964. 110-14.

2128

Vondersmith, Bernard J. "Suppose There Is an Epilogue? Dramatic Structure in *Shr.*" *College Language Association Journal.* 1981. 24: 329-35.

2129

Wayne, Valerie. "Refashioning the Shrew." *Shakespeare Studies.* 1985. 17: 159-87.

2130

West, Michael. "The Folk Background of Petruchio's Wooing Dance: Male Supremacy in *Shr.*" *Shakespeare Studies.* 1974. 7: 65-73.

2131

Woodbridge, Linda. *Women and the English Renaissance.* Urbana and Chicago: University of Illinois Press; Brighton: Harvester. 1984. 201-7, 221-2.

See also works listed under *Comedy: General Studies*, especially by Ralph Berry, Hawkins, and Stevenson, and under *Comedy: The Middle and Romantic Comedies*, especially by Leggatt.

The Tempest

2132

Allen, Don Cameron. "William Shakespeare: *Tmp.*" *Image and Meaning: Metaphoric Traditions in Renaissance Poetry.* Baltimore: Johns Hopkins University Press. 1960.

2133

Auden, W. H. "The Sea and the Mirror." *The Collected Poetry of W. H. Auden.* New York: Random House. 1945. 351-404.

2134

Awoonor, Kofi. "Caliban Answers Prospero: The Dialogue Between Western and African Literature." *Obsidian: Black Literature in Review.* 1981. 7: 75-98.

2135

Barker, Francis, and Hulme, Peter. "Nymphs and Reapers Heavily Vanish: the Discursive Con-Texts of *Tmp.*" *Alternative Shakespeares.* Drakakis, John, ed. London and New York: Methuen. 1985. 191-205.

2136

Berger, Karol. "Prospero's Art." *Shakespeare Studies.* 1977. 10: 211-39.

2137

Bergeron, David M. "The Tempest/*Tmp.*" *Essays in Literature.* (Western Illinois University) 1980. 7: 3-9.

2138

Brailow, David G. "Prospero's 'Old Brain': The Old Man as Metaphor in *Tmp.*" *Shakespeare Studies.* 1981. 14: 285-303.

2139

Brockbank, Philip. "*Tmp:* Conventions of Art and Empire." *Later Shakespeare.* Brown, John Russell, and Harris, Bernard, eds. Stratford upon Avon Studies 8. London: Arnold. 1966. 183-201.

2140

Brower, Reuben A. "The Heresy of Plot." *English Institute Essays 1951.* 1952. 44-69.

2141

Brower, Reuben A. "The Mirror of Analogy: *Tmp.*" *The Fields of Light: An Experiment in Critical Reading.* New York: Oxford University Press. 1951. 95-122.

2142

Brown, Paul. "'This Thing of Darkness I Acknowledge Mine': *Tmp* and the Discourse of Colonialism." *Political Shakespeare.* Dollimore, Jonathan, and Sinfield, Alan, eds. Manchester: Manchester University Press. 1985. 48-71.

2143

Cantor, Paul A. "Prospero's Republic: The Politics of Shakespeare's *Tmp.*" *Shakespeare as Political Thinker*. Alvis, John, and West, Thomas G., eds. Durham, N. C.: Carolina Academic Press. 1981. 239-55.

2144

Cantor, Paul A. "Shakespeare's *Tmp*: The Wise Man as Hero." *SQ.* 1980. 31: 64-75.

2145

Comito, Terry. "Caliban's Dream: The Topography of Some Shakespeare Gardens." *Shakespeare Studies*. 1981. 14: 23-54.

2146

Corfield, Cosmo. "Why Does Prospero Abjure his 'Rough Magic?'." *SQ.* 1985. 36: 31-48.

2147

Curry, Walter C. "Sacerdotal Science in Shakespeare's *Tmp.*" *Shakespeare's Philosophical Patterns*. Baton Rouge: Louisiana State University Press. 1937. 163-99.

2148

Dobrée, Bonamy. *"Tmp."* *Essays and Studies by Members of the English Association*. 1952. N.S. 5: 13-25.

2149

Dorsinville, Max. *Caliban Without Prospero*. Erin, Ontario: Press Porcépic. 1974.

2150

Driscoll, James P. "The Shakespearean Metastance: The Perspective of *Tmp.*" *Shakespeare: Contemporary Critical Approaches*. Garvin, Harry R., ed. Lewisburgh, Pa.: Bucknell University Press; London and Toronto: Associated University Presses. 1980. 154-69.

2151

Estrin, Barbara L. "Telling the Magician from the Magic in *Tmp.*" *Shakespeare: Contemporary Critical Approaches*. Garvin, Harry R., ed. Lewisburgh, Pa.: Bucknell University Press; London and Toronto: Associated University Presses. 1980. 170-87.

2152

Felperin, Howard. "Romance and Romanticism." *Critical Inquiry*. 1980. 6: 691-706.

2153

Fitz, L. T. "Mental Torment and the Figurative Method of *Tmp.*" *English Miscellany*. 1975-76. 25: 135-62.

2154

Fitz, L. T. "The Vocabulary of the Environment in *Tmp.*" *SQ*. 1975. 26: 42-7.

2155

Frey, Charles. "*Tmp* and the New World." *SQ*. 1979. 30: 29-41.

2156

Garber, Marjorie. "The Eye of the Storm: Structure and Myth in Shakespeare's *Tmp.*" *Hebrew University Studies in Literature*. 1980. 8: 13-43.

2157

Gesner, Carol. "*Tmp* as Pastoral Romance." *SQ* . 1959. 10: 531-9.

2158

Gilman, Ernest B. "'All Eyes': Prospero's Inverted Masque." *Renaissance Quarterly*. 1980. 33: 214-30.

2159

Grant, R. A. D. "Providence, Authority, and the Moral Life in *Tmp.*" *Shakespeare Studies*. 1983. 16: 235-63.

2160

Grazia, Margreta de. "*Tmp*: Gratuitous Movement or Action Without Kibes and Pinches." *Shakespeare Studies*. 1981. 14: 249-65.

2161

Hartwig, Joan. *Shakespeare's Tragicomic Vision*. Baton Rouge: Louisiana State University Press. 1972.

2162

Hoeniger, F. D. "Prospero's Storm and Miracle." *SQ*. 1956. 7: 33-8.

2163

Howard, Jean E. "Shakespeare's Creation of a Fit Audience for *Tmp.*" *Shakespeare: Contemporary Critical Approaches*. Garvin, Harry R., ed. Lewisburgh, Pa.: Bucknell University Press; London and Toronto: Associ-ated University Presses. 1980. 142-53.

2164

Hulme, Peter. "Hurricanes in the Caribbees: The Constitution of the Discourse of English Colonialism." *1642: Literature and Power in the Seventeenth Century*. Barker, Francis, et al, eds. Colchester: University of

Essex. 1981. 55-83.

2165

Hunt, Maurice. "Contrary Comparisons in *Tmp.*" *Shakespeare: Contemporary Critical Approaches.* Garvin, Harry R., ed. Lewisburgh, Pa.: Bucknell University Press; London and Toronto: Associated University Presses. 1980. 132-41.

2166

Hunt, Maurice. "'Stir' and Work in Shakespeare's Last Plays." *Studies in English Literature.* 1982. 22: 285-304.

2167

James, D. G. *The Dream of Prospero.* Oxford: Oxford University Press. 1967.

2168

Knight, G. Wilson. "Caliban as a Red Man." *Shakespeare's Styles: Essays in Honour of Kenneth Muir.* Edwards, Philip, et al, eds. Cambridge: Cambridge University Press. 1980. 205-20.

2169

Knox, Bernard. "*Tmp* and the Ancient Comic Tradition." *English Institute Essays 1954.* 1955. 52-73.

2170

Leininger, Lorie Jerrell. "Cracking the Code of *Tmp.*" *Shakespeare: Contemporary Critical Approaches.* Garvin, Harry R., ed. Lewisburgh, Pa.: Bucknell University Press; London and Toronto: Associated University Presses. 1980. 121-31.

2171

Leininger, Lorie Jerrell. "The Miranda Trap: Sexism and Racism in Shakespeare's *Tmp.*" *The Woman's Part.* Lenz, Carolyn Ruth Swift, et al, eds. Urbana, Chicago, and London: University of Illinois Press. 1980. 285-94.

2172

Loughrey, Bryan, and Taylor, Neil. "Ferdinand and Miranda at Chess." *Shakespeare Survey.* 1982. 35: 113-18.

2173

McGovern, D. S. "'Tempus' in *Tmp.*" *English.* (London) 1983. 32: 201-14.

2174

MacHovec, Frank J. "Shakespeare on Hypnosis: *Tmp.*" *American Journal of Clinical Hypnosis.* 1981. 24: 73-8.

2175

McPeek, James A. S. "The Genesis of Caliban." *Philological Quarterly.* 1946. 25: 378-81.

2176

Martz, William J. *The Place of* Tmp *in Shakespeare's Universe of Comedy.* Lawrence, Kansas: Coronado Press. 1978.

2177

Marx, Leo. "Shakespeare's American Fable." *The Machine in the Garden: Technology and the Pastoral Ideal in America.* New York: Oxford University Press. 1964. 34-72.

2178

Miko, Stephen J. "Tempest." *English Literary History.* 1982. 49: 1-17.

2179

Moser, Fernando de Mello. "The Island and the Vision: English Renaissance Approaches to the Problem of Perfection." *Studia Anglica Posnaniensia.* 1979. 11: 155-62.

2180

Mowat, Barbara A. "Prospero, Agrippa, and Hocus Pocus." *English Literary Renaissance.* 1981. 11: 281-303.

2181

Neill, Michael. "Remembrance and Revenge: *Ham, Mac, Tmp.*" *Jonson and Shakespeare.* Donaldson, Ian, ed. Canberra: Australian National University; Atlantic Highlands, N. J.: Humanities Press. 1983. 35-56.

2182

Nuttall, A. D. *Two Concepts of Allegory: A Study of Shakespeare's* Tmp *and the Logic of Allegorical Expression.* London: Routledge and Kegan Paul; New York: Barnes and Noble. 1967.

2183

Orgel, Stephen K. "New Uses of Adversity: Tragic Experience in *Tmp.*" *In Defense of Reading.* Brower, Reuben A., and Poirier, Richard, eds. New York: Dutton. 1962. 110-32.

2184

Orgel, Stephen K. "Prospero's Wife." *Representations.* 1984. 8: 1-13.

2185

Palmer, D. J., ed. *Shakespeare,* Tmp: *A Casebook.* London: Macmillan. 1968.

2186

Pearson, D'Orsay W. "'Unless I Be Reliev'd by Prayer': *Tmp* in Perspective." *Shakespeare Studies.* 1974. 7: 253-82.

2187

Peterson, Douglas L. "*Tmp* and Ideal Comedy." *New York Literary Forum.* 1980. 5-6: 99-110.

2188

Peterson, Douglas L. *Time, Tide, and Tempest: A Study of Shakespeare's Romances.* San Marino, California: Huntington Library Press. 1973.

2189

Petry, Alice Hall. "Knowledge in *Tmp.*" *Modern Language Studies.* 1980-81. 11: 27-32.

2190

Phillips, James E. "*Tmp* and the Renaissance Idea of Man." *SQ.* 1964. 15: 147-59.

2191

Platt, Michael. "Shakespeare's Apology for Poetic Wisdom." *Shakespeare and the Arts.* Cary, Cecile Williamson, and Limouze, Henry S., eds. Washington, D. C.: University Press of America. 1982. 231-44.

2192

Sharp, Sister Corona. "Caliban: The Primitive Man's Evolution." *Shakespeare Studies.* 1981. 14: 267-83.

2193

Srigley, Michael. *Images of Regeneration: A Study of Shakespeare's* Tmp *and Its Cultural Background.* Uppsala: Almqvist and Wiksell. 1985.

2194

Still, Colin. *Shakespeare's Mystery Play: A Study of* Tmp. London: Palmer. 1921. Enlarged and clarified as *The Timeless Theme.* London: Nicholson and Watson, 1936.

2195

Stoll, Elmer Edgar. "*Tmp.*" *PMLA.* 1932. 47: 699-726.

2196

Strachey, Lytton. "Shakespeare's Final Period." *Books and Characters, French and English.* London: Chatto and Windus; New York: Harcourt,

Brace. 1922. 49-69. First published 1906.

2197

Sundelson, David. "'So Rare a Wonder'd Father': Prospero's *Tmp.*" *Representing Shakespeare.* Schwartz, Murray M., and Kahn, Coppélia, eds. Baltimore and London: Johns Hopkins University Press. 1980. 33-53.

2198

Tovey, Barbara. "Shakespeare's Apology for Imitative Poetry: *Tmp* and *The Republic.*" *Interpretation.* 1983. 11: 275-316.

2199

Traversi, Derek A. "*Tmp.*" *Scrutiny.* 1949. 16: 127-57.

2200

Walter, James. "From Tempest to Epilogue: Augustine's Allegory in Shakespeare's Drama." *PMLA.* 1983. 98: 60-76.

2201

William, David. "*Tmp* on the Stage." *Jacobean Theatre.* Brown, John Russell, and Harris, Bernard, eds. Stratford-upon-Avon Studies 1. London: Arnold. 1960. 133-58.

2202

Wilson, J. Dover. *The Meaning of* Tmp. Newcastle upon Tyne: Literary and Philosophical Society. 1936.

See also works listed under *Comedy: The Late Romances*, especially by Frye, Gesner, Kay, Mowat, and Yates.

Timon of Athens

2203

Bergeron, David M. "Alchemy and *Tim.*" *College Language Association Journal.* 1970. 13: 364-73.

2204

Bergeron, David M. "*Tim* and Morality Drama." *College Language Association Journal.* 1967. 10: 181-8.

2205

Bradbrook, Muriel C. "The Comedy of Timon: A Reveling Play of the Inner Temple." *Renaissance Drama.* 1966. 9: 83-103.

2206

Bradbrook, Muriel C. *The Tragic Pageant of* Tim. Cambridge: Cambridge University Press. 1966. Reprinted as "Blackfriars: The Pageant of *Tim*." *Shakespeare the Craftsman*. New York: Barnes and Noble. London: Chatto and Windus, 1969. 144-67.

2207

Butler, Francelia. *The Strange Critical Fortunes of Shakespeare's* Tim. Ames: Iowa State University Press. 1966.

2208

Campbell, Oscar James. *Shakespeare's Satire*. New York: Oxford University Press; London: Milford. 1943. 168-97.

2209

Collins, A. S. "*Tim*: A Reconsideration." *Review of English Studies*. 1946. 22: 96-108.

2210

Cook, David. "*Tim*." *Shakespeare Survey*. 1963. 16: 83-94.

2211

Davidson, Clifford. "*Tim*: The Iconography of False Friendship." *Huntington Library Quarterly*. 1980. 43: 181-200.

2212

De Alvarez, Leo Paul S. "*Tim*." *Shakespeare as Political Thinker*. Alvis, John, and West, Thomas G., eds. Durham, N. C.: Carolina Academic Press. 1981. 157-79.

2213

Ellis-Fermor, Una. "*Tim*: An Unfinished Play." *Review of English Studies*. 1942. 18: 270-83.

2214

Empson, William. "Timon's Dog." *The Structure of Complex Words*. London: Chatto and Windus; Toronto: Clarke Irwin; New York: New Directions. 1951. 175-84.

2215

Erlich, Avi. "Neither to Give nor to Receive: Narcissism in *Tim*." *CUNY English Forum*. Brody, Saul N., and Schecter, Harold, eds. New York: AMS Press. 1985. Vol. I. 215-30.

2216

Farnham, Willard E. "The Beast Theme in Shakespeare's *Tim*." *Essays and Studies by Members of the Department of English, University of California*.

(University of Calif. Publications in English vol. 14). Berkeley and Los
Angeles: University of California Press. 1943. 49-56.

2217

Goldstein, Leonard. "Alcibiades' Revolt in *Tim.*" *Zeitschrift für Anglistik
und Amerikanistik*. 1967. 15: 256-78.

2218

Honigmann, E. A. J. "*Tim.*" *SQ*. 1961. 12: 3-20.

2219

Kernan, Alvin. *The Cankered Muse: Satire of the English Renaissance*. New
Haven and London: Yale University Press. 1959. 198-205.

2220

Knight, G. Wilson. "*Tim* and Buddhism." *Essays in Criticism*. 1980. 30:
105-23.

2221

Knight, G. Wilson. "*Tim* and its Dramatic Descendants." *Review of English
Studies*. 1961. 2: 9-18.

2222

Knights, L. C. "*Tim.*" *The Morality of Art: Essays Presented to G. Wilson
Knight*. Jefferson, D. W., ed. New York: Barnes and Noble; London:
Routledge and Kegan Paul. 1969. 1-17.

2223

Lancashire, Anne. "*Tim*: Shakespeare's *Dr. Faustus*." *SQ*. 1970. 21: 35-44.

2224

Levin, Harry. "Shakespeare's Misanthrope." *Shakespeare Survey*. 1973. 26:
89-94.

2225

Levitsky, Ruth. "*Tim*: Shakespeare's *Magnyfycence* and an Embryonic *Lr*."
Shakespeare Studies. 1978. 11: 107-21.

2226

Maxwell, J. C. "*Tim.*" *Scrutiny*. 1948. 15: 195-208.

2227

Merchant, W. Moelwyn. "*Tim* and the Conceit of Art." *SQ*. 1955. 6:
249-57.

2228

Morsberger, Robert E. "*Tim:* Tragedy or Satire?" *Shakespeare in the Southwest*. Stafford, T. J., ed. El Paso: Texas Western Press of the University
of Texas. 1969. 56-70.

2229

Muir, Kenneth. "*Tim* and the Cash-Nexus." *Modern Quarterly Miscellany.* 1946. 1: 67-76.

2230

Nowottny, Winifred M. T. "Acts IV and V of *Tim*." *SQ.* 1959. 10: 493-7.

2231

Pettet, E. C. "*Tim*: The Disruption of Feudal Morality." *Review of English Studies.* 1947. 23: 321-36.

2232

Ross, Daniel W. "'What a Number of Men Eats Timon': Consumption in *Tim*." *Iowa State Journal of Research.* 1985. 59: 273-84.

2233

Ruszkiewicz, John J., comp. Tim: *An Annotated Bibliography.* New York: Garland. 1986.

2234

Scott, William O. "The Paradox of Timon's Self-Cursing." *SQ.* 1984. 35: 290-304.

2235

Soellner, Rolf. Tim: *Shakespeare's Pessimistic Tragedy. With a Stage History by Gary Jay Williams.* Columbus: Ohio State University Press. 1979.

2236

Spencer, Terence J. B. "Shakespeare Learns the Value of Money: The Dramatist at Work on *Tim*." *Shakespeare Survey.* 1953. 6: 75-8.

2237

Walker, Lewis. "Fortune and Friendship in *Tim*." *Texas Studies in Literature and Language.* 1977. 18: 577-600.

2238

Walker, Lewis. "Money in *Tim*." *Philological Quarterly.* 1978. 57: 269-71.

2239

Woods, Andrew H. "Syphilis in Shakespeare's Tragedy of *Tim*." *American Journal of Psychiatry.* 1934. 91: 95-107.

See also works listed under *Tragedy*, especially by Farnham and Wilson.

2240

Barroll, J. Leeds. "Shakespeare and Roman History." *Modern Language Review.* 1958. 53: 327-43.

2241

Bolton, Joseph S. G. "*Tit*: Shakespeare at Thirty." *Studies in Philology.* 1933. 30: 208-24.

2242

Bowers, Fredson T. *Elizabethan Revenge Tragedy, 1587-1642.* Princeton: Princeton University Press. 1940.

2243

Bryant, J. A., Jr. "Aaron and the Pattern of Shakespeare's Villains." *Renaissance Papers.* 1984. 29-36.

2244

Broude, Ronald. "Four Forms of Vengeance in *Tit*." *Journal of English and Germanic Philology.* 1979. 78: 494-507.

2245

Brucher, Richard T. "'Tragedy, Laugh On': Comic Violence in *Tit*." *Renaissance Drama.* 1979. N.S. 10: 71-91.

2246

Calderwood, James L. "*Tit:* Word, Act, Authority." *Shakespearean Metadrama.* Minneapolis: University of Minnesota Press. 1971. 23-51.

2247

Cutts, John P. "Shadow and Substance: Structural Unity in *Tit*." *Comparative Drama.* 1968. 2: 161-72.

2248

Desmonde, William H. "The Ritual Origin of Shakespeare's *Tit*." *International Journal of Psycho-Analysis.* 1955. 36: 61-5.

2249

Ettin, Andrew V. "Shakespeare's First Roman Tragedy." *English Literary History.* 1970. 37: 325-41.

2250

Fawcett, Mary Laughlin. "Arms/Words/Tears: Language and the Body in *Tit*." *English Literary History.* 1983. 50: 261-77.

2251

Ford, P. Jeffrey. "Bloody Spectacle in Shakespeare's Roman Plays: The Politics and Aesthetics of Violence." *Iowa State Journal of Research.* 1980. 54: 481-9.

2252

Forker, Charles R. *"Tit, Ham,* and the Limits of Expressibility." *Hamlet Studies.* 1980. 2: 1-33.

2253

Hamilton, A. C. *"Tit:* The Form of Shakespearian Tragedy." *SQ.* 1963. 14: 201-13.

2254

Hastings, William T. "The Hardboiled Shakespeare." *Shakespeare Association Bulletin.* 1942. 17: 114-25.

2255

Hunter, G. K. "Shakespeare's Earliest Tragedies: *Tit* and *Rom."* *Shakespeare Survey.* 1974. 27: 1-9.

2256

Hunter, G. K. "Sources and Meanings in *Tit." Mirror up to Shakespeare: Essays in Honour of G. R. Hibbard.* Gray, J. C., ed. Toronto, Buffalo, and London: University of Toronto Press. 1984. 171-88.

2257

Law, Robert Adger. "The Roman Background of *Tit." Studies in Philology.* 1943. 40: 145-53.

2258

Sommers, Alan. "'Wilderness of Tigers': Structure and Symbolism in *Tit."* *Essays in Criticism.* 1960. 10: 275-89.

2259

Tricomi, Albert H. "The Aesthetics of Mutilation in *Tit." Shakespeare Survey.* 1974. 27: 11-19.

2260

Waith, Eugene M. "The Ceremonies of *Tit." Mirror up to Shakespeare: Essays in Honour of G. R. Hibbard.* Gray, J. C., ed. Toronto, Buffalo, and London: University of Toronto Press. 1984. 159-70.

2261

Waith, Eugene M. "The Metamorphosis of Violence in *Tit." Shakespeare Survey.* 1957. 10: 39-49.

2262

West, Grace Starry. "Going by the Book: Classical Allusions in Shakespeare's *Tit*." *Studies in Philology*. 1982. 79: 62-77.

2263

Williams, Jimmy Lee. "Thematic Links in Shakespeare's *Tit* and *Oth:* Sex, Racism and Exoticism, Point and Counterpoint." *Identity and Awareness in the Minority Experience: Past and Present*. Carter, George E., and Mouser, Bruce, eds. La Crosse: Institute for Minority Studies, University of Wisconsin - La Crosse. 1975. 158-90.

2264

Wilson, J. Dover. "*Tit* on the Stage in 1595." *Shakespeare Survey*. 1948. 1: 17-22.

See also works listed under *Tragedy*, especially by Brooke, Brown, and Harris, Danson, Maxwell, Spencer, and Spivack.

Troilus and Cressida

2265

Adamson, Jane. "Drama in the Mind: Entertaining Ideas in *Tro*." *Critical Review*. 1985. 27: 3-17.

2266

Berger, Harry, Jr. "*Tro*: The Observer as Basilisk." *Comparative Drama*. 1968. 2: 122-36.

2267

Bradbrook, Muriel C. "What Shakespeare Did to Chaucer's *Troilus and Criseyde*." *SQ*. 1958. 9: 311-19.

2268

Burns, M. M. "*Tro*: The Worst of Both Worlds." *Shakespeare Studies*. 1980. 13: 105-30.

2269

Cole, Douglas. "Myth and Anti-Myth: The Case of *Tro*." *SQ*. 1980. 31: 76-84.

2270

Cox, John D. "The Error of Our Eye in *Tro*." *Comparative Drama*. 1976. 10: 147-71.

2271

Dollimore, Jonathan. "Marston's *Antonio* Plays and Shakespeare's *Tro*: The Birth of a Radical Drama." *Essays and Studies (English Association)*. 1980. N.S. 33: 48-69.

2272

Dusinberre, Juliet. "*Tro* and the Definition of Beauty." *Shakespeare Survey*. 1983. 36: 85-95.

2273

Everett, Barbara. "The Inaction of *Tro*." *Essays in Criticism*. 1982. 32: 119-39.

2274

Farnham, Willard. "Troilus in Shapes of Infinite Desire." *SQ*. 1964. 15: 257-64.

2275

Fiedler, Leslie A. "Shakespeare's Commodity-Comedy: A Meditation on the Preface to the 1609 Quarto of *Tro*." *Shakespeare's "Rough Magic": Renaissance Essays in Honor of C. L. Barber*. Erickson, Peter, and Kahn, Coppélia, eds. Newark: University of Delaware Press; London and Toronto: Associated University Presses. 1985. 50-60.

2276

Flannery, Christopher. "*Tro:* Poetry or Philosophy?" *Shakespeare as Political Thinker*. Alvis, John, and West, Thomas G., eds. Durham, N. C.: Carolina Academic Press. 1981. 145-56.

2277

Fly, Richard D. "Monumental Mockery: *Tro* and the Perversities of Medium." *Shakespeare's Mediated World*. Amherst: University of Massachusetts Press. 1976. 27-51.

2278

Foakes, R. A. "*Tro* Reconsidered." *University of Toronto Quarterly*. 1963. 32: 142-54.

2279

Freund, Elizabeth. "'Ariachne's Broken Woof': The Rhetoric of Citation in *Tro*." *Shakespeare and the Question of Theory*. Parker, Patricia, and Hartman, Geoffrey, eds. New York and London: Methuen. 1985. 19-36.

2280

Gagen, Jean. "Hector's Honor." *SQ*. 1968. 19: 129-37.

2281

Girard, René. "The Politics of Desire in *Tro.*" *Shakespeare and the Question of Theory.* Parker, Patricia, and Hartman, Geoffrey, eds. New York and London: Methuen. 1985. 188-209.

2282

Greene, Gayle. "Language and Value in Shakespeare's *Tro.*" *Studies in English Literature.* 1981. 21: 271-85.

2283

Greene, Gayle. "Shakespeare's Cressida: 'A Kind of Self'." *The Woman's Part.* Lenz, Carolyn Ruth Swift, et al, eds. Urbana, Chicago, and London: University of Illinois Press. 1980. 133-49.

2284

Helton, Tinsley. "Paradox and Hypothesis in *Tro.*" *Shakespeare Studies.* 1977. 10: 115-31.

2285

Jagendorf, Zvi. "All Against One in *Tro.*" *English.* (London) 1982. 31: 199-210.

2286

Jago, David M. "The Uniqueness of *Tro.*" *SQ.* 1978. 29: 20-7.

2287

Kaufmann, R. J. "Ceremonies for Chaos: The Status of *Tro.*" *English Literary History.* 1965. 32: 139-59.

2288

Kaula, David. "Will and Reason in *Tro.*" *SQ.* 1961. 12: 271-83.

2289

Kermode, Frank. "Opinion, Truth, and Value." *Essays in Criticism.* 1955. 5: 181-7.

2290

Kimbrough, Robert. *Shakespeare's Tro and Its Setting.* Oxford: Oxford University Press; Cambridge, Mass.: Harvard University Press. 1964.

2291

Knights, L. C. "*Tro* Again." *Scrutiny.* 1951. 18: 144-57.

2292

Langman, F. H. "*Tro.*" *Jonson and Shakespeare.* Donaldson, Ian, ed. Canberra: Australian National University; London: Macmillan; Atlantic Highlands, N. J.: Humanities Press. *Jonson and Shakespeare.* 1983. 57-73.

2293

Lawrence, W. W. "Troilus, Cressida, and Thersites." *Modern Language Review*. 1942. 37: 422-37.

2294

Lynch, Stephen J. "Shakespeare's Cressida: 'A Woman of Quick Sense'." *Philological Quarterly*. 1984. 63: 357-68.

2295

McAlindon, T. "Language, Style, and Meaning in *Tro*." *PMLA*. 1969. 84: 29-43.

2296

Medcalf, Stephen. "Epilogue: From *Troilus* [Chaucer's] to *Tro*." *The Later Middle Ages*. Medcalf, Stephen, ed. London: Methuen; New York: Holmes and Meier. 1981. 291-305.

2297

Muir, Kenneth. "*Tro*." *Shakespeare Survey*. 1955. 8: 28-39.

2298

Newlin, Jeanne T. "The Modernity of *Tro*: The Case for Theatrical Criticism." *Harvard Library Bulletin*. 1969. 17: 353-73.

2299

Nowottny, Winifred M. T. "'Opinion' and 'Value' in *Tro*." *Essays in Criticism*. 1954. 4: 282-96.

2300

Oates, J. C. "The Ambiguity of *Tro*." *SQ*. 1966. 17: 141-50.

2301

Okerlund, Arlene N. "In Defense of Cressida: Character as Metaphor." *Women's Studies*. 1980. 7: 1-17.

2302

Presson, Robert K. *Shakespeare's* Tro *and the Legends of Troy*. Madison: University of Wisconsin Press. 1953.

2303

Rabkin, Norman. "*Tro*: The Uses of the Double Plot." *Shakespeare Studies*. 1965. 1: 265-82.

2304

Richards, I. A. "*Tro* and Plato." *Hudson Review*. 1948. 1: 362-76.

2305

Robertson, Hugh. "*Tro* and *MM* in Their Age: Shakespeare's Thought in Its Context." *Self and Society in Shakespeare's* Tro *and* MM. Jowitt, J. A.,

and Taylor, R. K. S., eds. Bradford: University of Leeds Centre for Adult
Education. 1982. 3-26.

2306

Rollins, Hyder E. "The Troilus-Cressida Story fom Chaucer to Shakespeare." *PMLA*. 1917. 32: 383-429.

2307

Shaw, William P. "*Tro*, V.iv-v, x: Giving Chaos a Name and a Local Habi-
tation." *Shakespeare and Renaissance Association of West Virginia:
Selected Papers*. 1977. 1: 24-48.

2308

Sinfield, Alan. "Kinds of Loving: Women in the Plays." *Self and Society in
Shakespeare's* Tro *and* MM. Jowitt, J. A., and Taylor, R. K. S., eds.
Bradford: University of Leeds Centre for Adult Education. 1982. 27-44.

2309

Smith, J. Oates. "Essence and Existence in Shakespeare's *Tro*." *Philological
Quarterly*. 1967. 46: 167-85.

2310

Snyder, Richard C. "Discovering a 'Dramaturgy of Human Relationships' in
Shakespearean Metadrama: *Tro*." *Shakespeare and the Arts*. Cary, Cecile
Williamson, and Limouze, Henry S., eds. Washington, D. C.: University
Press of America. 1982. 199-216.

2311

Soellner, Rolf. "Prudence and the Price of Helen: The Debate of the Tro-
jans in *Tro*." *SQ*. 1969. 20: 255-63.

2312

Southall, Raymond. "*Tro* and the Spirit of Capitalism." *Shakespeare in a
Changing World*. Kettle, Arnold, ed. London: Lawrence and Wishart.
1964. 217-32.

2313

Stafford, T. J. "Mercantile Imagery in *Tro*." *Shakespeare in the Southwest*.
Stafford, Tony J., ed. El Paso: Texas Western Press of the University of
Texas. 1969. 36-42.

2314

Stamm, Rudolf. "The Glass of Pandar's Praise: The Word-Scenery, Mirror
Passages, and Reported Scenes in Shakespeare's *Tro*." *Essays and Studies
(English Association)*. 1964. N.S. 17: 55-77.

2315

Stein, Arnold. "*Tro*: The Disjunctive Imagination." *English Literary History*. 1969. 36: 145-67.

2316

Takada, Yasunari. "How to Do Things With 'Fall-Out' Systems in *Tro*." *Shakespeare Studies*. 1981-82. 20: 33-58.

2317

Taylor, George C. "Shakespeare's Attitude Towards Love and Honor in *Tro*." *PMLA*. 1930. 45: 781-6.

2318

Thomson, Patricia. "Rant and Cant in *Tro*." *Essays and Studies*. (English Association) 1969. n.s. 22: 33-56.

2319

Traversi, Derek A. "*Tro*." *Scrutiny*. 1938. 7: 301-19.

2320

West, Thomas G. "The Two Truths of *Tro*." *Shakespeare as Political Thinker*. Alvis, John, and West, Thomas G., eds. Durham, N. C.: Carolina Academic Press. 1981. 127-43.

2321

Wilson, Douglas B. "The Commerce of Desire: Freudian Narcissism in Chaucer's *Troilus and Criseyde* and Shakespeare's *Tro*." *English Language Notes*. 1983. 21: 11-22.

2322

Yoder, R. A. "'Sons and Daughters of the Game': An Essay on Shakespeare's *Tro*." *Shakespeare Survey*. 1972. 25: 11-25.

See also works listed under *Comedy: The Problem Comedies*, especially by Lawrence and Rossiter.

2323

Barnet, Sylvan. "Charles Lamb and the Tragic Malvolio." *Philological Quarterly*. 1954. 33: 178-88.

2324

Barton, Anne. "*AYL* and *TN:* Shakespeare's Sense of an Ending." *Shakespearian Comedy*. Bradbury, Malcolm, and Palmer, David J., eds. Stratford-upon-Avon Studies 14. London: Arnold. 1972. 160-80.

2325

Berry, Ralph. "*TN*: The Experience of the Audience." *Shakespeare Survey*. 1981. 34: 111-19.

2326

Booth, Stephen. "*TN* 1.1: The Audience as Malvolio." *Shakespeare's "Rough Magic": Renaissance Essays in Honor of C. L. Barber*. Erickson, Peter, and Kahn, Coppélia, eds. Newark: University of Delaware Press; London and Toronto: Associated University Presses. 1985. 149-67.

2327

Carroll, William C. "The Ending of *TN* and the Tradition of Metamorphosis." *New York Literary Forum*. 1980. 5-6: 49-61.

2328

Downer, Alan S. "Feste's Night." *College English*. 1952. 13: 258-65.

2329

Eagleton, Terence. "Language and Reality in *TN*." *Critical Quarterly*. 1967. 9: 217-28.

2330

Everett, Barbara. "Or What You Will." *Essays in Criticism*. 1985. 35: 294-314.

2331

Greif, Karen. "Plays and Playing in *TN*." *Shakespeare Survey*. 1981. 34: 121-30.

2332

Hartman, Geoffrey H. "Shakespeare's Poetical Character in *TN*." *Shakespeare and the Question of Theory*. Parker, Patricia, and Hartman, Geoffrey, eds. New York and London: Methuen. 1985. 37-53.

2333

Hartwig, Joan. "Feste's 'Whirligig' and the Comic Providence of *TN*." *English Literary History.* 1973. 40: 501-13.

2334

Hollander, John. "*TN* and the Morality of Indulgence." *Sewanee Review.* 1959. 67: 220-38.

2335

Jenkins, Harold. "Shakespeare's *TN*." *Rice Institute Pamphlet.* 1959. 45: 19-42.

2336

Kimbrough, Robert. "Androgyny Seen Through Shakespeare's Disguise." *SQ.* 1982. 33: 17-33.

2337

Langman, F. H. "Comedy and Saturnalia: The Case of *TN*." *Southern Review* (Australia). 1974. 7: 102-22.

2338

Leech, Clifford. TN *and Shakespearian Comedy.* Halifax: Dalhousie University Press; Toronto: University of Toronto Press. 1968.

2339

Levin, Richard A. "*TN, MV*, and Two Alternate Approaches to Shakespearean Comedy." *English Studies.* 1978. 59: 336-43.

2340

Levin, Richard A. "Viola: Dr. Johnson's 'Excellent Schemer'." *Durham University Journal.* 1979. N.S. 40: 213-22.

2341

Lewalski, Barbara K. "Thematic Patterns in *TN*." *Shakespeare Studies.* 1965. 1: 168-81.

2342

Logan, Thad Jenkins. "*TN*: The Limits of Festivity." *Studies in English Literature.* 1982. 22: 223-38.

2343

Markels, Julian. "Shakespeare's Confluence of Tragedy and Comedy: *TN* and *Lr*." *SQ.* 1964. 15: 75-88.

2344

McAvoy, William C., comp. TN: *A Bibliography to Supplement the New Variorum Edition of 1901.* New York: Modern Language Association. 1984.

2345

Palmer D. J. "Art and Nature in *TN.*" *Critical Quarterly.* 1967. 9: 201-12.

2346

Salingar, L. G. "The Design of *TN.*" *SQ.* 1958. 9: 117-39.

2347

Schleiner, Winfried. "Orsino and Viola: Are the Names of Serious Characters in *TN* Meaningful?" *Shakespeare Studies.* 1983. 16: 135-41.

2348

Schwartz, Elias. "*TN* and the Meaning of Shakespearean Comedy." *College English.* 1967. 28: 508-19.

2349

Seiden, Melvin. "Malvolio Reconsidered." *University Review.* 1961. 28: 105-14.

2350

Siegel, Paul N. "Malvolio: Comic Puritan Automaton." *New York Literary Forum.* 1980. 5-6: 217-30.

2351

Slights, Camille W. "The Principle of Recompense in *TN.*" *Modern Language Review.* 1982. 77: 537-46.

2352

Slights, William W. E. "'Maid and Man' in *TN.*" *Journal of English and Germanic Philology.* 1981. 80: 327-48.

2353

Summers, Joseph H. "The Masks of *TN.*" *University Review.* 1955. 22: 25-32.

2354

Tilley, Morris P. "The Organic Unity of *TN.*" *PMLA.* 1914. 29: 550-66.

2355

Trousdale, Marion. "Semiotics and Shakespeare's Comedies." *Shakespearean Comedy.* Charney, Maurice, ed. New York: New York Literary Forum. 1980. 245-55.

2356

Williams, Porter, Jr. "Mistakes in *TN* and Their Resolution: A Study in Some Relationships of Plot and Theme." *PMLA.* 1961. 76: 193-9.

2357

Woodbridge, Linda. "'Fire in Your Heart and Brimstone in Your Liver': Towards an Unsaturnalian *TN.*" *Southern Review* (Australia). 1984. 17:

270-91.

Yearling, Elizabeth M. "Language, Theme, and Character in *TN*." *Shakespeare Survey*. 1982. 35: 79-86.

See also works listed under *Comedy: General Studies*, especially by Barber, Brown, and Salingar, and under *Comedy: The Middle and Romantic Comedies*, especially by Leggatt.

The Two Gentlemen of Verona

2359

Brooks, Harold F. "Two Clowns in a Comedy (to Say Nothing of the Dog): Speed, Launce (and Crab) in *TGV*." *Essays and Studies* (English Association). 1963. N.S. 16: 91-100.

2360

Cook, Ann Jennalie. "Shakespeare's Gentlemen." *Jahrbuch der Deutschen Shakespeare-Gesellschaft West*. 1985. 9-27.

2361

Craig, Hardin. "Shakespeare's Development as a Dramatist in the Light of His Experience." *Studies in Philology*. 1942. 39: 226-338.

2362

Danby, John F. "Shakespeare Criticism and *TGV*." *Critical Quarterly*. 1960. 2: 309-21.

2363

Godshalk, William Leigh. "The Structural Unity of *TGV*." *Studies in Philology*. 1969. 66: 168-81.

2364

Holmberg, Arthur. "*TGV*: Shakespearean Comedy as a Rite of Passage." *Queen's Quarterly*. 1983. 90: 33-44.

2365

Lindenbaum, Peter. "Education in *TGV*." *Studies in English Literature*. 1975. 15: 229-44.

2366

Perry, Thomas A. "Proteus, Wry-Transformed Traveller." *SQ* . 1954. 5: 33-40.

2367

Price, Hereward T. "Shakespeare as a Critic." *Philological Quarterly.* 1941. 20: 390-9.

2368

Rossky, William. "*TGV* as Burlesque." *English Literary Renaissance.* 1982. 12: 210-19.

2369

Slights, Camille Wells. "*TGV* and the Courtesy Book Tradition." *Shakespeare Studies.* 1983. 16: 13-31.

2370

Vyvyan, John. *Shakespeare and the Rose of Love.* London: Chatto and Windus; New York: Barnes and Noble; Toronto: Clarke Irwin. 1960.

2371

Weimann, Robert. "Laughing with the Audience: *TGV* and the Popular Tradition of Comedy." *Shakespeare Survey.* 1969. 22: 35-42.

2372

Wells, Stanley. "The Failure of *TGV*." *Shakespeare-Jahrbuch.* 1963. 99: 161-73.

See also works listed under *Comedy: General Studies*, especially by Ralph Berry, Charlton, Evans, R. G. Hunter, Pettet, and Salingar, and the works listed under *Comedy: The Middle and Romantic Comedies*, especially by Leggatt.

Venus and Adonis

2373

Allen, Don Cameron. "On *Ven.*" *Elizabethan and Jacobean Studies Presented to Frank Percy Wilson in Honor of His Seventieth Birthday.* Davis, Herbert, and Gardner, Helen, eds. Oxford: Clarendon. 1959. 100-11.

2374

Allen, Michael J. B. "The Chase: The Development of a Renaissance Theme." *Comparative Literature.* 1968. 20: 301-12.

2375

Asals, Heather. "*Ven*: The Education of a Goddess." *Studies in English Literature.* 1973. 13: 31-51.

2376

Beauregard, David N. *"Ven*: Shakespeare's Representation of the Passions."
Shakespeare Studies. 1975. 8: 83-98.

2377

Bowers, R. H. "Anagnorisis, or the Shock of Recognition in Shakespeare's
Ven." Renaissance Papers 1962. 1963. 3-8.

2378

Bradbrook, Muriel C. "Beasts and Gods: Greene's *Groats-Worth of Witte*
and the Social Purpose of *Ven." Shakespeare Survey.* 1962. 15: 62-72.

2379

Cantelupe, Eugene B. "An Iconographical Interpretation of *Ven,* Shakespeare's Ovidian Comedy." *SQ.* 1963. 14: 141-51.

2380

Daigle, Lennet J. *"Ven*: Some Traditional Contexts." *Shakespeare Studies.*
1980. 13: 31-46.

2381

Doebler, John. "The Many Faces of Love: Shakespeare's *Ven." Shakespeare*
Studies. 1983. 16: 33-43.

2382

Hamilton, A. C. *"Ven." Studies in English Literature.* 1961. 1: 1-15.

2383

Hatto, A. T. *"Ven* -- and the Boar." *Modern Language Review.* 1946. 41:
353-61.

2384

Jahn, J. D. "The Lamb of Lust: The Role of Adonis in Shakespeare's *Ven."*
Shakespeare Studies. 1972. 6: 11-25.

2385

Kahn, Coppélia. "Self and Eros in *Ven." Centennial Review.* 1976. 20:
351-71.

2386

Keach, William. *Elizabethan Erotic Narratives: Irony and Pathos in the Ovid-*
ian Poetry of Shakespeare, Marlowe, and Their Contemporaries. New
Brunswick, N. J.: Rutgers University Press; Hassocks, Sussex: Harvester
Press. 1977. 52-84.

2387

Leech, Clifford. "Venus and Her Nun: Portraits of Women in Love by
Shakespeare and Marlowe." *Studies in English Literature.* 1965. 5: 247-68.

2388

Lever, J. W. "Venus and the Second Chance." *Shakespeare Survey.* 1962.
15: 81-8.

2389

Miller, Robert P. "Venus, Adonis, and the Horses." *English Literary History.* 1952. 19: 249-64.

2390

Muir, Kenneth. *"Ven:* Comedy or Tragedy?" *Shakespearean Essays.* Thaler,
Alwin, and Sanders, Norman, eds. Knoxville: University of Tennessee
Press. 1964. 1-13.

2391

Price, Hereward T. "Function of Imagery in *Ven." Papers of the Michigan
Academy of Science, Arts and Letters.* 1945. 31: 275-97.

2392

Prince, F.T. *William Shakespeare: The Poems.* London: Longmans, Green.
1963. 7-11.

2393

Putney, Rufus. "Venus 'Agonistes'." *University of Colorado Studies in Language and Literature.* 1953. 4: 52-66.

2394

Putney, Rufus. *"Ven:* Amour with Humour." *Philological Quarterly.* 1941.
20: 533-48.

2395

Rabkin, Norman. *"Ven* and the Myth of Love." *Pacific Coast Studies in
Shakespeare.* McNeir, Waldo F., and Greenfield, Thelma N., eds. Eugene:
University of Oregon Press. 1966. 20-32.

2396

Rebhorn, Wayne A. "Mother Venus: Temptation in Shakespeare's *Ven."
Shakespeare Studies.* 1978. 11: 1-19.

2397

Sheidley, William E. "'Unless It Be a Boar': Love and Wisdom in
Shakespeare's *Ven." Modern Language Quarterly.* 1974. 35: 3-15.

2398

Streitberger, W. R. "Ideal Conduct in *Ven." SQ* . 1975. 26: 285-91.

2399

Truax, Elizabeth. "Venus, Lucrece, and Bess of Hardwick: Portraits to
Please." *Shakespeare and the Arts.* Cary, Cecile Williamson, and Limouze,

Henry S., eds. Washington, D. C.: University Press of America. 1982.
35-56.

2400

Uhlmann, Dale C. "Red and White Imagery in *Ven.*" *Shakespeare and Renaissance Association of West Virginia: Selected Papers.* 1983. 8: 15-20.

2401

Vessey, D. W. Thomson. "Venery and Sophistication: Shakespeare's *Ven* and Marlowe's *Hero and Leander.*" *The Bard* (London). 1981. 3: 74-91.

2402

Williams, Gordon. "The Coming of Age of Shakespeare's Adonis." *Modern Language Review.* 1983. 78: 769-76.

The Winter's Tale

2403

Barber, C. L. "'Thou That Beget'st Him That Did Thee Beget': Transformation in *Per* and *WT.*" *Shakespeare Survey.* 1969. 22: 59-67.

2404

Barber, Charles. "*WT* and Jacobean Society." *Shakespeare in a Changing World.* Kettle, Arnold, ed. London: Lawrence and Wishart. 1964. 233-52.

2405

Barkan, Leonard. "'Living Sculptures': Ovid, Michelangelo, and *WT.*" *English Literary History.* 1981. 48: 639-67.

2406

Bartholomeusz, Dennis. WT *in Performance in England and America, 1611-1976.* Cambridge: Cambridge University Press. 1982.

2407

Barton, Anne. "Leontes and the Spider: Language and Speaker in Shakespeare's Last Plays." *Shakespeare's Styles: Essays in Honour of Kenneth Muir.* Edwards, Philip, et al, eds. Cambridge: Cambridge University Press. 1980. 131-50.

2408

Battenhouse, Roy. "Theme and Structure in *WT.*" *Shakespeare Survey.* 1980. 33: 123-38.

2409

Bergeron, David M. "Hermione's Trial in *WT.*" *Essays in Theater.* 1984. 3: 3-12.

221

2410

Bethell, S. L. WT: *A Study*. London, New York and Toronto: Staples. 1947.

2411

Biggins, Dennis. "'Exit Pursued by a Beare': A Problem in *WT*." *SQ*. 1962. 13: 3-13.

2412

Bonjour, Adrien. "The Final Scene of *WT*." *English Studies*. 1952. 33: 193-208.

2413

Bonjour, Adrien. "Polixenes and the Winter of His Discontent." *English Studies*. 1969. 50: 206-12.

2414

Bryant, J. A., Jr. "Shakespeare's Allegory: *WT*." *Sewanee Review*. 1955. 63: 202-22.

2415

Bryant, Jerry H. "*WT* and the Pastoral Tradition." *SQ*. 1963. 14: 387-98.

2416

Coghill, Nevill. "Six Points of Stage-Craft in *WT*." *Shakespeare Survey*. 1958. 11: 31-41.

2417

Cox, Lee Sheridan. "The Role of Autolycus in *WT*." *Studies in English Literature*. 1969. 9: 283-301.

2418

Curtis, Harry, Jr. "The Year Growing Ancient: Formal Ambiguity in *WT*." *College Language Association Journal*. 1980. 23: 431-7.

2419

Cuvelier, Eliane. "'Perspective' in *WT*." *Cahiers Elisabéthains*. 1983. 23: 35-46.

2420

Davidson, Clifford. "The Iconography of Illusion and Truth in *WT*." *Shakespeare and the Arts*. Cary, Cecile Williamson, and Limouze, Henry S., eds. Washington, D. C.: University Press of America. 1982. 73-91.

2421

Ellis, John. "Rooted Affection: The Genesis of Jealousy in *WT*." *College English*. 1964. 25: 545-7.

2422

Engel, Wilson F., III. "Sculpture and the Art of Memory in Elizabethan and Jacobean Drama." *Modern Language Studies.* 1980. 10: 3-9.

2423

Erickson, Peter B. "Patriarchal Structures in *WT.*" *PMLA.* 1982. 97: 819-29.

2424

Ewbank, Inga-Stina. "The Triumph of Time in *WT.*" *Review of English Literature.* 1964. 5: 83-100.

2425

Felperin, Howard. "'Tongue-tied our Queen?': The Deconstruction of Presence in *WT.*" *Shakespeare and the Question of Theory.* Parker, Patricia, and Hartman, Geoffrey, eds. New York and London: Methuen. 1985. 3-18.

2426

Foakes, R. A. "Character and Dramatic Technique in *Cym* and *WT.*" *Studies in the Arts: Proceedings of the St. Peter's College Literary Society.* Warner, Francis, ed. Oxford: Blackwell. 1968. 116-30.

2427

Frey, Charles. *Shakespeare's Vast Romance: A Study of* WT. Columbia and London: University of Missouri Press. 1980.

2428

Frye, Northrop. "Recognition in *WT.*" *Essays on Shakespeare and Elizabethan Drama in Honor of Hardin Craig.* Hosley, Richard, ed. Columbia: University of Missouri Press. 1962. 235-46.

2429

Gurr, Andrew. "The Bear, The Statue, and Hysteria in *WT.*" *SQ.* 1983. 34: 420-5.

2430

Hardman, C. D. "Theory, Form, and Meaning in Shakespeare's *WT.*" *Review of English Studies.* 1985. 36: 228-35.

2431

Hartwig, Joan. "The Tragicomic Perspective of *WT.*" *English Literary History.* 1970. 37: 12-36.

2432

Hillman, Richard W. "The 'Gillyvors' Exchange in *WT.*" *English Studies in Canada.* 1979. 5: 16-23.

223

2433

Hoeniger, F. David. "The Meaning of *WT.*" *University of Toronto Quarterly.* 1950-51. 20: 11-26.

2434

Hughes, Merritt Y. "A Classical vs. a Social Approach to Shakespeare's Autolycus." *Shakespeare Association Bulletin.* 1940. 15: 219-26.

2435

Laroque, Francois. "Pagan Ritual, Christian Liturgy, and Folk Customs in *WT.*" *Cahiers Elisabéthains.* 1982. 22: 25-33.

2436

Latimer, Kathleen. "The Communal Action of *WT.*" *The Terrain of Comedy.* Cowan, Louise, ed. Dallas: Dallas Institute of Humanities and Culture. 1984. 125-42.

2437

Lindenbaum, Peter. "Time, Sexual Love, and the Uses of Pastoral in *WT.*" *Modern Language Quarterly.* 1972. 33: 3-22.

2438

Livingston, Mary L. "The Natural Art of *WT.*" *Modern Language Quarterly.* 1969. 30: 340-55.

2439

McDonald, Russ. "Poetry and Plot in *WT.*" *SQ* . 1985. 36: 315-29.

2440

Martz, Louis L. "Shakespeare's Humanist Enterprise: *WT.*" *English Renaissance Studies Presented to Dame Helen Gardner in Honour of her Seventieth Birthday.* Carey, John, ed. Oxford: Clarendon. 1980. 114-31.

2441

Matchett, William H. "Some Dramatic Techniques in *WT.*" *Shakespeare Survey.* 1969. 22: 93-108.

2442

Mowat, Barbara A. "A Tale of Sprights and Goblins." *SQ* . 1969. 20: 37-46.

2443

Muir, Kenneth. "The Conclusion of *WT.*" *The Morality of Art: Essays Presented to G. Wilson Knight.* Jefferson, D. W., ed. New York: Barnes and Noble; London: Routledge and Kegan Paul. 1969. 87-101.

2444

Muir, Kenneth, ed. *Shakespeare --* WT: *A Casebook.* London: Macmillan. 1968.

2445

Nathan, Norman. "Leontes' Provocation." *SQ*. 1968. 19: 19-24.

2446

Neely, Carol Thomas. "*WT*: The Triumph of Speech." *Studies in English Literature*. 1975. 15: 321-38.

2447

Nuttall, A. D. *Shakespeare:* WT. London: E. Arnold. 1966.

2448

Pafford, John H. P. "Music, and the Songs in *WT*." *SQ*. 1950. 10: 161-75.

2449

Palmer, Daryl W. "Entertainment, Hospitality, and Family in *WT*." *Iowa State Journal of Research*. 1985. 59: 253-61.

2450

Partridge, A. C. "*WT* in the Theatre: Structure and Interpretation." *Unisa English Studies*. 1982. 20: 1-5.

2451

Proudfoot, Richard. "Verbal Reminiscence and the Two-Part Structure of *WT*." *Shakespeare Survey*. 1976. 29: 67-78.

2452

Pyle, Fitzroy. WT: *A Commentary on the Structure*. London: Routledge and Kegan Paul; New York: Barnes and Noble. 1969.

2453

Rico, Barbara Roche. "From 'Speechless Dialect' to 'Prosperous Art': Shakespeare's Reca ling of the Pygmalion Image." *Huntington Library Quarterly*. 1985. 48: 285-95.

2454

Schanzer, Ernest. "The Structural Pattern of *WT*." *Review of English Literature*. 1964. 5: 72-82.

2455

Siegel, Paul N. "Leontes a Jealous Tyrant." *Review of English Studies*. 1950. 1: 302-7.

2456

Siemon, James Edward. "'But It Appears She Lives': Iteration in *WT*." *PMLA*. 1974. 89: 10-16.

2457

Smith, Jonathan. "The Language of Leontes." *SQ*. 1968. 19: 317-27.

2458

Taylor, Michael. "Innocence in *WT*." *Shakespeare Studies*. 1982. 15: 227-42.

2459

Tinkler, F. C. "*WT*." *Scrutiny*. 1937. 5: 344-64.

2460

Williams, John A. *The Natural Work of Art: The Experience of Romance in Shakespeare's* WT. Cambridge, Mass.: Harvard University Press; Oxford: Oxford University Press. 1967.

See also works listed under *Comedy: The Late Romances*, especially by Felperin, Hartwig, Kay, Knight, and Mowat; under *Comedy: the Problem Comedies*, especially by Foakes; and under *Comedy: General Studies*, especially by R. G. Hunter.

ARTHOS, John 515, 643, 1385, 1747, 1841
ASALS, Heather 2375
ASP, Carolyn 1386
ATKINS, G. Douglas 1293
AUBERLEN, Eckhard 1072
AUDEN, W[ystan] H[ugh] 900, 1387, 2133
AWOONOR, Kofi 2134
AYCOCK, Wendell M. 1491, 1682, 2091
BABB, Lawrence 599
BACHE, William B. 1478
BADY, David 1573
BAINES, Barbara J. 1897
BALD, R[obert] C[ecil] 1189
BALDO, Jonathan 756
BALDWIN, Dean R. 1159
BALDWIN, T[homas] W[hitfield] 15, 644, 2046
BAMBER, Linda 16
BARBER, Benjamin R. 1672
BARBER, C[esar] L[ombardi] 168, 269, 600, 645, 901, 1842, 2403
BARBER, Charles L. 902, 1001, 2404
BARISH, Jonas A. 17, 903, 1190, 1714
BARKAN, Leonard 2405
BARKER, Francis 2135, 2164
BARKER, Gerard A. 1843
BARNET, Sylvan 601, 1191, 1574, 2323
BARROLL, J[ohn] Leeds 544, 2240
BARRY, Jackson G. 2047
BARTHOLOMEUSZ, Dennis 1388, 2406
BARTLETT, John 18
BARTON, Anne 169, 602, 662, 1002, 1098, 1636, 1898, 2324, 2407
BASS, Eben 904
BATES, Paul A. 1844, 2048
BATTENHOUSE, Roy W. 757, 1160, 1479, 2408
BAUER, Robert J. 1192
BAWCUTT, N. W. 1480
BAXTER, John 1899
BAYLEY, John 391

BAYLEY, Peter 1393
BEAN, John C. 2103
BEAUCHAMP, Gorman 1039
BEAUREGARD, David N. 2376
BECK, Richard J. 905
BECKERMAN, Bernard 19
BEINER, G. 1350
BELLRINGER, A.W. 1099
BELSEY, Catherine 170, 392
BENNETT, Josephine Waters 516, 758, 1117, 1193, 1481
BENNETT, Kenneth C. 171
BENNETT, Robert B. 603
BENTLEY, Gerald Eades 20, 270
BEREK, Peter 1351
BERGER, Harry, Jr. 308, 906, 1194, 1389, 1390, 1575, 1715, 1900, 2266
BERGER, Karol 2136
BERGERON, David M[oore] 232, 271, 353, 474, 517, 712, 1901, 1929, 2104,
    2137, 2203, 2204, 2409
BERGGREN, Paula S. 21
BERKELEY, David 907
BERLIN, Normand 393
BERMAN, Ronald S. 1, 1003, 1040, 1073, 1161, 1482
BERNAD, Miguel A. 1391
BERRY, Edward I. 172, 309, 604, 908, 1074
BERRY, Francis 22, 1845
BERRY, Ralph 23, 173, 663, 664, 759, 1100, 1195, 1352, 1664, 1962, 2325
BERTRAM, Paul 1075
BETHELL, Samuel L[eslie] 24, 310, 1748, 2410
BETHURUM, Dorothy 1665
BEVINGTON, David M 2, 25, 660, 1041, 1963
BIGGINS, Dennis 2411
BILTON, Peter 26
BIRENBAUM, Harvey 1196, 1392
BIRJE-PATIL, J. 1483
BLACK, James 909, 1197, 1666, 1901, 1997
BLACK, Matthew W. 394, 395, 1902
BLACK, Michael 1393

BLACKER, Carmen 779
BLAKE, N[orman] F[rancis] 27
BLANPIED, John W. 311, 910
BLAYNEY, Peter W.M. 1198
BLIGH, John 28, 1101
BLISS, Lee 1076
BLISSETT, William 1394
BLISTEIN, Elmer M. 132, 219, 913, 1436
BLITS, Jan H. 1102
BLOOM, Alan 1903
BLOOM, Allan 1576
BLOOM, E. A. 2127
BLOOM, Edward A. 421, 1201, 1292
BOAS, Frederick S 1042
BODKIN, Maud 1749
BOGARD, Travis 1904
BOLTON, Joseph S. G 2241
BONAZZA, Blaze Odell 233
BOND, Ronald B. 1998
BONHEIM, Helmut W. 1199
BONHEIM, Jean 1969
BONI, John 1484
BONJOUR, Adrien 760, 761, 1103, 1162, 1163, 2412, 2413
BONNARD, Georges A. 1750, 1905
BONO, Barbara J. 545
BOOTH, Stephen 546, 762, 1200, 1395, 2049, 2326
BOOTH, Wayne C. 1396
BORIS, Edna Zwick 312
BOUGHNER, Daniel C. 911, 912, 1004, 1353, 1354, 1637
BOWDEN, William R. 1104
BOWERS, A. Robin 1874
BOWERS, Fredson T. 396, 547, 763, 764, 913, 2242
BOWERS, R. H. 2377
BOYER, Clarence Valentine 1964
BRACHER, Mark 605
BRADBROOK, Muriel C[lara] 518, 1355, 1485, 1486, 2205, 2206, 2267, 2378
BRADBURY, Malcolm 174, 390, 602, 810, 2324

BRADDY, Haldeen 765, 1005

BRADEN, Gordon 397

BRADLEY, A[ndrew] C[ecil] 398, 548, 665, 914

BRAILOW, David G. 2138

BRAND, Alice Glarden 549

BRASHEAR, Lucy 1397

BRASHEAR, William R. 766

BRENNAN, Anthony 1006

BRENNER, Gerry 1999

BRERETON, Geoffrey 399

BREYER, Bernard R. 1105

BRIGGS, K[atharine] M[ary] 1667

BRINTON, Laurel J. 2050

BRISTOL, Michael D. 29

BRITTIN, Norman A. 666

BROCKBANK, [John] Philip 713, 1043, 1846, 1906, 2139

BROCKMAN, B.A. 667

BRODY, Saul N. 2215

BROMLEY, Laura G. 1875

BRONSON, B. H., et al. 1498

BRONSTEIN, Herbert 1577

BROOKE, Nicholas 400, 1201, 1202, 1965

BROOKS, Cleanth 1398

BROOKS, Harold F. 646, 1966, 2359

BROUDE, Ronald 2244

BROWER, Reuben A. 401, 1075, 1186, 2140, 2141, 2183

BROWN, Beatrice D. 1578

BROWN, John Russell 30, 175, 196, 302, 403, 442, 459, 646, 720, 767, 929, 1043, 1082, 1407, 1419, 1424, 1426, 1429, 1451, 1457, 1467, 1845, 2139, 2201

BROWN, Paul 2142

BROWNING, Ivor R. 668

BRUCHER, Richard T. 768, 2245

BRUNVAND, Jan H. 2105

BRUYN, Lucy de. 1579

BRYANT, J. A., Jr. 915, 1638, 1907, 2243, 2414

BRYANT, James C. 2000

BRYANT, Jerry H. 2415
BRYSON, Norman 1475
BULLOUGH, Geoffrey 31, 313
BULMAN, James C. 314, 402
BURCKHARDT, Sigurd 32, 1044, 1164, 1580
BURDEN, Dennis H. 315
BURKE, Kenneth 550, 1106, 1203, 1751
BURNS, Margie 606, 2268
BURROW, J.A. 916
BURT, Richard A. 2106
BURTON, Dolores M. 669, 1967
BUSH, Douglas 33
BUTLER, Francelia 2207
BUTLER, Guy 1204
BUTTING, Gary 835
CAIN, H. Edward 917
CALDERWOOD, James L. 34, 316, 519, 520, 670, 769, 770, 1045, 1165,
    1356, 1357, 1399, 1400, 1668, 1908, 2246
CAMDEN, Carroll C. 714, 771, 1752
CAMPBELL, Josie P. 918
CAMPBELL, Lily B[ess] 317
CAMPBELL, Oscar James 35, 36, 1205, 2208
CANDIDO, Joseph 919, 1007, 1046, 1077
CANTELUPE, Eugene B. 2379
CANTOR, Paul A[rthur] 404, 2143, 2144
CAPUTI, Anthony 551, 1487
CAREY, Anna Kirwans 1368
CAREY, John 750, 1332, 2440
CARLISLE, Carol Jones 37
CARNOVSKY, Morris 1581
CARR, W.I. 671
CARROLL, D[aniel] Allen 1669
CARROLL, William C 176, 1358, 1639, 2001, 2327
CARTELLI, Thomas 521
CARTER, Albert H. 522
CARTER, George E. 2263
CARTER, Ronald 1839

233

COMTOIS, M. E. 1671
CONKLIN, Paul 775
CONNOLLY, Thomas F 1108
COOK, Ann Jennalie 44, 1491, 1754, 2360
COOK, David 1716, 2210
COOK, Elizabeth 2052
COOKE, Katharine 45
COOPER, Marilyn M. 2107
COOPERMAN, Stanley 776
CORFIELD, Cosmo 2146
COUCHMAN, Gordon W. 553
COULTER, Cornelia C. 180, 648
COURSEN, Herbert R., Jr. 181, 322, 1109, 1211, 1212, 1359, 1402, 1403
COWAN, Louise 1909, 2436
COWHIG, Ruth 1755
COX, John D. 1492, 2270
COX, Lee Sheridan 2417
COX, Richard H. 1672
CRAIG, Hardin 323, 675, 777, 778, 1213, 2361
CRAIG, Terry Ann 2108
CRAIK, T. W. 1717
CRANE, Mary Thomas 324
CRANE, Milton 572
CREWE, Jonathan V 649
CRIBB, T. J. 2003
CROCKER, Lester G. 1587
CROSS, Gerald 922
CRUTTWELL, M. J. Patrick 272, 2053
CUNLIFFE, John W. 410
CUNNINGHAM, Dolora G. 1404
CUNNINGHAM, J[ames] V[incent] 411
CURRY, Walter Clyde 1405, 1406, 2147
CURTIS, Harry, Jr. 2418
CUTTS, John P. 1080, 1848, 2247
CUVELIER, Eliane 2419
DABYDEEN, David 1755
DAIGLE, Lennet J. 2380

235

ELLIS, John 2421
ELSON, John 1167
ELTON, William R. 5, 1220
EMPSON, William 787, 927, 928, 1221, 1416, 1499, 1760, 2056, 2214
ENGEL, Wilson F., III. 2422
ENRIGHT, D.J. 678
ERICKSON, Peter B. 59, 60, 167, 186, 480, 612, 1194, 1374, 1362, 1403, 1608, 1636, 2033, 2275, 2326, 2423
ERLICH, Avi 2215
ERLICH, Bruce 1591
ESTRIN, Barbara L. 559, 2005, 2151
ETTIN, Andrew V. 2249
EVANS, Bertrand 183, 417, 2006
EVANS, Gareth Lloyd 929
EVANS, K. W. 1761
EVANS, Malcolm 61, 184, 1363
EVANS, Robert O. 2007
EVERETT, Barbara 1222, 1719, 1762, 2008, 2273, 2330
EWBANK, Inga-Stina 1851, 1852, 2424
FABER, M.D. 679
FAIRCHILD, Hoxie N 1500
FALK, Doris V. 788
FALK, Florence 1675
FARLEY-HILLS, David 2109
FARNHAM, Willard E. 185, 418, 419, 2216, 2274
FAWCETT, Mary Laughlin 2250
FEDER, Lillian 1223
FELDMAN, Harold 1111
FELHEIM, Marvin 247, 1112, 1640, 2110
FELPERIN, Howard 275, 420, 1081, 1224, 1225, 1853, 2152, 2425
FENDER, Stephen 1676
FERGUSON, Margaret W. 789
FERGUSSON, Francis 1417
FERRIS, David S. 1226
FERRUCCI, Franco 1418
FERRY, Anne 2057
FIEDLER, Leslie A. 62, 186, 2275

FIENBERG, Nona 1854
FINCH, G. J. 1677
FINEMAN, Joel 2058, 2111
FINK, Zera S. 613
FINKE, Laurie A. 930
FISH, Charles 931
FISH, Stanley 680
FITCH, Robert E. 560
FITZ, L. T. 561, 1501, 2153, 2154
FLAHIFF, F[rederick J.] 1210
FLANNERY, Christopher 2276
FLEISSNER, Robert F. 1013, 1641
FLEMING, Keith 790
FLY, Richard D. 1227, 1502, 2277
FOAKES, R[eginald] A 87, 257, 421, 716, 791, 1113, 1419, 2278, 2426
FODOR, A. 1592
FORD, P. Jeffrey 2251
FOREMAN, Walter C., Jr. 422
FORKER, Charles R. 328, 423, 792, 1007, 2252
FORTIN, René E. 614, 1114
FRAIL, David 615
FRANK, Mike 276
FRANKE, Wolfgang 1678
FRASER, Russell A. 1228
FRAZIER, Harriet C. 63
FREEDMAN, Barbara 651, 1642
FRENCH, A. L. 1048, 1049, 1050, 1916, 1971
FRENCH, Carolyn S. 1229
FRENCH, Marilyn 64
FRENCH, Tita 1878
FREUD, Sigmund 1230, 1420, 1593
FREUND, Elizabeth 932, 2279
FREY, Charles 2155, 2427
FRIESNER, Donald Neil 65
FROST, William 1231
FRYE, Dean 681, 1232
FRYE, Northrop 187, 188, 189, 258, 277, 329, 424, 2428

FRYE, Roland M. 793, 1421
FUJIMURA, Thomas H. 1594
FUZIER, Jean 530
GAGEN, Jean 2280
GALLENCA, Christiane 1643
GARBER, Marjorie B. 66, 67, 190, 1679, 1868, 2156
GARDINER, Judith Kegan 2059
GARDNER, C[olin] O[xenham] 1917
GARDNER, Helen 33, 385, 794, 1233, 1422, 1763, 1764, 2373
GARNER, Shirley Nelson 1595, 1680
GARRETT, John 363, 1733
GARVIN, Harry R. 1209, 1602, 1893, 2150, 2151, 2163, 2165, 2170
GAUDET, Paul 1918, 1919
GERARD, Albert S. 1766, 1767
GEARY, Keith 1596
GELLER, Lila 717
GELVEN, Michael 1765
GENT, Lucy 1423
GESNER, Carol 278, 718, 2157
GIANKARIS, C.J. 1115
GILBERT, A. J. 2060
GILLILAND, Joan F. 719
GILMAN, Ernest B. 2158
GIRARD, René 652, 1597, 1681, 1682, 2281
GLESS, Darryl J. 1503
GODSHALK, William Leigh 525, 1014, 1364, 2363
GOHLKE, Madelon 425, 426, 1768
GOLDBERG, Jonathan 68
GOLDBERG, S.L. 1234
GOLDEN, Leon 427
GOLDMAN, Michael 69, 428, 682, 933, 1235, 1424
GOLDSMITH, Ulrich K 2061
GOLDSTEIN, Leonard 2217
GOLDSTIEN, Neal L. 1365
GOLL, August 1972
GOLLANCZ, Israel 1598
GOMEZ, Christine 795

HALLSTEAD, R. N. 1772
HALSTEAD, William L. 1773, 1920
HAMILTON, A[lbert] C[harles] 236, 2253, 2382
HAMILTON, Donna B. 563
HAMILTON, William 800
HAMMOND, Antony 1716
HAMMOND, Gerald 1869
HANCHER, Michael 2064
HANHAM, Alison 1973
HANKISS, Elemér 431
HAPGOOD, Robert 76, 330, 331, 432, 527, 801, 936, 1118, 1601, 1646, 1774, 1921
HARARI, Josué V. 1681
HARBAGE, Alfred 77, 78, 79, 80, 81, 433, 1367
HARBAGE, Alfred. [pseud. Thomas Kyd] 564
HARCOURT, John B. 2010
HARDIN, Richard F. 1647
HARDING, D. W. 1428
HARDING, Davis P. 1504
HARDISON, O.B., Jr. 434, 802, 1238, 1335
HARDMAN, C. D. 2430
HARGROVE, Nancy D. 1239
HARRIS, Bernard 196, 302, 403, 442, 459, 646, 720, 767, 929, 1043, 1082, 1845, 2139, 2201
HARRIS, Laurie Lanzen 82
HARRISON, John L. 1505
HARRISON, Thomas P. 326, 1887, 2011
HARTLEY, Lodwick 1720
HARTMAN, Geoffrey H. 68, 124, 308, 789, 804, 868, 885, 1236, 1247, 1809, 1894, 1900, 2062, 2111, 2279, 2281, 2332, 2425
HARTSOCK, Mildred E. 1119
HARTWIG, Joan 83, 279, 2161, 2333, 2431
HARVEY, Nancy Lenz 1368
HASSEL, R[udolph] Chris, Jr. 248, 1974, 1975
HASTINGS, William T. 2254
HATLEN, Burton 1120, 1602
HATTAWAY, Michael 84

HATTO, A. T. 2383
HAWKES, Terence 85, 435, 803, 804, 1686, 1775
HAWKINS, Harriett 86, 1506, 1776
HAWKINS, Michael 1429
HAWKINS, Peter S. 67
HAWKINS, Sherman H 193, 937
HAYS, Janice 1721
HEDRICK, Donald K. 805
HEIFETZ, Jeanne 1603
HEILMAN, Robert Bechtold 1240, 1430, 1777, 1976, 2114
HEINZELMAN, Kurt 1604
HELTON, Tinsley 2284
HEMINGWAY, Samuel B. 938, 1648
HENDERSON, W.B. Drayton 1241
HENINGER, Simeon K., Jr. 1369, 1922
HENKLE, Roger B. 939
HENNING, Standish, et al. 2017
HENSLOWE, Philip 87
HERBERT, T[homas] Walter 2065
HERNDL, George C. 436
HERRICK, Marvin T. 437
HERRNSTEIN, Barbara 2066
HERTZBACH, Janet S. 806
HERZFELD, Michael 895
HESTER, M. Thomas 1968
HEXTER, J[ack] H. 1923
HIBBARD, George R[ichard] 88, 1242, 1666, 1778
HIGHFILL, Philip H., Jr. 1098
HILL, R. F. 438, 684, 2012
HILLMAN, Richard W. 1856, 2432
HINCHCLIFFE, Judith 1054
HINCHLIFFE, Michael 1243
HINELY, Jan Lawson 1649
HIRSH, James E. 89, 807
HOBDAY, C. H. 2067
HOCKEY, Dorothy C 1244, 1924
HODGE, R.I.V. 1245

242

HOENIGER, F. David 721, 1857, 2162, 2433
HOFLING, Charles K. 685, 722
HOGG, James 273, 1271
HOLADAY, Allan 1605
HOLDERNESS, Graham 332
HOLE, Sandra 1246
HOLLAND, Norman N. 90, 439, 1247, 1687, 2013
HOLLANDER, John 2334
HOLLOWAY, John 440
HOLMBERG, Arthur 2364
HOLMER, Joan Ozark 1606
HOLSTUN, James 686
HOLZBERGER, William G. 896
HOMAN, Sidney R. 280, 1688, 1779, 2065
HONIG, Edwin 687
HONIGMANN, E. A. J. 91, 441, 2218
HOOVER, Claudette 1248
HOSLEY, Richard 1674, 2014, 2115, 2428
HOTSON, Leslie 940, 1650
HOWARD, Jean E. 92, 1507, 2163
HOWLAND, Anne 67
HOY, Cyrus 1370
HUBLER, Edward L. 1780, 2068
HUEBERT, Ronald 1651
HUFFMAN, Clifford Chalmers 688
HUGENBERG, Lawrence W., Sr. 1977
HUGHES, Merritt Y. 2434
HULBERT, James 826
HULME, Hilda 93
HULME, Peter 2135, 2164
HULSE, S. Clark 1879, 1880
HUMPHREYS, Arthur R. 1925
HUMPHRIES, Jefferson 1249
HUNT, Maurice 723, 1858, 2165, 2166
HUNTER, G. K. 237, 281, 333, 442, 443, 808, 941, 942, 1371, 1431, 1781,
    2255, 2256
HUNTER, Robert Grams 194, 444, 1372

JORDAN, Hoover H. 1784
JORDAN, William Chester 1607
JORGENS, Jack L. 96
JORGENSEN, Paul A. 336, 565, 690, 813, 814, 944, 1016, 1017, 1257, 1435,
    1436, 1722, 1785, 1786, 1927
JOSEPH, Bertram 815, 816
JOSIPOVICI, Gabriel 1787
JOWITT, J. A. 1531, 1555, 2305, 2308
JUMP, John D. 817
KAHN, Coppélia 60, 97, 167, 186, 480, 739, 830, 1194, 1374, 1403, 1608,
    1632, 1636, 1687, 1881, 2015, 2033, 2118, 2197, 2275, 2326, 2385
KAHN, Sholom J. 1258
KANTAK, V. Y. 195, 1437
KANTOROWICZ, Ernst H. 337, 1928
KANZER, Mark 1259
KAPPELER, Susanne 1475
KASTAN, David Scott 98, 283, 528
KAUFMANN, R. J. 1510, 2287
KAUL, Mythili 1859
KAULA, David 566, 1121, 1260, 1788, 2070, 2288
KAVANAGH, James H. 99
KAY, Carol McGinnis 284, 726, 1789
KAY, Dennis 100
KAYSER, John R. 1122
KEACH, William 2386
KEAST, W.R. 1261
KEIGHTLEY, Thomas 1689
KELLY, Henry A. 338
KERMODE, Frank 196, 285, 1083, 1084, 1262, 2289
KERNAN, Alvin B. 339, 621, 945, 1055, 1263, 1264, 2219
KERNBERG, Otto F. 2016
KERNODLE, George R. 1265
KERRIGAN, William 818
KESTENBAUM, Clarice J. 1266
KETTLE, Arnold 448, 1034, 1797, 2312, 2404
KIEFER, Frederick 449
KIERNAN, Michael 946

245

LUKES, Timothy J. 1275
LYNCH, Amy 1022
LYNCH, Stephen J. 2294
MACCARY, W. Thomas 200
MACDONALD, Andrew 1023
MACDONALD, Gina 1023
MACDONALD, Ronald R. 347, 571, 1933
MACHOVEC, Frank J. 2174
MACINTYRE, Alasdair 835
MACINTYRE, Jean 693, 836, 1024, 1279
MACK, Maynard 443, 459, 460, 572, 837
MACKAY, Maxine 1615
MACLEAN, Hugh 348, 1280
MACLURE, Millar 461, 694
MAHOOD, M[olly] M[aureen] 108, 252
MAJORS, G. W. 1886
MALLETT, Phillip 1979
MANHEIM, Michael 349, 1057
MANLEY, Frank 964
MANSELL, Darrel, Jr. 1523
MARCUS, Mordecai 1694
MARES, F[rancis] H[ugh] 1725
MARGESON, John M.R. 463
MARIENSTRAS, Richard 109
MARKELS, Julian 573, 1130, 1283, 2343
MARKS, Carol L. 1284
MARSH, Derick R[upert] C[lement] 464, 732, 965, 1447, 1524
MARSHALL, David 1695
MARTZ, Louis L. 2440
MARTZ, William J. 201, 1525, 2176
MARX, Joan C. 733
MARX, Leo 2177
MARX, Steven 626
MASON, Harold A. 465, 1285
MASSEY, Irving 1226
MATCHETT, William H. 1171, 2441
MATTHEWS, G. M. 1797

249

MATTSSON, May 1172
MAXWELL, James C. 466, 695, 1286, 1526, 2226
MAY, James E. 1173
MCALINDON, Thomas 1131, 2295
MCAVOY, William C. 2344
MCCANLES, Michael 692
MCCOLLOM, William G. 1726
MCCOMBIE, Frank 1276
MCCULLEN, Joseph T. 1277, 1795
MCDONALD, Russ 834, 2439
MCELROY, Bernard 457
MCFARLAND, Thomas 202, 458, 1278
MCGEE, Arthur R. 1796
MCGOVERN, D. S. 2173
MCGRATH, Michael J. Gargas 1672
MCGUIRE, Philip C. 110, 1527, 2021
MCGUIRE, Richard L. 959
MCLAVERTY, J. 960
MCLAY, Catherine M. 1375
MCLUHAN, Herbert M. 961
MCLUSKIE, Kathleen 1281, 1528, 2119
MCMANAWAY, James G. 6, 323, 595, 607, 633, 981, 1167, 1189, 1465, 1824
MCMILLIN, Scott 1934
MCNAMARA, Anne M. 962
MCNEAL, Thomas H. 462, 1058
MCNEIR, Waldo F. 343, 389, 675, 718, 744, 963, 1282, 1774, 2028, 2395
MCPEEK, James A. S. 2175
MCROBERTS, Paul 7
MCTAGUE, Michael J. 1616
MCVEAGH, John 1617
MEAGHER, John C. 111
MEBANE, John S. 1696
MEDCALF, Stephen 2296
MELCHIORI, Barbara Arnett 1448
MELCHIORI, Giorgio 1798, 2078
MELLAMPHY, Ninian 1449
MENDILOW, A.A. 1025

MENDONCA, Barbara Heliodora C. de. 1799
MERCER, Peter 1800
MERCHANT, William Moelwyn 1026, 1287, 1450, 1529, 2227
MERRILL, Robert 203
MERRIX, Robert P. 966
MESZAROS, Patricia K. 1861
METZ, G[eorge] Harolds 1902
MICHAEL, Nancy 1862
MICHELI, Linda 1086
MIDGLEY, Graham 1618
MIKO, Stephen J. 2178
MILES, Rosalind 1530
MILLARD, Barbara C. 617
MILLER, Anthony 1132
MILLER, David L. 838
MILLER, Robert P. 2389
MILLS, John A. 839
MILLS, Laurens J. 574
MILLS, Paul 1531
MINCOFF, Marco 467, 468, 627, 1059, 1060, 1087, 1532
MINER, Madonne M. 1980
MIOLA, Robert S. 112, 239, 1133
MIRIAM JOSEPH, Sister 113, 840, 841
MITCHELL, Charles 696, 1619
MITCHELL, Giles R. 967
MIZENER, Arthur 2079
MOFFET, Robin 734
MOISAN, Thomas E. 2022
MONAGHAN, James 968
MONEY, John 1801
MONTGOMERY, Robert L. 1887, 1935
MONTROSE, Louis Adrian 1376, 1697
MOONEY, Michael E. 1288
MOORE, James A. 1981
MOORE, John R. 575, 1802
MOORE, Nancy 1134
MOORE, Olin H. 2023

PARIS, Bernard J. 1458, 1538, 1808, 1983
PARK, Clara Claiborne 630
PARKER, Douglas H. 2027
PARKER, Patricia 68, 124, 308, 655, 789, 804, 868, 885, 1236, 1809, 1894,
   1900, 2062, 2111, 2279, 2281, 2332, 2425
PARKER, R.B. 535
PARROTT, Thomas Marc 210
PARSONS, Philip 1377
PARTEN, Anne 1621, 1654
PARTRIDGE, Eric 125
PARTRIDGE,A. C. 2450
PAUL, Henry N. 1459
PEARLMAN, E. 1460
PEARSON, D'Orsay W. 2186
PEAT, Derek 1298
PECHTER, Edward 974
PECK, Russell A. 1299
PEQUIGNEY, Joseph 2083
PERRET, Marion 2120
PERRY, Thomas A. 2366
PERRY, T[heodore] Anthony 1300
PERRYMAN, Judith C. 1378
PETERSON, Douglas L. 1137, 1864, 2028, 2084, 2187, 2188
PETRONELLA, Vincent F. 1936
PETRY, Alice Hall 2189
PETTET, Ernest C. 211, 1175, 1622, 2029, 2231
PHIALAS, Peter G. 253, 852, 1027, 1937, 1938
PHILLIPS, James Emerson, Jr. 477, 2190
PINCISS, G.M. 1138
PIPER, William Bowman 2085
PIRIE, David 1301
PLATT, Michael 2086, 2191
PLOWMAN, Max 1623
POIRIER, Richard 1075, 1186, 2183
POLLIN, Burton R. 853
POPE, Elizabeth Marie 1539
POPE, Randolph D. 733

PORTER, Joseph A. 354
POTTS, Abbie Findlay 1540
POZNAR, Walter 1624
PRATT, Samuel M. 1062
PRESSON, Robert K. 1302, 2302
PRICE, Hereward T. 1063, 2367, 2391
PRICE, Jonathan R. 1541
PRICE, Joseph G. 536, 1002
PRIESTLEY, J[ohn] B[oynton] 1701
PRINCE, F[rank] T[empleton] 1889, 2392
PRIOR, Moody E. 355, 478, 854, 1139, 1625, 1810
PROSER, Matthew N. 479, 702, 855
PROSSER, Eleanor A. 856
PROUDFOOT, Richard 2451
PROVOST, Foster 1939
PUTNEY, Rufus 2393, 2394
PYLE, Fitzroy 2452
QUILLER-COUCH, Arthur 292
QUINN, Edward G. 36
QUINN, Michael 356, 1940
RABKIN, Norman 126, 127, 480, 703, 762, 1028, 1140, 1626, 2303, 2395
RACKIN, Phyllis 481, 704, 1064, 1176, 1941
RADOFF, M. L. 1029, 1655
RAMSEY, Paul 2087
RANALD, Margaret Loftus 1811
RANSOM, John Crowe 2088, 2089
REBHORN, Wayne A. 212, 2396
REED, Robert Rentoul, Jr. 357, 1942
REED, Victor B. 2100
REESE, Max M. 358
REGAN, Mariann Sanders 2090
REIBETANZ, John 1303
REID, B. L. 1461
REID, S.W. 1304
REIK, Theodor 1656
REIMAN, Donald H 1943
REISS, Timothy J. 482

RENO, Raymond 975
REYNOLDS, George F. 857
REYNOLDS, Jack A. 1773, 1920
REYNOLDS, James A. 1944
RIBNER, Irving 359, 737, 1141, 1462, 1945
RICHARDS, I. A. 2304
RICHARDSON, W.M. 1030
RICHMOND, Hugh M. 213, 360, 1089, 1984
RICKERT, R.T. 87
RICKS, Don 1065
RICO, Barbara Roche 1542, 2121, 2453
RIDLER, Anne 235
RIEFER, Marcia 1543
RIEMER, A.P. 214, 579, 976
RIFFATERRE, Michael 1702
RIGGS, David 361
RIGHTER, Anne 128
RINGBOM, Hakan, et al. 1313
RISH, Shirley 1142
RISTINE, Frank Humphrey 293
ROBBIN, Robin 1871
ROBERTS, Jeanne Addison 6, 215, 216, 1657, 1658, 2122
ROBERTSON, D[urant] W[aite], Jr 858
ROBERTSON, Hugh 2305
ROBINSON, James E. 1305, 1703
ROBINSON, Randal F. 859
ROCHE, Thomas P., Jr. 1306, 2091
ROESEN, Bobbyann 1379
ROESSNER, Jane 2092
ROGERS, Robert 1812
ROGERS, William Hudson 362
ROLLINS, Hyder E. 2306
ROSAND, David 1890
ROSCELLI, William J. 1544
ROSE, Jacqueline 860, 1545
ROSE, Mark 129, 861, 1813
ROSE, Paul L. 580

ROSE, Steven 1731
ROSEN, William 483
ROSENBERG, Marvin 484, 1307, 1463, 1814
ROSENHEIM, Judith 1546
ROSINGER, Lawrence 1308
ROSMARIN, Adena 2093
ROSS, Charles 1053
ROSS, Daniel W. 2232
ROSS, Gordon N. 1946
ROSSITER, A[rthur] P[ercival] 130, 262, 363, 1985
ROSSKY, William 2368
ROUDA, F.H. 705
ROZETT, Martha Tuck 485, 581, 2030
RUSCHE, Harry 1309
RUSSELL, G. W. 1815
RUSZKIEWICZ, John J. 2233
RUTELLI, Romana 2094
SACCIO, Peter 364, 2123
SACKS, Elizabeth 1547
SAHEL, Pierre 1090
SAID, Edward W. 1597, 1770
SALE, Roger 1548
SALGADO, Gamini 656
SALINGAR, Leo 217, 862, 977, 2346
SALOMON, Brownell 1031
SALTER, F.M. 1177
SANDERS, Norman 365, 813, 1143, 2390
SANDERS, Wilbur 366, 486, 1947, 1986
SANFORD, Wendy C 863
SCHAEFERMEYER, Mark J. 1977
SCHANZER, Ernest 263, 1144, 1145, 1549, 1704, 1705, 2454
SCHAUM, Melita 1310
SCHECTER, Harold 2215
SCHEFF, Thomas J. 864
SCHELL, Edgar 1311
SCHELLING, Felix E. 367
SCHLEINER, Louise 1508, 1550

SCHLEINER, Winfried 2347
SCHOENBAUM, Samuel 131, 132, 133, 1884, 1948, 2095
SCHOFF, Francis G. 537, 1312
SCHUCKING, Levin L. 134, 487
SCHUELLER, Herbert M. 884
SCHWARTZ, Elias 488, 1816, 2348
SCHWARTZ, Helen J. 1032
SCHWARTZ, Murray M. 739, 830, 1632, 1687, 2197
SCHWARTZ, Robert 160, 865
SCHWINDT, John 489
SCOTT, Margaret 1551
SCOTT, Mark W. 82
SCOTT, William O. 218, 2234
SCOUFOS, Alice L. 978, 979
SCOUTEN, Arthur H. 1552
SCRAGG, Leah 1817
SEIDEN, Melvin 2349
SELL, Roger D. 1313
SELTZER, Daniel 1818
SEMON, Kenneth J. 294
SENG, Peter J. 866, 980
SERPIERI, Alessandro 135, 1314
SEWALL, Richard B. 1315
SEWELL, Elizabeth 1706
SHAABER, M[atthias] A[dam] 219, 981, 982
SHAHEEN, Naseeb 738
SHAPIRO, Michael 582
SHAPIRO, Stephen A. 583, 1819
SHARP, Sister Corona 2192
SHAW, Catherine M. 657, 1820
SHAW, George Bernard 136
SHAW, John 631, 983
SHAW, William P. 2307
SHEIDLEY, William E. 2397
SHELL, Marc 1627
SHERIDAN, Alan 1769
SHERIFF, William E. 1987

SHIRLEY, John W. 984, 1659
SHOWALTER, Elaine 868
SHUCHTER, J.D. 985
SHULMAN, Jeff 1380
SHURGOT, Michael W 2124
SIBLY, John 1178
SIDER, John W. 221
SIEGEL, Paul N. 490, 1317, 1553, 1707, 1821, 2031, 2350, 2455
SIEMON, James Edward 2456
SIMMONS, Joseph L. 491, 584, 1179
SIMONDS, Peggy Muñoz 706
SIMPSON, Lucie 585
SINFIELD, Alan 50, 137, 869, 1011, 1281, 1495, 1528, 2142, 2308
SISSON, C[harles] J[asper] 264, 492, 870
SKULSKY, Harold 871, 1318, 1554
SKURA, Meredith 139, 739
SLIGHTS, Camille Wells 1628, 1660, 2351, 2369
SLIGHTS, William W. E 2352
SMIDT, Kristian 368, 1464
SMITH, Don 1555
SMITH, Fred M. 1988
SMITH, Gordon Ross 10, 369, 565, 855, 1033, 1146, 1556, 2013, 2032
SMITH, Hallett 2096
SMITH, J. Oates 2309
SMITH, James C. 632, 1732
SMITH, John Hazel 1629
SMITH, Jonathan 2457
SMITH, Rebecca 872
SMITH, Robert M. 1319
SMITH, Warren D. 740
SNOW, Edward A. 1822, 2033, 2097
SNYDER, Karl E. 1557
SNYDER, Richard C. 2310
SNYDER, Susan 222, 586, 1320, 1321, 1823, 2034
SOELLNER, Rolf 2235, 2311
SOMERSET, J.A.B. 140, 223
SOMMERS, Alan 2258

SOUTHALL, Raymond 873, 1558, 2312

SOYINKA, Wole 141

SPARGO, John Webster 1465

SPEAIGHT, Robert 493

SPENCER, Terence J[ohn] B[ew] 578, 494, 495, 2236

SPENCER, Theodore 142, 496, 633, 874, 1824

SPENDER, Stephen 1466

SPEVACK, Marvin 143, 144, 497, 875

SPIVACK, Bernard 145, 498, 986, 987, 1825

SPLITTER, Randolph 1826

SPRAGUE, Arthur Colby 146, 224, 370, 988

SPROAT, Kezia Vanmeter 1827

SPURGEON, Caroline F.E. 147

SRIGLEY, Michael 2193

STAEBLER, Warren 634

STAFFORD, Tony J. 1277, 2228, 2313

STALLYBRASS, Peter 1467

STAMM, Rudolf 741, 2314

STAMPFER, J. 1322

STAMPFER, Judah 499, 1322

STANISLAVSKY [ALEKSEEV, Konstantin S.] 1828

STANSBURY, Joan 1708

STATES, Bert O. 500, 876, 1323, 1468

STEAD, C[hristian] K[arlson] 1559

STEADMAN, John M. 1661

STEIN, Arnold 1469, 2315

STEMPEL, Daniel 587

STEPHENSON, A.A. 742

STEPPAT, Michael 588

STETNER, S.C.V. 1324

STEVENSON, David Lloyd 225, 1560

STEVENSON, Warren 1325

STEVICK, Robert D. 1180

STEWART, Douglas J. 989

STEWART, J[ohn] I[nnes] M[ackintosh] 148, 1326

STEWART, William F. 1829

STILL, Colin 2194

STIMPSON, Catharine R. 1891
STIRLING, Brents 501, 589, 1147, 1470, 1830, 1949, 2098
STOCKHOLDER, Katherine 707, 877, 1327, 1328, 1865
STOLL, Elmer E[dgar] 149, 226, 590, 635, 990, 1329, 1471, 1630, 1831, 1832, 1833, 1989, 2195
STONE, George Winchester 1330
STONE, P.W.K. 1331
STONEX, Arthur Birens 1631
STOREY, Graham 130, 262, 1733
STRACHEY, James 1230, 1420, 1593
STRACHEY, Lytton 296, 2196
STRAUCH, Edward H. 2035
STREITBERGER, W. R. 2398
STRIBRNY, Zdenek 1034
STROUP, Thomas B. 591
STUGRIN, Michael A. 1690
STUMP, Donald V., et al. 898
SUBLETTE, Jack R. 991, 1950
SUHAMY, Henri 878
SUMMERS, Joseph H. 150, 1332, 2353
SUNDELSON, David 1561, 2197
SUTHERLAND, James 313
SUZMAN, Arthur 1951
SWANDER, Homer D. 743, 744, 1066
SWAYNE, Mattie 1067
SWINBURNE, Algernon Charles 1333, 1834, 1952
SWINDEN, Patrick 227
SYLVESTER, Bickford 1892
SYPHER, Wylie 1562, 1734, 2036
SZENCZI, Miklos 371
SZYFMAN, Arnold 1334
TABORSKI, Boleslaw 825
TAKADA, Yasunari 2316
TALBERT, Ernest William 240, 372, 1335
TANNER, Tony 297
TANSELLE, G. Thomas 2037
TAVE, Stuart M. 992

TAYLOR, Gary 151, 1336, 1337, 1872
TAYLOR, George C[offin] 2317
TAYLOR, Mark 152
TAYLOR, Michael 538, 708, 745, 879, 1508, 1709, 1735, 1866, 2458
TAYLOR, Neil 2172
TAYLOR, R. K. S. 1531, 1555, 2305, 2308
TENNENHOUSE, Leonard 153, 1563, 1632
TEODORESCU-BRINZEU, Pia 1835
TEODORESCU, Anda 880
TEY, Josephine 1990
THALER, Alwin 813, 2390
THAYER, C[alvin] G[raham] 373
THOM, Martha Andresen 2125
THOMAS, Sidney 1991
THOMPSON, Karl F. 1953
THOMSON, Patricia 2318
THOMSON, Peter 154
THORNDIKE, Ashley H. 298
THORNE, William B. 746, 2126
TILLEY, Morris P. 2354
TILLYARD, E[ustace] M[andeville] W[etanhall] 228, 241, 265, 299, 374, 375,
    1091, 2127
TINKLER, F. C. 747, 2459
TOBIAS, Richard C. 276
TOLIVER, Harold E. 993, 994
TOLMAN, Albert H. 636, 1035
TOMPKINS, J. M. S. 1867
TOOLE, William B. 266, 1148, 2038
TOVEY, Barbara 1633, 2198
TRACE, Jacqueline 1181
TRACI, Philip J. 247, 592, 637, 1640, 1736, 2110
TRAFTON, Dain A. 1954
TRASCHEN, Isadore 881
TRAUGOTT, John 1737
TRAVERSI, Derek A. 155, 242, 300, 376, 502, 709, 1338, 1339, 1564, 2199,
    2319
TRICOMI, Albert H. 2259

TROUSDALE, Marion 229, 658, 1955, 2355
TRUAX, Elizabeth 1893, 2399
TURNER, Robert Y. 243, 377, 378, 379, 539, 748
TYSDAHL, Bjorn 1692
UHLMANN, Dale C. 2400
UPHAUS, Robert W. 301
URE, Peter 1956
URKOWITZ, Steven 1340
UTTERBACK, Raymond V. 1068, 2039
VAN DE WATER, Julia C. 1182
VAN DEN BERG, Kent 156, 638
VAN TASSEL, David E. 1565
VANDER MOTTEN, J. P. 2099
VAUGHAN, Virginia Mason 1183
VAWTER, Marvin L. 1149, 1150
VELZ, John W. 503, 504, 1151, 1152, 1153, 1154, 1155
VESSEY, D. W. Thomson 2401
VESZY-WAGNER, L. 1472
VICKERS, Brian 157, 158, 1341
VICKERS, Nancy 1894
VINCENT, Barbara C. 593
VON ROSADOR, K. Tetzeli 244
VONDERSMITH, Bernard J. 2128
VYVYAN, John 254, 1381, 2370
WAAGE, Frederick O., Jr. 1092
WAIN, John 1738
WAINGROW, Marshall 1190
WAITH, Eugene M. 380, 505, 1184, 2260, 2261
WALDOCK, Peter B. 896
WALKER, Lewis 2237, 2238
WALKER, Marshall 230
WALKER, Roy 882
WALLEY, Harold R. 1895
WALTER, James 2200
WALTON, James K. 1342, 1836
WARHAFT, Sidney 883
WARMBROD, Nancy Compton 2040

264

WIDDOWSON, Peter 107
WILCHER, Robert 256
WILDERS, John 384
WILEY, Paul L. 1095
WILKINSON, Andrew M. 1156
WILLEN, Gerald 2100
WILLIAM, David 2201
WILLIAMS, Arnold 1319
WILLIAMS, Gary Jays 1669
WILLIAMS, George Walton 2025
WILLIAMS, Gordon 2402
WILLIAMS, Gwyn 659
WILLIAMS, Jimmy Lee 2263
WILLIAMS, John A. 2460
WILLIAMS, Mary C. 1741
WILLIAMS, Paul V. A. 1979
WILLIAMS, Philip 1993
WILLIAMS, Porter, Jr. 2356
WILLIAMS, Raymond 1475
WILLIAMSON, C.F. 1345
WILLIAMSON, Claude C.H. 889
WILLIAMSON, Marilyn L. 594, 640, 1037, 2042
WILLSON, Robert F., Jr. 511, 1840
WILSON, Douglas B. 2321
WILSON, Edwin 136
WILSON, Elkin Calhoun 595
WILSON, Emmett 710
WILSON, F[rank] P[ercy] 385, 386
WILSON, Harold S. 512, 542, 751, 1569
WILSON, John Dover 231, 890, 995, 996, 1038, 1958, 2202, 2264
WILSON, Rawdon 641
WILSON, Robert R. 891
WILT, Judith 892
WIMSATT, William K. 596
WINCOR, Richard 304
WINEKE, Donald R. 1070
WINNY, James 387, 2101

WINSTON, Mathew 1570
WITT, Robert W. 997
WITTREICH, Joseph 1346
WOOD, Alice I. P. 1994
WOOD, Frederick T. 513
WOODBRIDGE, Linda 165, 597, 1742, 2131, 2357
WOODS, Andrew H. 2239
WORMHOUDT, Arthur 893
WRAY, William R. 894
WRIGHT, Eugene P. 967
WRIGHT, George T. 166
WYNNE, Lorraine 895
YATES, Frances A. 305, 1383
YEARLING, Elizabeth M 2358
YEATS, W[illiam] B[utler] 1959
YODER, R. A. 1157, 2322
YOUNG, David 642, 896, 1347
YOUNG, David P. 1712
YOUNG, H. McClure 2102
ZAGORIN, Perez 1923
ZANDVOORT, R.W. 1158
ZEEVELD, W. Gordon 388, 711, 998, 1071
ZELICOVICI, Dvora 1348
ZENDER, Karl F. 1476
ZIEGELMAN, Lois 897
ZITNER, Sheldon P. 898, 999, 1713, 1960
ZOLBROD, Paul G. 276